RECOVERING NATURE

Ralph McInerny
Michael P. Grace Professor of Medieval Studies
Director of the Jacques Maritain Center
University of Notre Dame

# RECOVERING NATURE
Essays in Natural Philosophy, Ethics, and
Metaphysics in Honor of Ralph McInerny

Edited by

THOMAS HIBBS AND JOHN O'CALLAGHAN

UNIVERSITY OF NOTRE DAME PRESS
Notre Dame, Indiana

University of Notre Dame Press
Notre Dame, IN 46556
All Rights Reserved

Copyright © 1999 by University of Notre Dame
Published in the United States of Americ

Paperback edition published in 2017

*Library of Congress Cataloging-in-Publication Data*

Recovering nature : essays in natural philosophy, ethics, and metaphysics in honor of Ralph McInerny / edited by Thomas Hibbs and John O'Callaghan.
p. cm.
Includes bibliographical references.
ISBN 978-0-268-16070-8 (paperback)
ISBN 978-0-268-01666-1 (hardback)
1. —Philosophy of nature. 2. Thomists. I. McInerny, Ralph M. II. Hibbs, Thomas S. III. O'Callaghan, John.
BD581.R39     1999
149'.91—dc21                                                99–38120

*The paper used in this publication meets the minimum requirements of the American National Standard for Information Sciences—Permanence of Paper for Printed Library Materials, ANSI Z39.48-1984.*

# CONTENTS

ACKNOWLEDGMENTS   vii

INTRODUCTION, *Thomas Hibbs and John O'Callaghan*   1

### I. Natural Philosophy

Quantification in Sixteenth-Century Natural Philosophy,
*William Wallace, O.P.*   11

The Failure of Positivism and the Enduring Legacy of Comte,
*Jude P. Dougherty*   25

The Philosophies of Mind and Nature, *John Haldane*   37

Persons and Things, *Thomas De Koninck*   53

### II. Ethics

John Case: An Example of Aristotelianism's Self-Subversion?,
*Alasdair MacIntyre*   71

Keeping Virtue in Its Place: A Critique of Subordinating Strategies,
*David Solomon*   83

Deliberation about Final Ends: Thomistic Considerations,
*Daniel McInerny*   105

Moral Terminology and Proportionalism, *Janet E. Smith*   127

The Gospels, Natural Law, and the American Founding,
*Michael Novak*   147

McInerny Did It, or Should a Pacifist Read Murder Mysteries?,
*Stanley Hauerwas*   163

### III. Metaphysics

Religious Pluralism and Natural Theology, *Laura Garcia*   179

Reid, Hume, and God, *Alvin Plantinga*   201

Two Roles for Catholic Philosophers, *Alfred J. Freddoso*   229

From Analogy of "Being" to the Analogy of Being, *David B. Burrell, C.S.C.*   253

Index   267

# ACKNOWLEDGMENTS

We have incurred a number of debts in the process of editing this volume. First, we would like to thank Mrs. Alice Osberger, longtime administrative assistant to Ralph McInerny, for her assistance and advice on numerous matters. Second, we wish to express our gratitude to the contributors, who have graciously and promptly responded to all of our requests. We especially wish to acknowledge one of the contributors, David Solomon. The idea for this volume was born in a conversation we had with David a few summers ago. Along the way, he has provided encouragement, wit, and prudential judgment. Third, we would like to thank Mr. Michael Joyce and Ms. Dianne Sehler of the Lynde and Harry Bradley Foundation. The Foundation generously provided a grant to defray the costs of the publication of this volume and to support a celebration in honor of the achievements of Ralph McInerny. Finally, we gratefully acknowledge the assistance of John McCudden, Ann Rice, and Jeffrey Gainey of the University of Notre Dame Press, who have made many helpful editorial corrections and suggestions and who have expressed enthusiasm about the project from the very beginning.

# INTRODUCTION

*Thomas Hibbs and John O'Callaghan*

The recovery of nature has been a unifying and enduring aim of the writings of the man to whom this book is dedicated, Ralph McInerny, Michael P. Grace Professor of Medieval Studies at the University of Notre Dame, director of the Jacques Maritain Center, former director of the Medieval Institute, and author of numerous works in philosophy, literature, and journalism. The list of achievements and accolades could go on and on. But, although we have come to praise not bury McInerny, we want to do so by showing what we have learned from his teaching and writing. Clearly, one of the central preoccupations of his brand of Thomism, as an Aristotelian-Thomist, has been attention to nature. In his persistent, clear, and creative defenses of natural theology and natural law, Ralph has appealed to nature in order to establish a dialogue between theists and nontheists, to contribute to the moral and political renewal of American culture, and particularly to provide philosophical foundations for Catholic theology.

While many of the fads that have plagued philosophy and theology during the last half-century have come and gone, recent developments suggest that Ralph's commitment to Aristotelian-Thomism has been boldly, if quietly, prophetic. Philosophers of religion and proponents of the ethics of virtue draw with increasing confidence upon premodern insights, arguments, and modes of inquiry. The rejuvenation of variants on Aristotle's conception of nature is now a pervasive feature of the philosophical landscape. Consider, for example, (a) the exploration of an anthropology to complement virtue ethics, (b) the reformulation of a variety of traditional arguments from nature for the existence of God, (c) the rehabilitation, even in discussions of evolutionary theory, of teleology, (d) the search for conceptions of the human person that avoid the reductionist alternatives of dualism and materialism, and (e) the renewed interest in the viability of natural law as a basis for political and legal reasoning.

This volume brings together essays by an impressive group of scholars. The contributors certainly do not all agree with one another nor on every point with the man whom their essays honor; nor, finally, do all the essays focus equally on the Aristotelian-Thomist conception of nature. Yet the topics and modes of inquiry in the essays complement one another nicely and all have been written with Ralph in mind. Indeed, it is a sign of the admiration that Ralph elicits in colleagues and friends that, when asked, a group of very busy scholars eagerly agreed to submit an essay and that they finished their pieces, if not in every case at the deadline, well in advance of what academic custom now considers punctual. Had we but world enough and time, we are convinced we could produce a number of lively and interesting volumes dedicated to the work and life of Ralph McInerny. As some small token of our gratitude, this one will have to suffice.

We have divided the essays into three categories, following the order of learning recommended by Aristotle: natural philosophy, ethics, and metaphysics.

### NATURAL PHILOSOPHY

The chief impediment to the recovery of the classical, Aristotelian conception of nature is undoubtedly the assumption that the modern sciences have decisively refuted the central tenets of Aristotle's natural philosophy, or at least that their rejection was a necessary prelude to the impressive and irreversible advances of the sciences. The essays by William Wallace ("Quantification in Sixteenth-Century Natural Philosophy") and Jude Dougherty ("The Failure of Positivism") treat, respectively, the sixteenth-century origins of modern science and nineteenth-century positivism. Wallace shows how the birth of the modern sciences did not occur *ex nihilo* in the seventeenth century, but rather grew out of the sixteenth-century development of "new techniques of quantification . . . of space, motion, and force." By demonstrating the medieval sources of these sixteenth-century developments, Wallace underscores the continuity between medieval and early modern science and suggests possibilities for integrating the new mathematical approach to nature with the older Aristotelian approach.

If Wallace shows how attention to the history of science undermines naive assumptions about the incompatibility of ancient and modern views of nature, Dougherty suggests that the actual practice of nineteenth- and twentieth-century science is incompatible with the interpretation of science most antithetical to Aristotle's natural philosophy: Comte's positivism. Positivism "not only ruled out metaphysics but ruled out theoretical physics as well." At the root of its failure is its denial of the efficacy of causal reasoning. Like Wallace, Dougherty thinks the time is ripe for seeing modern science in a more Aristotelian light: "Volumes of contemporary work in the philosophy of science... have taken a realist turn as many philosophers have recovered a realist perspective often directly inspired by Aristotle in their attempt to remain true to actual practice in the natural sciences."

As Dougherty observes, the lingering effects of positivism can still be seen in the human sciences. Perhaps the most striking way in which the Aristotelian order of this volume displays itself is in the inclusion of the papers by John Haldane and Thomas De Koninck under the heading of philosophy of nature. One lasting inheritance of positivism is the sense that philosophy and in particular metaphysics deal with all the problems left over after natural science has had its way. According to positivism, metaphysics will have a role to play only so long as conceptual difficulties about the mind and personal identity remain. Nothing could be further from the Aristotelian study of being-qua-being or the study of human nature as an area within the philosophy of nature. And yet, as John Haldane urges in "Mind and Nature," recent developments in philosophy of mind provide starting points for a fruitful dialogue between the Aristotelian-Thomistic philosophy of nature and analytic philosophical writing on thought and agency. With attention to the recent work of Davidson and Putnam, Haldane argues that physicalist reductionism is a lingering but now outdated prejudice. The key to his argument is the revival of formal causality as distinct from efficient causality. Form, which is evident in structures and patterns of behavior, "brings order, but not by pushing things this way or that." In philosophy of mind, we are at a "significant juncture"; we can move toward physicalism and reduction or away from it and toward hylomorphic personalism.

Another vexed question in contemporary philosophy concerns the nature of personhood. In his study of the "miracle of human persons, unique, indivisible... yet composites of mind and body," Thomas De Koninck ("Persons and Things") criticizes accounts of personhood that exclude part of the human population. These views rest on "abstract definitions set forth in complete defiance of concrete reality." Lacking in these definitions is any serious attention to the embodied nature of human persons. Aristotle's doctrine of the soul as the first actuality of an organic body potentially having life is helpful here. Aristotle's distinction between first and second actuality allows us to see that actuality does not exclude potentiality but rather is its basis. The consequence for personhood is clear: we can't take as the criterion of human dignity the actual or even potential exercise of the higher functions of second actuality, since they are only human as derived from the first actuality of the human being. At conception we have not a potential but an actual person. If one considers the recent facile use to which the Aristotelian account of "delayed hominization" has been put by writers otherwise uninterested in the substance of Aristotelian natural philosophy, DeKoninck's essay is an impressive example of Aristotelian natural philosophy in practice. It reflects critically upon and integrates advances in the modern sciences. It blends these with the insights of Sophocles and Levinas on the ethical capacity for recognition of the human body, especially in its most destitute and defenseless forms.

ETHICS

We have reason, then, to put into question the standard story about how Aristotle fell into desuetude in the early modern period. Alasdair MacIntyre suggests a different and hitherto unexplored reason for decline: the self-subversion of Renaissance Aristotelians ("John Case: An Example of Aristotelian Self-Subversion?"). MacIntyre begins with Sir Philip Sidney's mocking depiction of the moral philosophers in his *Apologie for Poetrie* (c. 1581). Posing the question of which of his contemporaries Sidney might have had in mind, MacIntyre suggests John Case, a renowned teacher of Aristotelian moral philosophy at Oxford. According to Case, "the teaching of moral philosophy . . . is the teaching of the moral virtues" and "the moral philosopher is preeminent . . . in making those whom he instructs virtuous." Case thus elevates the status of universities as educators in virtue for those who would serve the Elizabethan state. From the perspective of Aristotle, Case's understanding of his pedagogy embodies a double failure: a failure to heed Aristotle's distinction between the theory and practice of moral virtue and his exclusion of youth from moral theory, and a failure to recognize the incompatibility between Aristotle's ethics and politics, on the one hand, and the social and political world of Case's students, on the other.

While MacIntyre is interested in the self-subversion of Aristotelians in the seventeenth century, David Solomon focuses upon how they are spirited away in the twentieth. The recent revival of interest in "virtue ethics" among analytic and anglophone moral philosophers is rightly regarded as one more sign of a resurgent Aristotelianism in contemporary philosophy. Solomon argues that the opponents of virtue ethics, after initially arguing directly against the viability of such theories, have recently attempted to undermine them more indirectly by arguing that their central insights can be accommodated by deontological and consequentialist theoretical structures. Solomon explores a number of efforts to bring the virtues to heel, and argues that one of the most popular attempts is bound to fail.

Essays by Janet Smith and Daniel McInerny address crucial issues in the interpretation of Aquinas and in contemporary debates over virtue and natural law. The latter considers the question whether deliberation is limited to means or "must include final ends within its scope." Prompted by the growing consensus among scholars of Aristotle for the latter position, McInerny sorts out the reasons for this preference, examines carefully the relevant texts of Aristotle, and puts into question the novel interpretation. An important motivation for the broad view of deliberation is that the narrow view seems to make practical reason merely instrumental, a slave to the passions. Basing himself on Aquinas's interpretation of Aristotle, McInerny argues that the narrow view of deliberation has no such consequence. In fact, it is the "best way of preserving ... the commitment to a non-reductive, non-technocratic, conception of practical reason."

In "Moral Terminology and Proportionalism," Janet Smith argues that the meaning of terms is especially crucial to the debate between contemporary proportionalists and those who defend a more robust action-guiding interpretation of Thomas on natural law. On a number of key terms, she shows that Thomas's meaning does not coincide with that of the proportionalists. Especially problematic is the latter's claim that, when Aquinas and the magisterium of the Church refer to intrinsically evil acts, they are speaking in merely "formal terms." According to the proportionalists, this makes any additional condemnation of the act tautologous. While not asserting a fact/value split in Aquinas, Smith argues that his references to intrinsically evil acts are initially descriptive rather than evaluative.

If Thomas's natural law teaching is more supple than many have thought, it remains to be considered to what extent it can be the basis of a common discourse. Building upon McInerny's interpretation of Maritain on "practical reason and ... first principles of the natural law," Michael Novak argues that Maritain's positive assessment of the American regime and his grounding of the universal declaration of human rights in an account of natural law "advance the tradition in a living, vital, and even lifegiving manner." In "The Gospels, Natural Law and the American Founding," Novak argues for the fundamental compatibility between Maritain and the American Founders on the nature of a good society, which according to Maritain must be personalist, communitarian, pluralist, and theist. But what sort of agreement on the natural law can a pluralist society have? Novak underscores the "difference between agreement in theory and agreement in practice." Even people who deny the existence of the natural law cannot help exemplifying it.

One of the most fruitful developments in recent ethics concerns the exploration of the connections between moral philosophy and literature.

Prompted by the unsettling spectacle of a mystery-writing philosopher, Stanley Hauerwas turned to mysteries and soon found himself hooked. With the help of McInerny, Chesterton, and Sayers, Hauerwas ("McInerny Did It, Or Should a Pacifist Read Murder Mysteries?") examines the significance of the genre of mystery and argues that it contains "an extraordinary metaphysical draft on the way things are. . . . a presumption that justice is deeper than injustice." Although mysteries give us no guarantee that justice will win out, they may convince us that we "are not irrational to hope that justice will be done." For all of us and especially for overly refined ethicists, mysteries provide a reminder of the "fundamental conviction that murder is wrong."

## METAPHYSICS

Drawing inspiration from McInerny's defense of the "capacity of human reason to arrive at a genuine, if partial, grasp of moral and religious truths," Laura Garcia argues that contemporary philosophers of religion have neglected an important resource in their encounters with unbelievers: natural theology. In "Religious Pluralism and Natural Theology," she grants to those who would defend religious belief as properly basic that this may be true for some believers some of the time. But the tendency to map all religious belief onto this model is misleading, especially in a modern world where nearly all believers are likely to confront plausible objections to their faith. One of the chief objections can be had from the fact of religious pluralism. In the absence of argument, we seem to be left with incommensurable basic beliefs held by members of different religions; philosophers like John Hick adduce this pluralism as an argument against the reasonableness of religious belief itself. As a way out of this difficulty, Garcia urges that we "take up the recently neglected projects of natural theology and apologetics and see if we can give Professor Hick a reason to believe."

Stressing the link between the reliability of our rational powers and theism, Alvin Plantinga opts for Thomas Reid, a "poor man's Aquinas," over David Hume on the issues of the reliability of our powers of sensation and cognition and of the reasonableness of believing in the existence of God ("Reid, Hume, and God"). Plantinga deploys Reid on behalf of the reasonableness of reposing prima facie trust in our senses and reasoning powers. As in Aristotle, so too "reasonable" here does not mean provable or amenable to the criteria of Cartesian certitude; as Reid notes, it was the inevitable failure of reason's attempt to prove its own reliability that got us into the modern epistemological mess in the first place. Hume's "multilayered reflexive skepticism" is the natural result of his succumbing to Cartesian assumptions and of his agnosticism. It turns out that only theism can account for the reliability of our faculties, since the view that our cognitive capacities have not been designed in a rational and benevolent manner, but instead have arisen by chance, puts the reliability of our faculties in serious question. Thus realism can be vindicated only by theism; and epistemological naturalism flourishes only in the context of supernatural theism.

If McInerny has consistently asserted that the "Catholic thinker can be expected to maintain the human mind's ability, even in a condition of sin, to grasp truths of the moral as well as speculative order" (*The Question of Christian Ethics*, p. 6), he has also stressed two other truths. First, "apart from the light and reinforcement it receives from a setting of grace and faith, natural reason is a feeble reed indeed on which to have to rely" ("On Behalf of Natural Theology," in *Being and Predication*, p. 257). Second, the activity of "philosophizing" is inseparable "from the moral context of the philosopher's life" (*The Question of Christian Ethics*, p. 60). The final two essays in the volume, by Freddoso and Burrell, investigate the latter truths. The metaphysics of pagan philosophy, Alfred Freddoso reminds us, aims at wisdom ("Two Roles for Catholic Philosophers"). But the pursuit of wisdom is also central to the Christian life. Indeed, medieval thinkers like Aquinas see "Christian wisdom as the real (albeit hidden) object of the quest for wisdom that the classical philosophical inquirers had initiated but had been incapable of bringing to fulfillment in the absence of Christian revelation." In light of this and without denying the distinction between faith and reason or between the natural and the supernatural, Freddoso argues that the first and chief role of the Catholic philosopher is to articulate and transmit Catholic wisdom in its entirety. A second role is to engage nonbelieving philosophers by using a variety of argumentative and rhetorical approaches. Since a more constricted view of philosophy is embodied in the curricula of Catholic universities, we must look for opportunities to subvert the institutionalized curricula.

David Burrell ("From the Analogy of 'Being' to the Analogy of Being") focuses on the topic of analogy, the topic on which McInerny wrote his first book and to which he has returned throughout his career. Crucial to the perfection of the natural operation of our reason is the habit of attending to the multiple, analogically related, senses of words. McInerny's great contribution is his insistence that analogy is for Aquinas primarily a logical doctrine. If we think of it first as a metaphysical doctrine, we are likely to confuse the order of naming with the order of being. Quoting McInerny, Burrell notes that what we "name last is ontologically first." The divine names reflect both the telos of our language and the gap between signifier and signified. They mark the "distinction" of God from creation and "remind us that there could be no such set of [analogous] terms were the universe not itself derived from a source from which all that is . . . flows." Since it is "never enough to identify a subset of terms which are susceptible of analogous usage," one must "always display them in use." Displaying in use involves, especially in the case of language about the unknown God, the judgment of a wise person who participates in a form of life that "does not reduce the 'unknowing' but rather offers a way of living with it." Burrell's essay marvelously confirms McInerny's observations about the importance of the existential setting of the life of philosophy. It also calls to mind—as do the lives and work of the other contributors to this volume—one of McInerny's favorite phrases from John of St. Thomas: *philosophandum in fide*.

For Ralph, *magister magistrorum*.

# Part I
# Natural Philosophy

# 1

# Quantification in Sixteenth-Century Natural Philosophy

*William A. Wallace, O.P.*

The thesis of this essay is that the scientific revolution of the seventeenth century grew directly out of progress made in the study of natural philosophy during the sixteenth century, particularly through the introduction of new techniques in quantification. This development had its beginnings at Oxford and Paris in the fourteenth and fifteenth centuries, but it reached its culmination in the Iberian peninsula and in Italy during the sixteenth century. It was in these regions that the obstacle presented by *metabasis*, that is, the use of mathematical principles in the study of nature, was successfully overcome.[1] Once *metabasis* ceased to be an obstacle, the way was prepared for a successful merging of the tradition of natural philosophy, which provided the main core of teaching in the universities, with the "quadrivial" tradition (including optics and Archimedean statics), then regarded as a necessary propaedeutic for university studies though playing a minor role in the curriculum. The main arena for this development was the study of motion and of force as the source of motion and of rest, although the study of light was also of some importance. In what follows I give most attention to the quantification of space, of motion, and of force; after this I offer briefer comments on the quantification of light as relevant to my thesis. I conclude with a more general reflection on the relation of the Aristotelian-Thomistic tradition to recent philosophy of science.

### THE QUANTIFICATION OF SPACE

Let me begin with the quantification of space. This would seem to be the least controversial, for Aristotle himself discussed space in the fourth book of his *Physics* and then dealt extensively with its quantitative parts in the sixth book, with his analysis of the continuum. Rather than focus on space, however, I would remark on Aristotle's definition of place, particularly as this was expounded by the sixteenth-century Dominican commentator, Domingo de Soto. Soto is a key figure in my thesis, for early in that century he had studied at the University of Paris and there learned all of the "calculatory" techniques worked out by the Oxford Mertonians and the *Doctores Parisienses* during the fourteenth and fifteenth centuries. Instead of using such techniques in solving *sophismata* or in exercises conceived only *secundum imaginationem,* as had been the fashion at Oxford, Soto applied them to problems in the real world. He once stated that he began his intellectual life at Paris among the nominalists, but that he was reared in Spain, as a Thomist, among the realists. Perhaps this explains why he spent most of his life working out the tensions between the nominalists and the realists, and in so doing made a significant contribution towards the development of a mathematical physics in the latter part of the century.[2]

Aristotle, as is well known, defined the place of an object as "the innermost motionless surface" of the medium containing it (212a 20–21). The problem this definition presents is one of understanding precisely what Aristotle meant by the term "motionless," since any physical medium can be, and usually is, in motion at any particular time. Soto exemplifies this with the air in his classroom, or the air surrounding Salamanca; these seem to change continually, although the place of the room and the city apparently do not.[3] His answer to the difficulty is that the "innermost surface" of the containing medium is not to be taken materially, as a surface of air or water or other matter, but rather formally, as a physical surface implying a relationship to the center of gravity and to the poles and the ultimate sphere of the universe. With such a frame of reference, the place of Salamanca can be specified in terms of latitude and longitude regardless of the particular medium surrounding it, and even were the city to change its place, say, in an earthquake, the new place, whatever the surrounding medium, would be "motionless" in the same reference frame. Essentially Soto interprets Aristotle's definition in terms of a system of polar coordinates, and this enables him to speak meaningfully about motion in a void between the sphere of the moon and the earth's surface, were God to annihilate the intervening matter, and so to identify positions throughout the entire universe.

The point may seem trivial, but let me jump some decades ahead to Rome, where the German Jesuit Christopher Clavius was teaching mathematics at the Collegio Romano.[4] Clavius had studied at Coimbra under Pedro Nuñez, and one of his colleagues was the Spaniard Francisco Toledo, who had been Soto's "favored disciple" at Salamanca. Both were imbued with the realist spirit then abroad on the Iberian peninsula, which encouraged them to take mathematics seriously when applied to nature. Well known is Clavius's interest in the physical reality of eccentrics or epicycles; perhaps less well known is his own determination of the place of the nova of 1572 beyond the sphere of the moon, and the implications he saw for this in understanding, and correcting, the *De caelo* of Aristotle, especially in its teaching on the incorruptibility of the heavens.

At this time controversy was abroad in Italy over the certitude of the mathematical sciences. Alessandro Piccolomini, who took issue with the mathematicians, denied that their disciplines could even be regarded as sciences in the strict sense of Aristotle's *Posterior Analytics*.[5] A few Jesuit philosophers at the Collegio, and Benito Pereira was one, embraced the anti-mathematical side in the controversy. In effect Pereira revived the *metabasis* prohibition of earlier centuries and attempted to proscribe the use of mathematical argument in natural philosophy. Clavius successfully overcame Pereira's opposition and influenced a series of young Jesuit professors at the Collegio—Antonius Menu, Paulus Vallius, Muzio Vitelleschi, and Ludovicus Rugerius—to incorporate his mathematical demonstrations into their treatises on the *Physics* and the *De caelo*. This they did, even though it enormously complicated their analyses of the alterability and the corruptibility of the heavens. The young Galileo, as I have argued elsewhere, appropriated their teaching notes, with interesting consequences, of which more later.[6]

Part of the Italian controversy over the mathematical sciences was about the validity of what I shall call "positional mechanics," the Renaissance treatment of statical problems similar to Jordanus Nemorarius's *Scientia de ponderibus*, though worked out more thoroughly in the tradition of Archimedes and the *Quaestiones mechanicae* of the Aristotelian school. Clavius left no treatises on this subject, but one of his students, Giuseppe Biancani, S.J., did. Biancani later taught at Parma, where the famous astronomer Giambattista Riccioli, S.J., was in turn his student. The treatises written by Biancani on the mathematical and the physico-mathematical sciences justify them as conforming to the norms of the *Posterior Analytics*.[7] Not only that, but commentaries on the *Posterior Analytics* by Vallius, Vitelleschi, and Rugerius expand greatly the space allocated to the foreknowledge required for demonstration, devoting particular attention to the *suppositiones* employed in the "mixed sciences" and how they come to be certified.[8] The young Galileo was acquainted with these commentaries also, and indeed copied out Vallius's lectures on *De praecognitionibus* and *De demonstratione* in his little-known logical treatises, which I published only in the last decade.[9]

## THE QUANTIFICATION OF MOTION

Positional astronomy and positional mechanics, based as they were on the quantification of physical space, advanced considerably in the sixteenth century. They were merely propaedeutic, however, to an even greater advance in the quantification of motion. The fourteenth century had seen important beginnings in this area with the introduction of the "mean-speed theorem" and various calculatory treatises on the ratios of motions. As far as we know, none of these progressed substantially beyond the status of imaginative mathematical exercises. At sixteenth-century Paris, however, a definite change took place. Natural philosophers there—John Major, John Dullaert of Ghent, Juan de Celaya, to name a few—incorporated these techniques of quantification into their commentaries and "questionaries" on Aristotle's *Physics*.[10] Domingo de Soto had studied under Celaya at Paris and brought these analytical methods back to Spain, and eventually to Salamanca, in his own teaching of natural philosophy. Soto is justly famous for being the first, as far as is known, to apply correctly the expression *uniformiter difformis* to falling motion.[11] Around 1550, in his questions on the *Physics*, he described the free fall of a heavy body as uniformly accelerated, and gave figures showing that he interpreted this as velocity increasing in direct proportion to the time of fall.[12]

There has been some question as to how widely diffused was Soto's teaching later in the sixteenth century. His *Physics* was reprinted seven times in Spain and Italy, and later in Douay, into the early seventeenth century, and thus was available for anyone to read. More significant, in my view, is the fact that his analysis of free fall was taken up and developed in a number of manuscripts by Jesuits at Coimbra and at Evora, in Portugal, and also cited approvingly by Rugerius at the Collegio Romano.[13] The teaching, therefore, was very much alive. The problem is whether or not it was ever experimentally verified, and how it came to be passed on to Galileo, if indeed it was.

Before coming to that, I would call attention to another development relating to the quantitative description of motion: the difference between rectilinear and circular motion and how this might be applied to the natural and violent motions of elemental bodies. With regard to rectilinear motion, the downward motion of a heavy body, i.e., that toward the center of gravity, would be natural, whereas its upward motion, that away from the center, would be violent. For fire, the lightest body, the opposite would be true, but here a more interesting case presents itself. As fire recedes naturally from the center of gravity toward the sphere of the moon, it ultimately comes to that sphere, and then can only move in a circle. This was not thought to be unusual by Aristotelians, for fire would then seem to be taking on a motion *praeter naturam*, one above its nature, yet similar to that of the heavenly bodies. Albert of Saxony even speculated that as fire approached the lunar sphere its motion would become composite, involving both a rectilinear natural motion and a circular preternatural motion, thereby adumbrating the "superposition theorem" of modern mechanics.

But the key question is this: granted that the motion of fire at the sphere of the moon is circular, is such a motion natural or violent? The question has a long history with Greek and Arab commentators, and among the Latins was discussed by Albertus Magnus,[14] Thomas Aquinas, Albert of Saxony, and Nicole Oresme. In northern Italy it occupied the attention of Paul of Venice and Pietro d'Abano, and then, in the sixteenth century, was discussed by Marcantonio Zimara, Jacopo Zabarella, and the Jesuits of the Collegio Romano. The general answer that emerged was that the circular motion of fire (and indeed of any element, whether at the sphere of the moon or not), is neither natural nor violent, but is actually a third type intermediate between the two, variously identified as neutral, indifferent, or middle motion. The Jesuit Vitelleschi even speculated that such *motus medius,* once started in a resistanceless medium, would be uniform and perpetual, since nature would neither increase it nor diminish it, so long as it maintained the same distance from the center of gravity. This comes close to the idea of "circular inertia," adumbrated in Galileo's early *De motu* manuscripts and long thought to have been completely original with him. What is remarkable is that Galileo's notes on *De caelo,* based on these Jesuit lectures, reveal a prior knowledge of this neutral motion, even apart from his reference to it in the *De motu antiquiora.*[15]

THE QUANTIFICATION OF FORCE

Having introduced the notion of nature acting to increase or diminish a motion, I pass from the quantification of space and of motion to the next consideration, the quantification of force. In positional mechanics, static forces had been quantified from the time of Archimedes onward, and they had received fuller development in the Middle Ages with the work of Jordanus and others. Here I wish to consider dynamic forces, those associated with motion, in the sense employed by Aristotle in the fourth and seventh books of his *Physics.* These had been considered in fourteenth-century Oxford and Paris, but mainly *secundum imaginationem* and without specific reference to real forces operative in the world of nature.

Here too Domingo de Soto provides a starting point for the sixteenth-century development. The setting in which he worked was different from that of the fourteenth century, for by this time John Philoponus's commentary on the *Physics* had become available in the Latin West. In this commentary Philoponus introduced the notion that nature itself was a *vis* or force operative from within a substance and causing it to have its characteristic activities.[16] Now Soto had adopted the nominalist solution to the projectile problem, which taught that the projectile was not moved by the surrounding medium (as Aristotle himself had held), but rather by an impetus placed in the projectile by an external agent, the projector. Thomists at the time were divided on Aquinas's teaching in this matter, for in some texts St. Thomas seems to employ impetus whereas in others he seems to reject it. Soto favored the former interpretation, attributing the impetus doctrine to Aquinas, and then explained it in the following way. Impetus was like a force impressed on the projectile, which, after it left the projector, moved the projectile from within in much the same way as the *gravitas*, or *vis gravitatis*, moves the heavy object from within during its fall towards the center of gravity.[17] During the fall of the object, Soto held, its natural gravity remains the same, but its accidental gravity, namely, that acquired through the impetus of its fall, gradually builds up, and this serves to explain why the body accelerates as it approaches the center of gravity.[18] Thus force came to be, for Soto, a key causal factor in explaining why bodies move the way they do in both natural and forced motion.

These ideas were assimilated by the Roman Jesuits, as I have pointed out elsewhere, for one can find references to motive forces, resistive forces, and even occult forces in their notes on the motion of heavy bodies.[19] They offered a variety of teachings on the nature of impetus or *virtus impressa*, and on how this type of force can be used to explain phenomena not otherwise explicable with Aristotelian principles. When accounting for velocity increase with time of fall, surely a difficult problem, they combined motive and resistive forces in a distinctive way. Vitelleschi, for example, rejected the explanation offered by Galileo in his *De motu antiquiora*, where the Pisan physicist held that the increase occurs only at the beginning of the motion because there it gradually overcomes a residual lightness, a *privatio gravitatis*, left in the body by reason of its position. One might regard this as a type of internal resistance that has to be overcome before the falling body can reach its terminal velocity. Following Zabarella, Vitelleschi invokes an external resistive force as well. In his view, the falling body impels the medium in such a way that it offers less and less resistance to the body's motion; thus, the farther the body falls the faster it moves. This comes about, in his account as in Zabarella's, because the velocity of any motion results from an excess of the motive force over the resistance encountered; therefore the velocity of fall increases as the *vis gravitatis* builds up and the resistance grows less.

Such quantification of force, admittedly proposed only in a general way, found echo in a contemporary development in northern Italy, that of the Venetian mathematician and physicist Giovan Battista Benedetti, who is generally thought to have influenced Galileo's early writings on motion.[20] Like Soto and late sixteenth-century Jesuits, Benedetti used internal forces to account for projectile and gravitational phenomena, and combined them in ways that suggest a knowledge of the superposition theorem. He argued, as did Galileo, that velocity of fall is dependent not on weight but on specific gravity, and that all bodies will fall with the same speed *in vacuo*, where buoyancy and resistive effects can be neglected. Gravity and levity became for Benedetti relative concepts, so that for him, as for Archimedes and the Jesuit Vallius, air has no weight in air, nor water in water. And he analyzed the case of a body falling through the center of the earth to conclude that it would oscillate about the center, on the analogy of the motion of the bob of a pendulum of exceedingly long length.

These discussions of falling bodies are of interest for the proportionalities they suggest between motive and resistive forces, but they do not address the more important problem of measurement and experimental confirmation. Here I return again to Domingo de Soto to bring out a point I have made in a study of Benedetti. Benedetti's father was a Spaniard, and Benedetti himself was the friend of a Spanish Dominican, Petrus Arches, whom he praises lavishly in his *Resolutio* of 1553 and his *Demonstratio proportionum motuum localium contra Aristotelem et omnes philosophos* of 1554. It was Arches, in fact, who told Benedetti that criticisms of Aristotle's dynamic laws were being discussed in Rome the summer before Benedetti prepared his *Demonstratio*. Perhaps Arches knew of a work then just published at Brescia, in which the author, Giovanni Battista Bellasco, inquired why a ball of iron and one of wood fall to the ground at the same time. Soto himself does not give experimental support for his *uniformiter difformis* doctrine, but it is noteworthy that around the time of his writing there was some discussion of empirical evidence. As early as 1544 tests were being performed to show that Aristotle was wrong in his claim that heavy bodies will fall to the ground at speeds directly proportional to their weights. Benedetto Varchi, in his *Questioni sull'Alchimia*, finished by that date, states that the Dominican Francesco Beato, a philosopher at Pisa, had disproved Aristotle's claim. Shortly thereafter, and before finishing his *Physics* "questionary," Soto himself was in northern Italy attending the Council of Trent. The fact that he, Beato, and Arches were all Dominicans enhances the possibility of their sharing knowledge of these results.[21] And, of course, in 1575, Girolamo Borro, who was later to teach Galileo at Pisa, had stated that his experiments showed that a piece of wood reached the ground before a piece of lead, when both were projected from a second-story window. Only a year later, at Padua, Galileo's predecessor there, Giuseppi Moletti, reported a test in which a lead ball and a wooden ball, both of the same size, were released from a height and seen to reach the ground at the same moment of time. Very rough measurements, one might say, yet sufficient to refute Aristotle as an authority in the matter of free fall, and to set the parameters for further research.

More important, in my view, was the discussion of the *suppositiones* one must employ to have demonstrations in a mathematical physics based on such experimental findings. These are touched on in the Jesuit logic notes,[22] but they are much further developed by Benedetti and Galileo in the context of their treatment of impediments presented by the earth's geometry and various resistive effects. To my knowledge Benedetti does not discuss neutral motion, i.e., that intermediate between natural and violent motion, but for him horizontal motion for limited distances on the earth's surface would answer to that description. His basic thesis was that the only truly natural motion must be circular, for this alone can be perpetual. But, he reasons, there is no noteworthy difference between a perfect sphere and a plane surface of small extent. This explains why one will encounter no difficulty in moving a sphere along a horizontal surface; indeed, it can be moved by "a force no matter how small." In another context he qualifies an argument to specify that it holds only "when all impediment is removed." These techniques are remarkably similar to Galileo's, as I have abundantly documented in my *Galileo and His Sources*.[23] The transition from impetus theory to the principle of inertia came about in Galileo's later writings, where he could regard motions in a circle of large radius or over short distances as rectilinear, and could state that they could be initiated and maintained by "a force smaller than any given force." Effectively Galileo was able to eliminate the horizontal *vis* in intermediate motion, maintain that a body moving uniformly in a horizontal direction would not be constrained either to increase or to decrease its velocity, and so would continue to move uniformly, thus anticipating what would later be called Newton's first law of motion.

### THE QUANTIFICATION OF LIGHT

This leads to my final topic, the quantification of light. It is not my intention to deal with theories of vision, as these have been adequately treated in the literature.[24] I intend merely to consider light under the aspect of the intensification of forms, to show how Soto's expression *uniformiter difformis* came to be applied by late sixteenth-century Jesuits to optical phenomena.

The first person of interest here is Andeas Eudaemon-Ioannes, S.J., who taught physics at the Collegio Romano in 1597–98, and who left treatises on action and passion and on the motion of projectiles, both written in the manner of the *Calculatores*.[25] His treatise on action and passion generalizes the expression *uniformiter difformis* so that it can be applied to all cases of physical agency. Aware that this is a work in mathematical physics, he first notes that some propositions from his physical disputations will be presupposed, and that here his immediate objective is to note and prove propositions pertaining to mathematics. His first *suppositio* is the key one: every natural agent acts *uniformiter difformis* on a quantified subject when applied to it. The justification for this is that physicists commonly concede it, because one sees that an agent when close acts more vehemently and when farther away less so; therefore, the closer the greater, the farther the lesser; therefore, as distance increases, action decreases; therefore the action itself is *uniformiter difformis*.

We need not enter into the mathematical details of the thirty-one propositions Eudaemon deduces from this, some with a substantial number of corollaries. Suffice it to mention that he retained his interest in impetus theory after leaving Rome and, while at Padua in the first decade of the seventeenth century, discussed the famous "ship's mast" experiment with Galileo. It was to this "Father Andreas" that Galileo confided that he actually performed the experiment, although he later denied that he had done so in the *Dialogue* of 1632 on the grounds that he did not have to experiment to be assured of its truth.[26]

I shall finally mention the work of Franciscus Aquilonis, a Belgian Jesuit who had completed his theology studies at Salamanca in the late 1590s.[27] Clavius had written a large number of treatises in applied mathematics but had never treated optics. Aquilonis set for himself the task of completing Clavius's *opera*, and out of this effort emerged his *Opticorum libri sex*, published at Antwerp in 1613. The fifth book of this work, dealing with the propagation of light, is written in the calculatory manner of Eudaemon's treatises, and shows the precise way in which light diminishes "uniformly difformly" as it is propagated from its source. This is the beginning of an important Jesuit tradition in optics, culminating in the *Physico-mathesis de lumine* of Francesco Mario Grimaldi, S.J., published in 1665 and now regarded as a key work in the modern development of that science.

### AN ARISTOTELIAN-THOMISTIC POSTSCRIPT

What I have given is a quick overview of quantification in sixteenth-century natural philosophy, with main attention to motion and briefer notes on light. By the end of the sixteenth century there seems little doubt that methodological canons and conceptual apparatus for a mathematical physics of motion and of light were already at hand. It remained, of course, for the mature Galileo, plus Kepler, Newton, and others to develop these ideas into the "new sciences" of mechanics and optics that came to flourish in seventeenth-century Europe. Scholars working in this later period of the scientific revolution frequently express doubt about its indebtedness to the sixteenth century. If one knows nothing about that century, surely it is easy to pass it over in silence. But for those acquainted with it, it can be seen and studied for what it truly was: a period of transition from the medieval to the early modern, one of singular value for the history and philosophy of science.

Another point should also be made. This is that much of what has just been presented emerged from the Aristotelian-Thomistic tradition, a tradition that historians and philosophers of science have much maligned in the past. Soto, of course, represents the Thomistic tradition at its best, and the Jesuits mentioned above, who worked mainly in the first decades of the society's existence, took seriously St. Ignatius's injunction to follow the teachings of both Aristotle and St. Thomas Aquinas. One could argue that their work, linked as it was to the methodological advances at Padua preserved in Zabarella's logical treatises, marked the zenith of that tradition's development—soon to come under attack and shunted aside, unfortunately, by the Jesuits' most famous student, René Descartes.

What was important about these sixteenth-century thinkers is that they recognized that the study of quantity pertains not only to mathematics but to natural philosophy and metaphysics as well. Quantity is an integral part of a thing's nature, and important for the fact that physical quantity is the intermediate through which the powers and sensible qualities proper to corporeal natures come to exist within their structures. In the sixteenth century little was known in detail about the powers that are proper to natural kinds—inorganic, plant, animal, and human. This was particularly true of the inorganic, though a start had been made on the *vis gravitatis,* the power or force of gravity. The application of mathematical reasoning to that power was Newton's supreme achievement and pointed the way to quantitative principles that would underlie the modern sciences of physics, astronomy, chemistry, geology, and ultimately molecular biology. In my *The Modeling of Nature* I have sketched the tortuous path that led from the power of gravity to the four forces of high-energy physics that ground all recent speculation about our cosmos, and then to the higher powers whereby these are related to the plant and animal kingdoms.[28] I have also sketched the major demonstrations that enabled us to progress from knowing mountains on the moon to knowing the

DNA molecule.[29] The middle terms of these demonstrations are in all cases quantitative, that is, based on physical quantity, but manipulated by mathematical reasoning to yield a result that is true in the world of nature.

The importance of the mathematical premises in this type of reasoning cannot be overstated. In the demonstrative regress (*regressus*), as developed by Zabarella and employed with consummate skill by Galileo, the same middle term appears in both the mathematical and the physical premise of each demonstration.[30] What is essential to the regressive process is showing that the middle term is convertible with the predicate in at least one of the premises. Aristotle's own example of how this is done is the proof of the moon's being a sphere from its having phases (*Posterior Analytics*, I, 13). That a spherical shape *alone*, of all possible solid surfaces that are externally illuminated, is able to produce the appearances of crescent, half, gibbous, and full phases may not be readily *seen* by the naturalist, but it can be quickly *demonstrated* by the mathematician in a branch of study known as projective geometry. Quantitative convertibility is far easier to see than convertibility in any other category. And it is precisely that type of convertibility that is manifested in the key demonstrations sketched in *The Modeling of Nature*.

Four hundred years ago these demonstrations, had they been available, *per impossibile*, to natural philosophers, would have been understood by them and provided the basis for substantial restructuring of the special books of Aristotle's *libri naturales*. In the present day, especially when Aristotle's foundational treatises, the *Physics* and *De anima*, are largely *terra incognita* to philosophers, one would be rash to think of such restructuring as readily feasible. The situation is exacerbated by the fact that scientists have been brainwashed for centuries to picture the world in Cartesian coordinates, to see it as quality-less, power-less, and nature-less, extended as far as one wishes in $n$-dimensions, not one of which differs essentially from any other. But the challenge of restoring four centuries of forgetfulness of this once fruitful tradition is now there. It has to be faced by anyone who would bring both philosophy and science back to the world of nature and to all the wonders it presents to the modern mind.

NOTES

1. For an explanation of this concept, see Steven J. Livesey, "*Metabasis:* The Interrelationship of the Sciences in Antiquity and the Middle Ages," Ph.D. dissertation, The University of California, Los Angeles, 1982. See also his "The Oxford Calculators,

Quantification and Qualities, and Aristotle's Prohibition of *metabasis*," *Vivarium* 24 (1986), 50–69.

2. Details are given in my "Domingo de Soto and the Iberian Roots of Galileo's Science," in *Hispanic Philosophy in the Age of Discovery*, ed. Kevin White, Studies in Philosophy and the History of Philosophy, 19 (Washington, D.C.: The Catholic University of America Press, 1997), 113–29. For introductory materials relating to Soto's commentary and questions on the *Physics* of Aristotle, see my "Domingo de Soto's 'Laws' of Motion: Text and Context," in *Texts and Contexts in Ancient and Medieval Science: Studies on the Occasion of John E. Murdoch's Seventieth Birthday*, ed. Edith Sylla and Michael McVaugh (Leiden: E. J. Brill, 1997), 271–304.

3. In his first question on Book IV of Aristotle's *Physics*, fols. 58v–61r of the 1555 edition.

4. A recent study that supplies basic information about Clavius is James M. Lattis's *Between Copernicus and Galileo: Christoph Clavius and the Collapse of Ptolemaic Astronomy* (Chicago and London: University of Chicago Press, 1994).

5. For the definitive study of this controversy, see Anna De Pace, *Le Matematiche e il Mondo: Ricerche su un dibattito in Italia nella seconda metà del Cinquecento* (Milan: FrancoAngeli, 1993), esp. 21–75.

6. The main conclusions are given in my *Galileo and His Sources: The Heritage of the Collegio Romano in Galileo's Science* (Princeton: Princeton University Press, 1984). Details of some of the appropriated texts will be found in my *Galileo's Early Notebooks: The Physical Questions: A Translation from the Latin, with Historical and Paleographical Commentary* (Notre Dame: University of Notre Dame Press, 1977).

7. *Galileo and His Sources*, esp. 126–48 and 202–16.

8. This development is described in my "Aristotle and Galileo: The Uses of *Hupothesis* (*Suppositio*) in Scientific Reasoning," in *Studies in Aristotle*, ed. D. J. O'Meara, Studies in Philosophy and the History of Philosophy, 9 (Washington, D.C.: The Catholic University of America Press, 1981), 47–77. This article has been reprinted as Essay 3 in my *Galileo, the Jesuits and the Medieval Aristotle*, Collected Studies Series. CS346 (Aldershot, U.K.: Variorum Publishing, 1991).

9. The Latin text is given in Galileo Galilei, *Tractatio de praecognitionibus et praecognitis* and *Tractatio de demonstratione*, transcribed from the Latin autograph by W. F. Edwards, with an introduction, notes, and commentary by W. A. Wallace (Padua: Editrice Antenore, 1988). This is translated in my *Galileo's Logical Questions: A Translation, with Notes and Commentary, of His Appropriated Latin Questions on Aristotle's* Posterior Analytics, Boston Studies in the Philosophy of Science, 138 (Dordrecht-Boston-London: Kluwer Academic Publishers, 1992).

10. I have sketched various aspects of this development in my *Prelude to Galileo: Essays on Medieval and Sixteenth-Century Sources of Galileo's Thought*, Boston Studies in the Philosophy of Science, 62 (Dordrecht-Boston: D. Reidel Publishing Company, 1981).

11. Details are given in my "The Enigma of Domingo de Soto: *Uniformiter difformis* and Falling Bodies in Late Medieval Physics," *Isis* 59 (1968), 384–401, reprinted in my *Prelude to Galileo* (note 10 above), 91–109.

12. Additional details relating to Soto's calculations will be found in my "Domingo de Soto's 'Laws' of Motion: Text and Context" (note 2 above).

13. The Portuguese manuscripts are discussed in my "Late Sixteenth-Century Por-

tuguese Manuscripts Relating to Galileo's Early Notebooks," *Revista Portuguesa de Filosofia* 51 (1995), 677–98. They are also analyzed in the essay cited in the previous note.

14. Albert the Great seems to have initiated treatments of this problem in the Latin West. See my "Galileo's Citations of Albert the Great," *Albert the Great: Commemorative Essays*, eds. F. J. Kovach and R. W. Shahan (Norman: University of Oklahoma Press, 1980), 261–83; reprinted in *Prelude to Galileo* (note 10 above), 264–85.

15. See *Prelude to Galileo*, 270–74, with the additional references cited therein.

16. Philoponus's teaching on nature is sketched in Essay 13 of *Prelude to Galileo* (note 10 above), entitled "Galileo and the Causality of Nature"; see p. 290.

17. In his questions on the *Physics* of Aristotle, Bk. 8, quest. 3. This teaching and that of other Thomists on the projectile problem are discussed by James A. Weisheipl in his *Nature and Motion in the Middle Ages*, ed. William E. Carroll, Studies in Philosophy and the History of Philosophy, 11 (Washington, D.C.: Catholic University of America Press, 1985), 68–69.

18. This teaching is touched on by Soto in his commentary on the *Physics* of Aristotle, Bk. 8, chap. 9, text 76, and by Jesuit commentators who appropriated his teachings; see my "Domingo de Soto's 'Laws' of Motion: Text and Context" (note 2 above), 303–4.

19. See my "Causes and Forces in Sixteenth-Century Physics," *Isis* 69 (1978), 400–412, reprinted in *Prelude to Galileo*, 110–26; also *Galileo and His Sources* (note 6 above), 191–202.

20. For Benedetti's views, see my "Science and Philosophy at the Collegio Romano in the Time of Benedetti," in *Cultura, Scienze et Techniche nella Venezia del Cinquecento*, Atti del Convegno Internazionale di Studio "G. B. Benedetti e il suo tempo" (Venice: Istituto Veneto di Scienze, Lettere ed Arti, 1987), 113–26; reprinted as Essay 8 in *Galileo, the Jesuits, and the Medieval Aristotle* (note 8 above).

21. For more particulars, see notes 66 and 67 to the essay cited in the previous note.

22. For the Jesuit teachings appropriated by Galileo, see *Galileo and His Sources* (note 6 above), 112–14; also "Aristotle and Galileo: The Uses of *Hupothesis* (*Suppositio*) in Scientific Reasoning" (note 8 above).

23. See pp. 230–54.

24. See David C. Lindberg, *Theories of Vision from al-Kindi to Kepler* (Chicago: University of Chicago Press, 1976).

25. On Eudaemon's "calculatory" treatises, see my "The Early Jesuits and the Heritage of Domingo de Soto," *History and Technology* 4 (1987), 301–20, esp. 306–8, reprinted as Essay 6 in *Galileo, the Jesuits, and the Medieval Aristotle* (note 8 above).

26. See *Galileo and His Sources* (note 6 above), 269–71.

27. The optical work of Aquilonis, better known as François de Aguilon, is sketched in "The Early Jesuits and the Heritage of Domingo de Soto" (note 23), 311–12. He is the subject of a monograph by August Ziggelaar, S.J., *François de Aguilon, S.J. (1567–1617)* (Rome: Institutum Historicum S.I., 1983).

28. This in the first five chapters. The full title of the work is *The Modeling of Nature: Philosophy of Science and Philosophy of Nature in Synthesis* (Washington, D.C.: Catholic University of America Press, 1996).

29. In chapters 9 and 10, after the necessary logical apparatus has been set up in chapters 7 and 8.

30. A concise explanation of the regress is given in *The Modeling of Nature*, 300–308. For a full account of the method in the history of science, see my "Galileo's Regressive Methodology: Its Prelude and Its Sequel" in *Method and Order in Renaissance Philosophy of Nature: The Aristotle Commentary Tradition*, ed. D. A. Lisca, Ekhard Kessler, and Charlotte Methuen (Aldershot, U.K.: Ashgate, 1997), 229–52. Also relevant is my "Circularity and the Demonstrative *Regressus:* From Pietro d'Abano to Galileo Galilei," *Vivarium* 33.1 (1995), 76–97.

# 2

# The Failure of Positivism and the Enduring Legacy of Comte

*Jude P. Dougherty*

I

A reader of the excellent recently published biography of Désiré Cardinal Mercier by David A. Boileau[1] may be struck by the volume's multiple references to Comte, who is cited on at least twenty-five pages. Comte's philosophy was the reigning philosophy of the day when Mercier began the study of theology in 1873 at Louvain. Directly challenging Mercier's vocation, Auguste Comte proclaimed that men must forgo theological and metaphysical speculation to concentrate on observation of facts if they are to arrive at intellectual maturity. Although Comte belonged to the first half of the nineteenth century, his gospel was promulgated in the latter half by his disciples, notably Taine and Durkheim. This is not the place to recount Mercier's professional struggle with the epistemological issues which led Comte to metaphysical agnosticism and Mercier himself to the philosophical realism of Aristotle and Aquinas.[2]

The aim of this essay is to suggest that Comte's positivism, grounded as it was in the British empiricism of the day, not only ruled out metaphysics but ruled out theoretical physics as well and both for the same reason—Comte's denial of the efficacy of causal reasoning. According to Comte, physics errs as does metaphysics when it postulates abstract entities as explanatory causes. We are reminded of Etienne Gilson's remark that metaphysics has a way of burying its undertakers. We can add to that the observation that the success of nineteenth- and twentieth-century theoretical physics has laid to rest positivism as a philosophy of science.

It needs to be said, however, that while events of the past century have undermined the empiricists' foundation of positivism, the outlook is apt to survive any and all critiques for reasons that have little to do with the philosophy of science. Comte, generally accorded the title "Father of Positivism," is also regarded as one of the progenitors of sociology. Influenced by Locke and

Hume and for a time materially supported by Mill, Comte recognized the social implications of the empiricism emanating from the British Isles, implications which led directly to a secular humanism which he codified in his "religion of humanity." Although Comte's interests led him away from the philosophy of science per se and into the field of sociology, the term he coined came to be used in the wider sense of a philosophy of knowledge which limited knowledge to sensory experience.

It is positivism in the wider sense and not Comte's social philosophy which is the subject of this enquiry, although the two are intertwined. It is the thesis of this essay that Comte's social philosophy rests on a philosophy of science long outmoded, but his influence, direct or indirect, remains formidable in the social sciences. In many respects Comte was a product of his age, unifying an outlook which had already gained acceptance among the intelligentsia. Ancient truths about nature, human nature, and cognitive ability had already been successfully challenged by eighteenth-century philosophers on both sides of the channel, ostensibly with the support of the newly ascendant mathematical sciences of nature.

II

Reflections on the nature and capacity of human knowledge did not await the advent of eighteenth-century mathematical physics. Plato's discussion of science and the claims to knowledge by the Greeks will forever remain a starting point for the philosophy of science. It was Plato who bequeathed to Western philosophy the insight that all science is of the universal. Aristotle concurred, but he found the universal not in some unseen realm of archetypes but in the nature common to members of the species. Aristotle taught that by a process of abstraction we come to know the essence, nature, or quiddity of a thing, prescinding from its accidental features, which it may or may not have while remaining the thing that it is. Such is the object of science, the nature of an entity, the structure of a process, their properties and potentialities. Yet to have scientific knowledge is not simply to know what is, not simply to have uncovered a law of nature. For Aristotle, to have scientific knowledge is to know the entity, process, or property in the light of its cause or causes. Presupposed by Aristotle are two principles: the principle of substance and the principle of causality, both principles rejected by the British empiricists.

Positivism, in whatever specific form it takes, in effect denies at once the intelligibility of nature and the power of intellect to grasp "the more" that is given in the sense report. A contemporary Aristotelian, by contrast, will affirm that there is more in the sense report than the senses themselves are formally able to appreciate. Locke, in denying the reality of substance, reduces what we call substance to a constellation of events or sense reports. According to Locke, we use terms which imply substances, but this usage is merely a shorthand way of pointing to something without repeating at length all the properties we associate with that something or constellation.

Hume's account of causality similarly limits knowledge to a simple sense report. We experience succession, Hume tells us, not causality. "Cause" is the name we give to the antecedent, contiguous in place, continuous in time, and habitually associated with the consequent which we designate "effect."

If there are no natures or substances independent of the mind's creating them, if there is no causality, the enterprise called metaphysics collapses. For after all, metaphysics is based on the assumption that the realm of being is greater or wider in designation than the being reported by the senses. If the material order reported by the senses is all there is, then the most general science of reality is natural philosophy or the philosophy of nature. If there is an immaterial order of being as well as the material world of sense, then the most general science is the philosophy of being, also known as metaphysics or ontology. One can conclude to or reach the immaterial order only by a process of reasoning. Such reasoning has led mankind through the ages to affirm the existence of God, to posit an immaterial component of human knowing and a spiritual or immaterial soul.

It is not the purpose of this essay to argue for the existence of a transcendent realm but to suggest that the same sort of reasoning that leads one to affirm the existence of God also leads one to affirm the existence of the submicroscopic. As Comte himself recognized, causal reasoning is common to both natural theology and theoretical physics. The efficacy of causal reasoning is dramatically seen in those sciences where the postulated entities of one generation become the encountered ones of another. It can be shown that limiting knowledge to the sense report has implications not only for the natural sciences but for law, the social sciences, and theology as well. On a strict positivist account, science is in effect reduced to description and prediction, the social sciences are denied their object, "human nature," and of course natural theology is denied its object since there is no way to reason to the existence of God.

The questions which Mercier addressed are these: Do the natural sciences actually limit themselves to or conform to the positivist equation of knowledge with the empirically given? Is there not more to physics, chemistry, biology, and astronomy than mere description and prediction? We attempt to show that there is. But first a remark on the success of positivism as a theory of knowledge. Perhaps, viewed historically, it would be better called a program.

Auguste Comte was not a socially disinterested philosopher of knowledge. Positivism is a form of materialism, and many philosophers of the eighteenth and nineteenth centuries were perfectly willing to shed the notions of "God," an "ordered nature," and an "immaterial realm" for social and political reasons. If man is not accountable to a nature created and ordered by a benevolent God, many strictures are removed, institutions even rendered obsolete. It is not that in times past philosophy taught all that ecclesial authorities proclaimed about the source and end of human life, but as long as philosophy claimed an ability to reason to a first efficient cause and an ultimate final cause, it served as a prolegomena, if not a prop, for theology and religion. Comte himself wished to replace an inherited Christianity with his own "religion of humanity." H. G. Wells is reputed to have said that what Comte wanted was Catholicism without Christianity.

In the rush to embrace an iconoclastic epistemology, many of Comte's disciples failed to pay much attention to actual practice in the sciences. Hume notwithstanding, reasoning on a causal basis from the observed to the unobserved was and is common practice in the natural sciences. The existence of bacteria was inferred long before the microscope displayed their reality. In physics and chemistry molecular structures were inferred long before electron microscopes and particle accelerators graphically confirmed their reality. It is not misleading to say that in physics causal explanation is taken for granted. The encountered is routinely explained by that which is not encountered. No one who looks at the course of nineteenth- and twentieth-century theoretical physics can affirm that science is simply description and prediction. Molecular biology is replete with examples of once-inferred structures falling within the range of the observable with the passage of time. Clearly there is more to causality than Hume would allow. To search for an explanation is to look for a cause. While Comte did not fully embrace the skepticism of Hume, he did hold that scientific theories are merely the coordination of observed facts. The sciences, he tells us, subsume phenomena as observed facts which are descriptive, not explanatory.

The status of theories and conceptual schema is the central issue between realism and positivism in the philosophy of science. Much of what we know in contemporary theoretical physics is known by inference. Molecules, atoms, electrons, protons, neutrons, mesons, and their activity are inferred. In talking about them we form conceptual schema which the positivist, heir to centuries-old nominalism, treats as convenient ways of handling complex data. On the positivist's account, the conceptual scheme of "atom" is a mere convenience. The data are real enough; they are given in measurements of one sort or another, but to posit a nonexperienced source is to make an unwarranted intellectual leap. To interpret data as flowing from a structure independent of the mind is to go beyond what is given in experience. Contrary to this scenario offered by the contemporary heirs of Auguste Comte, Henri Poincaré, and Ernst Mach such as Hilary Putnam and Larry Laudan, it can be argued that Aristotle's philosophy of knowledge provides us with the basis for a realistic interpretation of our scientific knowledge of nature.

At the root of the positivist's account of science is the acceptance of Hume's notion of causality. Science, on Hume's principles, is reduced to description and prediction. But contemporary philosophy of science has a difficult time holding on to a Humean conception of causality. No physicist is content with merely describing sequence. The inquisitive mind looks for explanations. Structures are inferred. The difference in kind among natural structures is said to account for difference in phenomena. In attempts at explanation, structures are usually given visual representation; data are usually expressed in equations and linked to an imagined structure. While much of what we know about atomic phenomena can be expressed mathematically, such knowledge lacks explanatory power unless it is linked to a mechanism thought to be responsible for that which is measured.[3] The inferred mechanism is presented diagrammatically, schematically, or pictorially by means of a model. Modeling requires images. Commonly recognized are two types of models, iconic and sentential. A picture, or a diagram, is an iconic model; an equation, like other statements, is a sentential representation of something judged to be the case. Not everything we know can be expressed sententially. That we also think by means of pictures and diagrams is something Aristotle recognized when he described thinking as consisting of both imagination and judgment.

III

For the purpose of illustration permit me to relate an episode in the history of science which I take to be a rich source of relevant material. In late December 1938, Lise Meitner and her nephew Otto Frisch, one a theoretical chemist, the other a physicist, walked in the woods near Göteborg, Sweden. The problem before them was one created by the German physicists Otto Hahn and Fritz Strassmann, namely, the seeming formation of barium from uranium. That the nucleus of the uranium atom could be split was at that time unthinkable. Attempting to understand the reports of Hahn and Strassman, Meitner and her nephew allowed their imagination full play. In the conversation which took place between them Meitner and Frisch recalled that Bohr had once suggested that the nucleus of an atom resembled a liquid drop. If a drop could divide itself into smaller drops by elongating until a constricted neck formed in the middle and then could tear itself apart into two drops, perhaps something like this could happen to the uranium nucleus. Strong forces would resist, just as surface tension resists such a breakup in a drop of water. But nuclei are electrically charged and this might diminish the effect of the surface tension. Lise Meitner began to do some calculations on the back of a letter and on some scraps of paper. Frisch followed her calculations. Yes, the charge of a uranium nucleus might be a "wobbly uncertain drop, ready to divide itself at the slightest provocation, such as the impact of a neutron." When the two drops parted they would fly apart with tremendous energy, an energy calculated by Meitner to be approximately 200 million electron-volts.

Lise Meitner remembered at this point how to compute the masses of nuclei from the so-called "packing fraction." If the uranium nucleus divided, the two particles formed would be lighter than the original nucleus by about one-fifth of the mass of the proton. With some quick arithmetic, she multiplied the lost one-fifth of mass by the speed of light squared. It came out almost exactly at 200 million electron-volts. The lost one-fifth would supply exactly the 200 million electron-volts of energy with which the drop would tear apart. The importance of their insight was not lost on them. "So here was the source of all that energy," said Frisch. It is reported that the two looked at each other with incredulity, and then again with triumph.

In a paper reporting their discovery for the British journal *Nature*, they described the division of the nucleus as "fission." The source of the term itself is interesting. As they were writing the paper, Frisch had asked a young biologist what he and his confreres called the splitting of a cell. "Fission," he replied, and Frisch had the word he needed. Ruth Moore, from whom this account is taken, writes "the process was simply, accurately and perceptively named for all time."[4] Next came the task of testing their theory by experimentation.

The first point I wish to make is that Meitner and Frisch were clearly searching for an explanation of something that begged to be understood. They were looking for the mechanism responsible for the phenomena reported by their German colleagues. Although the data they were attempting to explain seemed implausible, they nevertheless accepted the data on the authority of Hahn and Strassman. Meitner and Frisch, as well as the scientific world on both sides of the Atlantic, believed the Hahn-Strassman report to be accurate. Need I note that the acceptance of the work of others is normal procedure in the sciences. Most theoretical physics is based on the authoritative reports of colleagues.

There is no doubt that, in their attempt to understand, Meitner and Frisch were looking for a cause. Their search led them to an imagined source. Note also the role of analogy or metaphor. The source of the energy released was imagined to be something like a drop of water, elongating and dividing. The nucleus was conceived in visual terms as a fluid. Clearly the mind was proceeding by analogy, from something better known to something less known. The familiar was serving as a model for the unfamiliar. The mechanism responsible for the phenomena was understood by means of an iconic model. The mind was not satisfied by a mere mathematical description of the phenomena reported. Not surprisingly the value of the Meitner/Frisch explanation was recognized universally. But was the explanation correct? If it were, it could not simply be checked by repeating the experiment which gave rise to it in the first place, although laboratories in Europe and North America eagerly repeated the experiment. For Aristotle, explanations are different than mere reports. For a contemporary mind schooled in Aristotelianism, an explanation in order to satisfy has to link a causal mechanism to the phenomena observed, phenomena which are initially reported as raw data, very often in equation form. Meitner, Frisch, Bohr, Fermi and the many others who quickly saw the implications of the explanation, began to integrate their new knowledge with other things they accepted. The plausible explanation became the accepted one as all that was known about the nature of uranium and its various isotopes cohered. Every attempt at interpretation was tested with every possible real or imagined experiment. The Meitner/Frisch explanation was dependent upon previous success in the construction of a model for the uranium atom. That model was initially constructed in an attempt to explain the cause of certain phenomena associated with the sensorially distinguishable and describable element uranium. Now the model was employed to explain something never intended, namely the breakup of the atom into barium and krypton.

There are several points which may be emphasized: (1) the implicit philosophical realism evident in the thought of Meitner and Frisch; (2) the fact that their model actually provided a plausible mechanism for the phenomena observed. By means of the model, properties were associated with their structural cause. The Meitner/Frisch mode of procedure followed what I take to be a realist account of scientific method. In attempting to understand the properties or activities encountered, the mind renders them intelligible by means of an imagined source. To provide a reasonable source is the function of the model. It is not simply a question of before and after, since the source is never directly experienced. There is a linking of behavior to that which is thought to behave by means of a plausible mechanism which can only be thought by means of a model. I stress, it is not simply a question of sequence, contiguity in place, continuity in time, and a habit of associating those events designated cause and effect; rather the mind is led to affirmation, because the inferred cause is thought to be responsible for the phenomena in question. The cause must be presented to the mind by means of an image, not just any image, but one rendering a plausible mechanism. The mind immediately rules out a multiplicity of images in favor of likely candidates. As mere logical possibility gives ground to material or real possibility, images are quickly discarded. The closer one comes to a true explanation, the fewer the images which can be entertained. Finally only one imaged source is regarded as plausible, and it is given the status of genuine cause. The imagined structure can be said to be, in Aristotelian language, "instantiated." I am using "structure" here not as a synonym for substantial form in the Aristotelian sense but as a quality consequent upon extension, certainly reflective of form, but not identical with form itself, nor with essence.

IV

The knowledge we have of the structures of the submicroscopic is by inference, yet the mental mechanism by which we attain and hold that knowledge is not much different from the everyday or commonsense knowledge we have of the world of sense experience.

There is one process of coming to know but, as Aristotle understood it, the awareness of commonality and the mental expression of that commonality seem to be distinguishable acts. Controlled knowing of the sort which takes place in the sciences is analogous to what may be taken as true of ordinary or commonsense awareness. I have in mind the deliberate focusing on commonality which takes place in controlled or scientific induction and the deliberate creation of images in order to understand that commonality and difference. It can be argued that, following Aristotle, controlled induction and model formation are but systematic attempts to do what the mind does naturally at a prior stage in coming to know. Through the process of induction the soul is "led to" or "brought to" the universal as present in the particular. When one of a number of logically indiscriminate particulars becomes the focus of interest, the earliest universal is present in the soul. In the flux of the particulars the soul is gradually able to perceive the first constant and unchanging universal. The plurality of individuals is required to focus the mind's vision gradually on that universal which is present in all individuals but is finally perceived as such by the mind in one particular instance. This is the intuition (*nous*) that apprehends the commonality of the nature under consideration and is the originative source of scientific knowledge.

Contemporary debates bring to mind ancient disputes, particularly those relating to Aristotle's *De Anima* III, 5. The terminology is sometimes new, but the age-old problem of universals haunts present discussion. This problem is sometimes framed in its contemporary setting as the problem of the relation of language to reality. W. Quine, for example, has argued that the referent of a term is not determinately fixed, and consequently reference is inscrutable in the sense that we can have no sure knowledge of what our speech is referring to.[5] Hilary Putnam holds that even an ideal theory, that is, one which is compatible with all possible observations and satisfies all theoretical and operational requirements, can employ different models. Since multiple models can satisfy all epistemic conditions, there is no nonarbitrary way of selecting one of them as the unique model representative of the posited structure. If there are alternative possible models of a theory, how can we know which approximates reality? Putnam maintains that reference cannot be fixed by the mind affirming a reality represented by the intentional model, since that would require the unintelligible notion of our minds's having access to reality that is unmediated by the theory whose reference is in question. Putman also rejects the view that reference is determined by a causal relation between a structure independent of the mind and the language user, since such a view would presuppose realism.[6]

In another text, Putman seems to be saying that the only reality to which we have access is "reality as it appears to us."[7] Putman is, of course, not alone in maintaining such a position. Idealists, such as Nicholas Rescher, maintain almost the same thing. The realist will counter that Putman's position is flawed by the fallacy of equivocation. In one sense to say that some item is mind-independent is to say that the item exists independently of the existence of any human mind. In another sense, to say that some item is mind-dependent is to say that it cannot be apprehended by the human mind in a way that is unmediated by some schema. The fact that some item is not mind-independent in the latter sense does not entail that it is not mind-independent in the former sense, and it is the former sense that is at issue in the realist conception of truth.

Neils Bohr recognized that theoretical concepts which are devoid of any perceptual content are problematic. He called them "idealizations," but, I think, in the mathematical sense that there is no such thing as a straight line or a triangle in sensorially experienced reality. If theoretical concepts are to have any genuine explanatory force, they cannot lose all connection with ordinary sense perception. Once science goes beyond the critical level where its concepts lose all connection with ordinary perceptual experience, it can no longer be regarded as providing a description of an actual mechanism. It should be noted that, in line with Bohr's description of scientific practice, Aristotelian realism does not require that true statements be regarded as conveying mental pictures which faithfully and completely depict the inherent properties of the object in itself. Science is always open-ended. There is always more to be known; there are always better representations to be attained. But the mind in achieving a better grasp of "what is" is not moving from the false to the true but from the less precise to the more precise. The progressive character of scientific enquiry is connected with its communal nature. Progress is usually the result of many minds working on the same problem with someone coming up with an idea no one articulated before.

In this context, P. F. Strawson's contemporary defense of an Aristotelian realism is worth noting. In Strawson's language the possibility of descriptive identification and reidentification of particulars implies not only a spatiotemporal world of external objects but intersubjective communication.[8] Material objects are ontologically basic from the point of view of particular identification. They are particulars which can be identified and reidentified without reference to particulars of a different sort. Basic particulars must be publicly observable objects of a sort that different observers can literally see, or hear, or touch. Other sorts of particulars are not basic in this respect.

V

To conclude, as Etienne Gilson has noted, "Being is neither intuited by a sensibility nor understood by an intellect; it is known by a *man*. An organic chain of mental operations links the sense perception of what is known as being to the abstraction and to the judgment through which man knows it as being."[9] We affirmed earlier the axiom "There is no intellection without accompanying sensation." But to recognize that principle is not to instantiate every image which accompanies thought. Some images are involuntary, spontaneously arising in the presence of their object, others are well-crafted, well-designed, themselves the product of much thought, created to represent as closely as conceivable the real. In the sciences we call them "models." A model is an idealized or postulated representation of an unobservable entity or process. Elements employed in their representation are analogous to entities at least partially understood from elsewhere. Associated with the model is a theory indicating how the envisaged mechanism is expected to behave and so permitting specific predictions to be made. The crafting of a model is not arbitrary. In their initial vagueness and generality the models are thrust upon us and held by us in a sensuous way by the imagination. But the intellect is not satisfied with vagueness. It wants precision even in the images it employs when judging and reasoning. If the images do not come, if they are not immediately evoked, it may be that the source of the phenomena indirectly grasped by statistical reports has not been truly identified; we do not yet know what to make of our finding. Sometimes the language we use may be misleading as, for example, when we talk about the "spin of a K meson." This does not militate against the realist position. It simply means that not all that is encountered is understood. We may for the time being have masses of data which require interpretation. Sometimes the mathematics may lag behind the data, sometimes the postulated mechanism behind the statistically expressed correlation. The whole thrust of the scientific enterprise is to render intelligible that which does not explain itself. The continuity between prescientific and scientific knowledge is assumed in a realist's account of knowing. In our own day, the globally distributed character of independent reports, the similar proffering of tentative explanations, the employment of common images to represent, indicate that the mind is not fabricating but discovering.

One often reads that scientific reports of nature supersede each other with remarkable frequency, that the reports to which we now subscribe have falsified previous reports taken to be true, and that we have reason to suspect that our present way of looking at things will give way to others. This is sometimes taken as evidence of the arbitrariness and unreliability of the conceptual schemes we currently employ. But the history of science discloses no such thing. In every period there have been false starts, but where explanations have been recognized as substantiated, they remain, sometimes as vague accounts which have been rendered more precise by the refinement of data or the rigor of explanation. Enhancement is not falsification. The advancement of our knowledge of nature does not refute the realist's description of the cognitive process but reinforces it. Explanatory notions such as "bacterium," "cell," "molecule," "atom," "circulatory system," "nerve fiber," were first theoretical entities before they became objects of direct or indirect perception.

To return to Comte, although the foundation of his theory of knowledge is seriously challenged by the march of events, his legacy in the social sciences remains. His law of stages is taken for granted by social theorists, many of whom have never directly encountered Comte.[10] His legacy remains in the work of Lucien Lévy-Bruhl, Emile Durkheim, and Hippolyte Taine, and their twentieth-century disciples. Few challenge the materialistic assumptions of contemporary anthropology, sociology, and psychology or look for the source of the relativism which pervades much contemporary educational theory.

The challenge which Mercier faced as a student remains, but with this difference. Today he could draw upon volumes of contemporary work in the philosophy of science which have taken a realist turn as many philosophers have recovered a realist perspective often directly inspired by Aristotle in their attempt to remain true to actual practice in the natural sciences. British empiricism may entail the materialism taken for granted by many social theorists, but it is rarely seen as an adequate philosophy of science.

NOTES

1. David A. Boileau, *Cardinal Mercier: A Memoir* (Leuven: Peeters, 1996).

2. One of Mercier's earliest works is entitled *Théorie de la connaissance certain* (1884). By 1923 it had gone through eight editions and was eventually translated into at least five languages.

3. For a fuller discussion of models in the natural sciences, see Rom Harré, *Principles of Scientific Explanation* (Chicago: University of Chicago Press, 1970), and William A. Wallace, *The Modeling of Nature: Philosophy of Science and Philosophy of Nature in Synthesis* (Washington, D.C.: Catholic University of America Press, 1996).

4. Ruth Moore, *Neils Bohr, The Man, His Science and the World They Changed* (Cambridge: The MIT Press, 1985).

5. William Quine, *Word & Object* (Cambridge: MIT Press, 1960); *The Roots of Reference* (LaSalle, Ill.: Open Court, 1974).

6. Hilary Putnam, *Realism and Reason: Philosophical Papers*, vol. 3 (Cambridge: Cambridge University Press, 1983), chap. 1, "Models and Reality."

7. Ibid. p. 207.

8. P. F. Strawson, *Individuals: An Essay in Descriptive Meta-physics* (London: Methuen, 1959), p. 38f.

9. Etienne Gilson, *Being and Some Philosophers*, 2d ed. (Toronto: Pontifical Institute of Medieval Studies, 1952), p. 206.

10. Comte's law of three stages may be stated simply. Everywhere in all matters, social phenomena begin in a theological stage, pass through a metaphysical stage, and terminate in a positivistic or scientific stage. *Cours de philosophie positive* was published in six volumes between 1830 and 1842. The influence of Comte is difficult to underestimate. Taine, Mill, and Durkheim were important early disciples. Later, so also were Lévy-Bruhl in France and John Dewey in the United States, although "disciple" may be too strong a word in the case of Dewey. Suffice it to say that Dewey accepted uncritically the "law of three stages."

# 3

# The Philosophies of Mind and Nature

## John Haldane

For over forty years Ralph McInerny has been a tireless, passionate, and witty advocate of the thought of Aquinas. Students and faculty in Catholic colleges and universities in North America have reason to be grateful for his fluent presentations of Thomas's ideas. But, of course, Ralph is no intellectual sectarian. He wishes all who seek wisdom to benefit from the insights of the *Summa* and other works. Also, he is not one to separate Thomas's philosophical thought from that of Aristotle. Quoting the old maxim *Sine Thoma, Aristoteles mutus esset* he balances it with another, *Sine Aristotele, Thomas non esset*. His recent translation of Aquinas in the Penguin Classics will bring the wisdom of Thomas's Catholic Aristotelianism to a wide readership throughout the English-speaking world.[1]

A major focus of Ralph's work has been ethics, where he has reaffirmed the necessity of invoking nature beyond convention, if convention is to be other than arbitrary. Indeed, this may prove to be his greatest gift to Catholic thought. Yet his appeal to the philosophy of nature as essential to the defeat of antirealism is by no means confined to the sphere of right action. He writes "Skepticism about the capacity of human beings to know reality . . . makes the philosophical task of recovery of natural principles a service to mankind"[2]

In what follows I deploy certain ideas drawn from Aristotelian-Thomistic philosophy of nature in order to address metaphysical problems concerning thought and agency. These problems have come to dominate contemporary philosophy of mind as that is practiced outside neoscholastic circles. In recent years there has been very little neo-Thomistic philosophy of mind, but a younger generation is beginning to show interest in the field. By implication, therefore, this essay is addressed to members of two constituencies, urging each to look at what the other has said and at how their largely isolated efforts might be brought together. I am confident Ralph will approve of the spirit of this intention. I find it less easy to predict his attitude to its embodiment, but I look forward to learning something of this when he arrives in Scotia to deliver the Gifford Lectures.

I

For the last quarter century the dominant view among analytical philosophers of mind has been that thought and action may be accounted for naturalistically, i.e., without reference to nonphysical entities. This, however, has not always been taken to require that psychological descriptions and explanations be reduced, by analysis or bridging laws, to descriptions and explanations couched in the vocabulary of physics. This relaxation of traditional materialism has been due, in large part, to the work of Donald Davidson, especially to his essay "Mental Events".[3] There, with great economy and elegance, Davidson argues that the (presumed) fact of mental/physical interaction, together with the assumptions that causation is lawlike, and that there are no laws linking the psychological and the physical, entails that mental events must be the terms of physical/physical laws, and hence that they must themselves be physical.

From the anomality of the psychological-qua-psychological to the physicality of the psychological-qua-causal was but two short steps. However it moved the subject on to new ground. Logical behaviorism and mind-body dualism having been set aside long ago, the chief building blocks of the new philosophy of mind are *physicalism* and *causalism*. The first is to be understood as the claim that every substance is a physical substance; the second as the thesis that the mind is a many-part operating system in which psychological items stand in relations of efficient causation to inputs from the environment, to one another and to behavioral outputs.

Given that physical causality was so prominent in Davidson's argument, it is ironic that this should have been invoked in what has recently become a fairly sustained attack on his position and on related versions of nonreductive physicalism. Davidson's critics differ between themselves but they are agreed that his insistence on the nonreducibility of the mental, combined with the claim that the laws under which mental/physical interaction occurs are physical ones, entails the inefficacy of mental attributes. Put another way, while Davidson's position allows that those events which are mental are causally related to inputs and outputs, the relations in question hold not in virtue of their mentality but on account of their physicality. The resulting options seem to be to accept epiphenomenalism, which contradicts the starting point of the theory, namely, that there is mental/physical interaction, or else to endorse the reduction of the mental to the physical, which contradicts the anomaly thesis. Reductionism is liable to prove victorious in that contest.

Davidson has responded forcefully to arguments of this sort, but I have to say that I find his responses implausible.[4] If we stand back from the detailed dialectic, it seems clear why the very enterprise was so appealing but also why it seemed doomed from the outset. Philosophy of mind from the early 1970s onwards moved towards a consensus around non-reductive physicalism. It did so because dualism seemed evidently false; yet old-fashioned mental/physical type identity faced counterexamples from the multiple physical-realizability of mental states, and efforts to secure reduction via disjunctive type-identification seem at best hopelessly ad hoc. What was wanted was the following: (1) *a duality of attributes;* (2) *a monism of bearers;* (3) *some sort of determination relation between the physicality of a bearer and the mentality of an attribute;* yet (4) *nonreducibility of the latter to the former.* In short, the benefits of dualism without its costs, or the virtues of physicalism without its liabilities.

If one thinks with Davidson's critics that these are impossible combinations, the question becomes one of where to move next, and the evident fact is that there is now no consensus on this issue. One may speak of the breaking out of a healthy pluralism, but it would be more accurate to characterize the situation as one of emerging disarray.

II

Philosophy of mind is composed of three overlapping issues: (1) *the nature of persons;* (2) *the nature of thought;* and (3) *the nature of action.* The first is the traditional locus of the mind-body problem, but when one considers sense-cognition it soon becomes evident that there is a difficulty about the connection between perception and sensation: are they distinct? identical? or is there a relationship of some other sort? and is thought a physical process? Likewise in asking about the relationship between action and movement very similar issues arise and one quickly faces an "agent-body problem."

Each of the three areas is the subject of extensive discussion in contemporary philosophy. Some authors make connections between them but many do not. Though I shall not pursue the issue further now, I think that the proper deployment of the ancient idea of hylomorphism suggests the integration of the three areas mentioned through the metaphysical priority of the first. Put another way, a correct account of the nature of persons will include, as essential aspects, accounts of the nature of thought and of action, since these are the primary modes of activity of those beings whose nature is that of persons. As the scholastic Aristotelians were wont to say, "acting follows upon being" and "things are specified by their powers."[5]

Before proceeding, let me say how I understand the notions of form and matter and the motivation for their introduction. My view is broadly Aristotelian though it invokes elements from Aquinas which are at least not explicit in Aristotle, and arguably may not be there at all. In allowing for their absence, however, I am not suggesting the possibility that they may be incompatible with Aristotle's conception. In fact the ideas in question are ones that predate Aristotle and are, I believe, what one arrives at if one thinks about the possibility of there being any things, or any thoughts of things.

The pre-Socratics asked very broad metaphysical questions and delivered equally wide-ranging answers. One such question is "what is the nature of reality?". Anaximander speculated that the original state of things was that of an undifferentiated mass; a vast extent of unstructured some-such. This he termed the "indefinite" or the "undifferentiated" (the *apeiron*). The question then became that of the source of the structure apparent in the world. Subsequently, Pythagoras, who adopted the notion of the *apeiron*, thought of emergent structure in mathematical terms. Thus he came to the view that the making of the *kosmos* involved the imposition of limit (*peras*) upon the undifferentiated, so as to produce the structured (*peperasmenon*). The pre-Socratics thought in terms of a genesis, but the general principle can be abstracted from any historical process of production. Moreover, no sense can be made of a something about which nothing can be said; a pure *apeiron* would resist any kind of subject/predicate description. This I take to show that a condition of there being something for thought to take hold of, is that the something has structure. Equivalently, a condition of there being thought is that there be relevant structuring principles (sortal and characterizing concepts plus logical constants).

So we arrive at hylomorphic analysis. Every particular may be understood in terms of the instantiation of a formal principle. Its form makes it to be the kind of thing it is, providing its definitive structure, its characteristic powers and liabilities, and so on. However, since, ex hypothesi, things of the same specific sort have formally identical principles, there arises the question of numerical difference. The analysis is completed by introducing the idea of matter as that which is structured and is the basis of numerical individuation within species. Their forms make two men alike (*qua* men); their matter makes them distinct (*qua* individual men). Speaking, as I just have, of the "matter" of living things it is tempting to proceed by iterative analysis so as to be led, via the form and matter of flesh and bones, and then of tissue fiber and chemical compounds, etc., to the infamous idea of *prime matter*—stuff of no kind.

This is avoidable. Think again of the Pythagorean principle: structure conjoined with absence of structure constituting something structured. Considered in the abstract it becomes clear that the unstructured, while not a something, is not a mere nothing. It is the possibility or potentiality for the reception of structure, and that structure stands to it as an actualizing principle. This, I suggest (employing Aquinas's potency/act distinction)[6] is how at the metaphysical level we should think of matter and form. The first is a potentiality for the reception of the second, the second a determinate actualization of this potentiality. Next, if we consider various kinds of forms we can ask about the kinds of possibility there are for their actualization or instantiation. In the case of concrete particulars the answer would appear to be "spatiotemporality," or whatever at the most fundamental level constitutes the empirical domain. But, of course, empirical reality always comes informed by some structure (and that necessarily, for recall the earlier remarks about the *apeiron*). So we need to distinguish between (a) matter as the condition of the possibility of the actuality of form (*materia prima*); and (b) matter as a particular empirical medium (*materia signata*). Matter in the first sense is not an empirical concept; matter in the second sense is the most general empirical concept.

One odd-sounding, but in fact coherent, implication of this is that it is an open question whether there is any immaterial matter. The initial impression of contradiction is removed when we see that this is now reformulable as asking whether there may be nonempirical potentialities for the reception of form. I will come to what I believe to be one such possibility shortly, but let me note that the analysis I have offered allows for a charitable interpretation of a view held in the Middle Ages. Peter Geach writes

> Some Scholastics held that just as two pennies or two cats differ by being different bits of matter, so human souls differ by containing different 'spiritual matter'. Aquinas regarded this idea as self-contradictory; it is at any rate much too obscure to count as establishing a possibility of distinct disembodied souls.[7]

Though he does not say so, I imagine Geach has in mind Aquinas's apparent disagreement with Bonaventure. In his *Commentary on the Sentences*, Bonaventure writes that "the rational soul is the principle and form of the human body" and then adds (following in a tradition begun a century earlier by Avicebron (Ibn Gebirol)) that the soul itself is hylomorphically composed of spiritual form and spiritual matter (*Super libros sententiarum*, 18). In the *Summa* Aquinas asks "whether the soul is composed of form and matter" and argues that it is not (*Summa Theologiae*, Ia, q. 75, a 5). His reasons are cogent so far as the possibility of a plurality of individual souls is concerned, but someone willing to countenace the old idea of a single universal soul might hold on to the idea that this is realized in "spiritual matter." I am not endorsing that proposal, but I do wish to prepare the ground for the suggestion that there are nonempirical modes of receiving forms.

### III

The problem of the nature of thought has several aspects of which two are prominent. What is the implication of the correct account of intentionality for the traditional issue of realism vs. representationalism? and what is the character and source of the components and the structure of thought (concepts and rationality, respectively)? It is characteristic of contemporary accounts of intentionality—be they internalist or externalist—that they view the originating relationship between object and thought in terms of the efficacy of the former in producing the latter. Crudely, we are to understand thoughts as prompted by the objects they are about, as those objects or their effects impinge upon our senses, or as facts about them are relayed by chains of communication going back to such impingements.

As one reflects upon this view it is hard not to feel the prospects of realism in cognition slipping away. In contemporary debates about intentionality it is possible to distinguish two positions which I shall label "old" and "new" versions of "representationalism". According to the first, the immediate objects of thought are images, ideas, or sentences. These are themselves foci of cognition and external reference is mediated by them (via a relationship of picturing [natural resemblance] or symbolism [whatever that might be and however it might be accounted for]). On standard interpretations Descartes and Locke are old-style representationalists, as, in some of their pronouncements, are Hartry Field and Jerry Fodor.[8] According to the second position, while mental representations mediate between the thinker and reality they are not themselves objects of cognition. So, while it may be that in order to think about some state of affairs it has to be the case that there is some proposition-like representation in the thinker's mind it does not follow that the thinker cognizes the state of affairs by entertaining a representation. Rather, the tokening of a propositional content by a mental sentence constitutes the thought, and reference is secured via the relationship between this and the external reality.[9]

Whatever the relative merits of these positions both have the consequence that mind is somewhat removed from the world. For even if a complete representationalist account of thought must make a connection between a subject's internal states and the external world (and not every theory of this sort accepts that requirement) the connection can only be *extrinsic,* a matter of efficient causation. In his Dewey Lectures, Hilary Putnam draws upon terminology adopted from John McDowell in order to make a similar critical point:

> McDowell argues persuasively that this picture [old representationalism], whether in its classical version or in its modern materialist version, is disastrous for just about every part of metaphysics and epistemology. In McDowell's terminology the key assumption responsible for the disaster is the idea that there has to be an interface [a causal not cognitive linkage] between our cognitive powers and the external world.... Accounts of perception that reject this claim are conventionally referred to as "direct realist" accounts.... But there is less to some versions of "direct realism" than meets the eye.... All one has to do to be a direct realist (in this sense) about visual experience, for example, is to say, "We don't perceive visual experiences, we have them".... "We perceive external things—that is, we are caused to have certain subjective experiences in the appropriate way by those external things," such a philosopher can say.[10]

What Putnam refers to here as "some versions of 'direct realism'" is what I have termed "new versions of representationalism." One may ask, however, what the alternative may be. Again following McDowell, but also under the influence of William James, Putnam advances what he calls *natural realism:* the view that "successful perception is just a seeing, or hearing, or feeling, etc., of things 'out there' and not a mere affectation of a person's subjectivity by those things."[11]

I agree with this, but what I find missing from Putnam's discussion (and indeed from McDowell's treatment of intentionality)[12] is any explicit account of how this is possible. Elsewhere I have urged the merit of the maxim "no epistemology without ontology"[13] and in this context the requirement is to say what else grounds the cognition of reality if not the effects of objects upon our senses, "the affectation of our subjectivity." Clearly input from the world is relevant and is in part at least a matter of efficient causation. However, if there is to be the sort of conformity of mind to thing which Putnam and McDowell seek, then I can see this being provided only according to an account of the sort developed by Aquinas when he writes that the intellect in act is the intelligible in act; or less scholastically, that the mind will be of a thing only when it is formally identical with it; when what we think and what is thought are the same.[14]

What does this mean? and how is it possible? It means that when I think of something, that which makes my thought to be the kind of thought it is—a dog thought, say—is formally identical to that which makes the object of my thought to be the kind of thing it is, a dog. Each actuality (thought and object) has a structuring principle (concept and substantial form); and these principles, though distinct in the modes of their actualization, are specifically alike. The form of dog exists naturally and substantially (*in esse naturale*) in the dog, and intentionally and predicatively (*in esse intentionale*) in the thought. To make full sense of this we need to extend standard Aristotelian ontology to include three different kinds of existents (1–3) and three kinds of relation, two being modes of exemplification (4 & 5), the other being one of instantiation (6):

1) *F-ness*—the universal, or form
2) *The f-ness of X*—a singular case, or instance
3) *X*—a particular subject
4) X *exemplifies* F-ness naturally, or is a natural *exemplification* of F-ness
5) X *exemplifies* F-ness intentionally, or is an intentional *exemplification* of F-ness
6) The f-ness of X is a natural *case* or *instance* of F-ness.

Contrary to some (mis)representations of the doctrine of intentional existence, when I think of a dog an individual animal does not come to exist in my thought; rather my thinking takes on a general feature dogness, which serves as a concept directing me to a particular or to the class. Accordingly, although successive thoughts of the same conceptual type involve numerically distinct exemplifications of the relevant form, these thoughts are not distinct instantiations of that form. For what it is to be an instantiation of F is to be a particularization of it—a case of F-ness, or the f-ness of a particular, the dogness-of-Lassie, say.

A merit of this view is that it explains what is otherwise a mystery, namely, how a thought can be intrinsically related to its object. They share the same form. It also serves, I believe, to save realism from the threat of conceptual relativism. In recent years Putnam has insisted upon an unmediated connection between mind and world. Yet without further specification and explanation this leaves scope for a different kind of skepticism to that traditionally associated with representationalism. He himself has maintained in a series of well-known publications that permutation arguments leave realism floundering so long as reference is thought of as something fixed objectively.[15] My own diagnosis of the deeper reasoning beneath these essays is that Putnam has presumed that reference-fixing from the side of the world could only be through lines of efficient causation from object to thinker. The problem for the realist, then, is not that such relations are insufficient, but that there are far too many of them with none standing out as the ground of reciprocal semantic relations between thinker and object of thought. Consider the vast number of causal lines extending from the world to me when I stand facing a dog and try to say which could constitute a privileged class sufficient to ground reference.

The difficulty is insurmountable so long as one is confined to efficient causation. But a further possibility is now before us. Form exemplified naturally makes the dog to be a dog. Form exemplified intentionally makes my thought of a dog to be a dog-type thought. To this we can add that the intentional exemplification has as a condition of its occurrence some prior natural exemplification. My thought is caused to have its content by the form of the dog.[16] There are, then, three cases of formal causation: *within the natural order, within the intentional order,* and *between the natural and the intentional orders*. It is very important at this point to make clear that formal causation is not a kind of efficient causation, or a rival to it. In late scholastic discussions one sometimes finds authors writing as if forms passed through the air in the manner of effluvia shed from the surfaces of objects. This invites empirical refutation and intellectual parody. But the proposal currently on offer does not require anything like this. We can say instead that the only effecting that goes on, as this is standardly conceived of, is that already known about, *but* that the effecting originates and terminates in formal structures. Efficient causation is the vehicle for the communication of form; form is what structures the object, the thought, and the movement between them. Efficient causation by itself failed to fix reference since what the idea of it omitted was the possibility that it carries form, or, as the scholastics would more accurately say, that it itself is "subject to formality." What makes it possible that there be dog-type thoughts is that there be dogs and that the form(s) of the latter has been communicated via effects originating in the animals themselves.

In cognition the person as subject receives forms, in action the person as agent expresses them. In both cases efficient causation is operating. Light hits the retina, it contracts, electrical impulses are set up in the afferent nerves, things happen in the brain. Things happen in the brain, impulses pass along efferent nerves, muscles contract, a hand moves. These matters are not in general dispute. The question is what is their relation to sight and action? I have argued above that if we are to make sense of perception, then we have to bring in formal causation and say that in the chain of efficient cause and effect the formal structure of the object is communicated to the sense, and in thought to the intellect. Perception is hylomorphically constituted with "sensibles" standing as forms to the matter of the sense organs.

Likewise action is hylomorphically constituted with intentions standing as forms to the matter of physiological movements. Efficient causation plays its part, but its part in these contexts is conditioned by the forms that govern it. This is why *action* explanation is not "causal" in the sense universally intended among analytical philosophers of mind and action. When I say that A stood up because he wanted to leave, I am not identifying (by hypothesis) something antecedent to a human movement which was the efficient cause of it. Rather I am identifying it formally (by observation of the agent in the circumstance) and saying that what he was doing was making to leave.

One way of interpreting what I have proposed is as claiming that intentionality plays a role in the production of action, additional to physical efficient causation. This formulation should be welcome to critics schooled in the current debates about mental causation, since it will seem to invite the well-rehearsed charge of causal overdetermination and raise the prospect of a retreat to epiphenomenalism of the sort of which Davidson stands accused. In the dock with him are other supervenience theorists and emergence revivalists. Let me recall the prosecution case by means of another diagram. Suppose we identify a sequence of events and are looking to attach two sets of properties to them, one mental (M) the other physical (P). Suppose further that we say that the mental properties supervene upon the physical ones or are emergent out of them (differences between supervenience and emergence are ultimately not relevant to the charge that is being pressed). Suppose next that we wish to allow that the physical properties in the sequence are causally related (P causes P* etc.). Suppose, finally, we want to say that the mental or more broadly the intentional properties of the events in sequence are also causally related. Then we can represent this in a style familiar from writings by Jaegwon Kim and others:

$$\text{Level 1} \quad M \text{---} c \text{---} M^* \text{---} c \text{---} M^{**} \text{---} c \text{---} M^{***}$$
$$\quad \quad \quad \quad | \quad \quad \quad \quad | \quad \quad \quad \quad | \quad \quad \quad \quad |$$
$$\text{Level 2} \quad P \text{---} c \text{---} P^* \text{---} c \text{---} P^{**} \text{---} c \text{---} P^{***}$$

Since, by hypothesis, P is naturally or metaphysically sufficient for M and P* is likewise sufficient for M*, and moreover P causes P*, it looks as if the attempt to find a role for M in relation to M* faces the dilemma of overdetermination or epiphenomenalism. How can M make a contribution as the advocate of supervenient causation might wish, since the occurrence of M* is already provided for from below? Emergentism envisages downward causation, so one might try the suggestion that M brings about M* not directly but by causing P*. That, however, involves denying the causal sufficiency of P for P* and violates the "causal closure of the physical" (*ccp*).

Much ink has already been printed on this topic and a number of imaginative suggestions have been canvassed. In a series of papers, Jonathan Lowe has explored the possibility of rejecting the argument (based upon the *ccp*) that if M has a cause it must be a wholly physical one.[17] There are certainly moves one can make here starting with the observation that the closure principle is question-begging and is not entailed by the conservation laws.

A related line of thought on the problem of emergence and downward causation has been described in a very useful and widely cited survey essay by Brian McLaughlin on emergentism in earlier British philosophy of mind and science.[18] Consideration of this will lead me to my conclusion. McLaughlin is concerned with the efforts of theorists in the earlier part of the century to combine a number of possibilities. First, everything is made of matter (for convenience let this be particulate). Second, there is no change without change in the basic particles. Third, however, there is a plurality of levels of organizational complexity and of causal powers proper to each level. Following on from the last, the organizational structures endow substances with causal powers additional to those of their particles. In particular, movements of multilevel substances are not due exclusively to motions of their microphysical particles. Structure-relative forces come into play as complexity emerges.

It hardly seems incoherent to suppose that there may be forces other than particle ones. The problem comes with the thought that these might begin to operate in addition to existing forces, for that may appear to be in violation of scientific laws. Movement conforms to the laws of motion, so if the emergent forces make a distinctive contribution to the dynamics of the substances in which they inhere, then dynamics will not be reducible to physics (assuming the latter to be confined to the properties of particles). Of itself that might be tolerable, but there is the issue of the conservation of mass and energy. As McLaughlin points out, however, the existence of structural forces can be rendered compatible with conservation principles, so long as it is not supposed that higher level structures have extra mass and so long as it is not assumed that additional energy is created (or destroyed). How, then, can they be effective, i.e. *forces*, at all? An answer lies in the possibility that the physical particles have potential energy that is only released as organizational structures emerge. McLaughlin allows the coherence of this earlier emergentist combination, and its compatibility with basic scientific principles, but is not disposed to believe that what it envisages is true. For he takes it that the empirical evidence shows that in accounting for chemical bonding and microbiology it is not necessary to appeal to forces other than particle ones.

Further detail or speculation about this possibility is unnecessary in the present context. Instead I wish to suggest how one might think about form, substance, and causality in a way related to but importantly different from what has just been described. As with the emergentists I maintain that structure makes a difference and that there are hierarchies of organizational complexity. In the case of a single unified substance (rather than an aggregate, say) these levels are successively subsumed. In hylomorphic terms there is in such a case only one actual substantial form, though there may be several virtual ones corresponding to lower-level unifications. Activities which in lower-level systems would be attributable to the presence of different kinds of structuring principles are taken under the governance of the higher form. Where I take leave of the earlier emergentism is in rejecting the idea that structure adds or releases force. When discussing cognition I maintained that my thought of a dog is given canine content by being caused to be such by the form of the dog. But I then stressed the importance of not thinking of formal determination as a type of efficient causation. Likewise, I wish to maintain that form may be a determinant of the substantial nature, including the characteristic activities, of a substance without that being a matter of efficiently constraining the location and behavior of basic particles. Intentionality plays an additional role but not by being an additional force (energy).

Some years ago Elizabeth Anscombe pointed out that the idea of (efficient) causation is not as such that of something deterministic or necessitating.[19] What it means to say that "c caused e" is that c made e happen. It does not follow from this that were there another situation alike in all relevant antecedent respects that the same would happen again. Anscombe's point is an important one but it can be carried further. She, I think, was still inclined to take for granted that causation was at least patterned if not invariable. So it is, but the possibility of that patterning is not something that can be got out of the idea of efficient causation as such, any more than could be got out the idea of invariability. There is nothing in the idea of physical particles standing in relations of cause and effect that implies, or provides a basis for, the idea of higher-level structures behaving in ways characteristic of their natures. Indeed, unless it is taken to be implied by the term "particles" that what is postulated at the basic level has structure, then order there seems unaccounted for as well.

I am not denying that there is organization at that level or that causal relations operating there do so in systematic ways, but I am urging that the possibility of this depends upon the existence of forms or structuring principles. Efficient causation neither implies determination nor excludes randomness, and without formal structure the latter is all that its contingencies could amount to. Once again, what form brings is order, but it does not to do so by pushing things this way or that. Its existence is testified to not by force detectors but by the fact that what exists, and how existents act, exhibits natural order. Without formal causation there would be no regularity, let alone any invariability, in the flow of events, for efficacy alone (or, equivalently, energy as *apeiron*) does not provide it. What forms there are is evident in the structures and patterns of behavior around us. That is the explanation of the old claim that the subject of science is substantial form.

In the present context the most important example of substantial form is that responsible for the nature and activity of human persons in whom a multitude of functions are brought under the unifying order of thought and action. The role of reason in agency is not as an efficient cause operating to produce movement by way of levels one or two in the M and P diagram. Rather, it makes a movement to be an action by bestowing upon it an intentional form. And if we ask what made the action happen, then so long as we are indeed dealing with an *action,* the answer is nothing other than the agent's power of actualizing the potential of his or her body by subsuming matter-energy already at work under the governance of living form and changing its (formal) character. Resistance to this possibility most likely will arise from the thought that the movement of an agent must already be determined (or probabilified) antecedently and from below—by the facts of physical causation—but I cannot see that this is anything other than a physicalist prejudice, and it is certainly question-begging. From the fact that physics is applicable to human movement it does not follow that action is reducible to it, or to it plus efficient mental causation. We stand at a significant juncture: two roads lead in opposite directions: towards and away from physicalism. The former now appears to lead back to reductionism, the latter moves towards hylomorphic personalism. Philosophers in the tradition contributed to by Ralph McInerny will know which route to follow. Their task must now be to persuade others to accompany them.[20]

NOTES

1. *Thomas Aquinas: Selected Writings,* edited, translated and introduced by Ralph McInerny (London: Penguin Books, 1998).

2. Ralph McInerny, "Second Hand Straw" (Aquinas Medalist Address) in M.

Baur, ed., *The Importance of Truth*, Proceedings of the American Catholic Philosophical Association, vol. 67, (1993).

3. Donald Davidson, "Mental Events," in *Essays on Actions and Events* (Oxford: Clarendon Press, 1980).

4. See, for example, Donald Davidson, "Problems in the Explanation of Action," in P. Pettit, R. Sylvan, and J. Norman, eds., *From Metaphysics to Morality* (Oxford: Blackwell, 1987); and "Thinking Causes" in John Heil and Alfred Mele, eds., *Mental Causation* (Oxford: Clarendon Press, 1993).

5. See, for example, Aristotle, *De Anima* book II, chap. IV and Aquinas's commentary. Both texts appear in Kenelm Foster and Silvester Humphries, translators, *Aristotle's De Anima in the Version of William of Moerbeke and the Commentary of St Thomas Aquinas* (London: Routledge and Kegan Paul, 1951).

6. See, for example, Aquinas, "On the Principles of Nature" in Timothy McDermott, *Thomas Aquinas: Selected Philosophical Writings* (Oxford: Oxford University Press, 1993): "Now just as anything potential can be called *material*, so anything that gives existence... can be called *form*," p. 68.

7. See Peter Geach, "Immortality" in *God and the Soul* (London: Routledge and Kegan Paul, 1969), p. 23.

8. See, for example, J. Fodor, *Representations: Philosophical Essays on the Foundations of Cognitive Science* (Brighton: Harvester, 1981); and "Mental Representation: An Introduction" in N. Rescher, ed., *Scientific Inquiry in Philosophical Perspective* (New York: University Press of America, 1987).

9. Such a view is canvassed by Robert Stecker in criticism of my interpretation and endorsement of Thomas Reid's opposition to the doctrine of ideas. See Robert Stecker, "Does Reid Reject/Refute the Representational theory of Mind?" *Pacific Philosophical Quarterly* 73 (1992). I reply in "Whose Theory? Which Representations?" *Pacific Philosophical Quarterly* 74 (1993).

10. See Hilary Putnam, "Sense, Nonsense, and the Senses: An Inquiry into the Powers of the Human Mind," *Journal of Philosophy* 91 (1994) pp. 453–54.

11. Putnam, "Sense and Nonsense," p. 454. Later in the lectures Putnam generously notes my own use of the distinction between representations as mental acts and as cognitive or causal intermediaries. See p. 505; also Haldane "Putnam on Intentionality," *Philosophy and Phenomenological Research* 52 (1992). I hope he might consider the suggestion that formal causation has to be part of a true account of cognition.

12. See John McDowell, *Mind and World* (Cambridge: Harvard University Press, 1994), Lectures I and II.

13. See Haldane, "Rational and Other Animals," in A. O'Hear, ed., *Verstehen and Humane Understanding* (Cambridge: Cambridge University Press, 1996).

14. Compare this with McDowell's Wittgensteinean version of cognitive identity: "there is no ontological gap between the sort of thing one can... think, and the sort of thing that can be the case," *Mind and World*, p. 27.

15. See, for example, Hilary Putnam, "Models and Reality," in *Realism and Reason* (Cambridge: Cambridge University Press, 1983), and "Model Theory and the Factuality of Semantics," in *Words and Life* (Cambridge: Harvard University Press, 1994).

16. Putnam worries about the invocation of substantial forms, using the example of dogs to make difficulty for it and to advance his own version of ontological relativity:

see "Aristotle after Wittgenstein," *Words and Life*. I respond to this in "On Coming Home to (Metaphysical) Realism," *Philosophy* 71 (1996).

17. See E. J. Lowe, "The Problem of Psychophysical Causation," *Australasian Journal of Philosophy*, 70 (1992); and "The Causal Autonomy of the Mental," *Mind* 102 (1993).

18. See B. McLaughlin, "The Rise and Fall of British Emergentism," in A. Beckermann, H. Flohr, and J. Kim, eds., *Emergence or Reduction?* (Berlin: De Guyter, 1992).

19. See G. E. M. Anscombe, "Causality and Determination" in her *Metaphysics and the Philosophy of Mind* (Oxford: Blackwell, 1981).

20. Another and longer version of this paper also appears in David Oderberg, ed., *Form and Matter* (Oxford: Blackwell, 1999).

# 4

# Persons and Things

*Thomas De Koninck*

What does Scripture mean when it speaks of the fire that "shall not be quenched," of the "eternal fire," "the lake of fire and sulphur" where the devil, the beast, and the false prophet "will be tormented day and night for ever and ever"?[1] In the course of a typically brilliant piece of speculation on that question, St. Augustine rules out neither immaterial nor material fire. But the main puzzle seems to be: If it is material fire, "then how will there be punishment in it for the evil spirits"? How can immaterial spirits "be tormented by the pain of material fire in a way which is real"? Still, such a contact could take place "in a wondrous manner that cannot be described"—another miracle of the omnipotent Creator. After all, "the spirit of man, which without doubt is immaterial also, can at this present time be shut up within the framework of a material body." There is, thus, "a different manner of contact of spirit with body, which produces a living being; and that conjunction is utterly amazing and beyond our powers of comprehension. I am speaking of man himself—*et hoc ipse homo est*."[2]

Quoting this last sentence from Augustine in a slightly abbreviated form, Pascal describes the so-called "mind-body problem" in a way that could not be bettered: "Who would not think, to see us compounding everything of mind and matter, that such a mixture is perfectly intelligible to us? Yet this is the thing we understand least; man is to himself the greatest prodigy in nature, for he cannot conceive what body is, and still less what mind is, and least of all how a body can be joined to a mind. This is his supreme difficulty, and yet it is his very being: *Modus quo corporibus adhaerent spiritus comprehendi ab hominibus non potest, et hoc tamen homo est.*" This last sentence, an abridgment of Augustine's, makes the central point: "The way in which minds are attached to bodies is beyond man's understanding, and yet this is what man is."[3]

But the chief enigma, surely, is each one of us, every single human being, different, unique, from the beginning till "the last syllable" of time. We can all share Augustine's wonder when he writes: "And yet the natural phenomena known to all men are no less wonderful, and would be a source of astonishment to all who observe them, if it were not man's habit to restrict his wonder at miracles to the rarities. For example, could anyone fail to see, on rational consideration, how marvelous it is that, despite the countless numbers of mankind, and despite the great similarity among men through their possession of a common nature, each individual has his unique individual appearance?"[4]

Indeed, one of the many great themes in Augustine is that marvels, "miracles" (from *miror, mirari:* to wonder) abound before our very eyes, so dulled by custom that we no longer see those marvels. Changing water into wine is fine, but what about water, what about nature? The power of a mere seed is for Augustine "a great thing" (*magna quaedam res est*) which ought to fill us with awe. One is reminded of the surprisingly similar wonder expressed by Hegel in his reflections on development (*Entwicklung*): one cannot see in the simple germ its provision for the entire tree, growth and all: branches, leaves, flowers, their color, odor, taste, and so forth. Or, more recently, of the observations of biologists who speak of cells as "miraculous" in quite the same sense as Augustine here: "Cells are the basic unity of life. They are the true miracle of evolution. Miracle in the figurative sense, since although we do not know how cells evolved, quite plausible scenarios have been proposed. Miraculous, none the less, in the sense that they are so remarkable."[5]

But the wonder of wonders must be the birth of humans. Augustine writes: "Someone rises from the dead, people are astonished; there are so many births every day, and no one wonders. Yet if we look at this with more discernment, it takes a greater miracle to give being to someone who was not, than to revive someone who was."[6] Again: "The births of so many humans who did not exist are each day greater miracles than the resurrections of humans who existed."[7] Finally: "Although the miracles of the visible world of nature have lost their value for us because we see them continually, still, if we observe them wisely they will be found to be greater miracles than the most extraordinary and unusual events. For man is a greater miracle than any miracle effected by man's agency."[8]

This is our topic: the everyday miracle of human persons, unique, indivisible—which is the original meaning, of course, of "individuals"—yet composites of mind and body. Contemporary debates, on the mind-brain relation, for instance, but even more so on issues concerning the human person and its dignity, in bioethics especially, would seem to offer sufficient proof, if it were still needed, that the person does appear to defy understanding. Bioethicists sometimes lend themselves to extreme views which are not unlike caricatures:

crude and simplistic, they are easy to grasp and may serve to bring out, by way of contrast, how much more complex and fascinating is the reality they miss. In what follows we will first stop to consider some such views briefly, and in the second place try to consider anew, in opposition to them, the wondrous nature of the human person.

ARE THERE "HUMAN NONPERSONS"?

*"Human" and "Person"*

According to established writers in the field of "applied ethics," there are "human persons" and "human nonpersons." For Michael Tooley, "in order to be a person, i.e., to have a serious right to life," an organism "must possess the concept of a self as a continuing subject of experiences and other mental states" and must believe "that it is itself such a continuing entity." Conclusion: "Everyday observation makes it perfectly clear, I believe, that a newborn baby does not possess the concept of a continuing self, any more than a newborn kitten possesses such a concept. If so, infanticide during a time interval shortly after birth must be morally acceptable."[9]

Along not dissimilar lines, H. Tristram Engelhardt Jr. claims that "Not all humans are equal.... Persons, not humans, are special. Adult competent humans have much higher intrinsic moral standing than human fetuses or adult frogs.... Only persons write or read books on philosophy." His argument is: persons are by definition capable of moral deliberation, they are self-conscious, rational, free to choose. Moral language reveals the *mundus intelligibilis* of Kant; it is after all to intellect that persons owe their freedom, their autonomy, their capacity for moral discourse. Those humans who do not meet such criteria, for instance the hopelessly comatose, the profoundly mentally retarded, the severely brain-damaged, fetuses, infants, are therefore "human nonpersons" devoid of "standing in the moral community," giving rise to what Engelhardt calls "morally relevant inequalities."[10]

As to the "appeal to a notion of potentiality in order to argue that since fetuses and children are potential persons, they must *eo ipso* be accorded the rights and standing of persons," Engelhardt calls upon Thomas Aquinas and the Catholic Church as his witnesses "that a sort of human life preceded the human life of persons," adding the following argument: "If X is a potential Y, it follows that X is not a Y. If fetuses are potential persons, it follows clearly that fetuses are not persons."[11]

The distinction between human and person appears to be gaining ground and, as one writer puts it not without candor, "will become even more significant as medical technology gallops ahead and resources shrink." For him as for other so-called "personalists," or defenders of "high standard personhood," "the possession of self-consciousness is a necessary and sufficient condition to be a person of full moral status"; those who contend "that all humans possess full moral status" belong to the "physicalist" or "low standard personhood camp," as do Aquinas and the Catholic Church. According to the same writer, "physicalism" was "first formulated by St. Thomas Aquinas."[12]

*Critical Remarks*

One striking feature of those uplifting accounts of "self-conscious," "rational beings," "moral agents" fully enjoying their "moral standing," and "the concept of a continuing self," is the absence of the human body—as if "these our actors ... were all spirits and are melted into air, into thin air" (*The Tempest* IV, 1, 148–50). The omission is the stranger for being addressed mainly to medical practitioners, particularly in a day and age when the wonderful discoveries of biology, neurophysiology especially, have done so much to rid us once and for all of crude dualism. In Engelhardt's account, for example, the human body turns up, to all practical purposes, only to disqualify one from the status of person, either because it is not yet fully formed or because it is in deep distress, as with the severely brain-damaged or the hopelessly comatose. Yet surely this inescapably implies, even on such a view, that when it belongs to an adult in perfect form, the human body *is* part of the person. How this can be must then be explained, as must indeed be the fact that its eventual malfunctioning would entail that it no longer *is* part of the person, since there would on such a view no longer be a person there owing to the body's distressed state.

Wittgenstein shared with Augustine, whom he revered, and with Aquinas, the concern to refute conceptions of the human ego which would sever it from the human body, as if it were in direct communication with itself, deciding on the world from within, from some detached, disengaged point of view. Such has to be the view of those who would oppose human to person, speaking of "our self-conscious minds" as "embodied in spatiotemporally extended brains and bodies." Fergus Kerr has very aptly criticized conceptions that reduce the human person to a dimensionless pinpoint round which everything turns, to a solitary, solipsist ego or I, wrapped in absolute immanence, endowed with divine attributes. Wittgenstein struggled to rid himself of such a conception, seemingly inherited from Descartes and Locke among others, by focussing upon ordinary experience.[13]

Now ordinary experience proves that all characteristic human activities involve the body in some way or other—which is not to say that they are all bodily. Being tired and unable, as a consequence, to think as clearly as one would like, has always supplied a plain manifestation of this, well before neuroscience was able to illustrate with greater precision our dependence on the brain and on our whole biological makeup and condition. None of the activities that we experience as human persons could ever be adequately described as activities of egos like pinpoints, "punctual selves" à la Locke, inside a body. And *pace* Mr. Tooley, one would need to be singularly remote not to be able to see that an infant is conscious of itself through the sense of touch, as we all are from day to day, including no doubt Mr. Tooley, well before anything like the *cogito* moves in and much more "continuously" than through any "concept." In *On Certainty*, Wittgenstein is particularly good on our debt to the sense of touch, which he uses to criticize the method of philosophical analysis practiced since Descartes as false, on the grounds that its presuppositions are false. To paraphrase him quickly, most certain is the fact, for instance, that I have two hands, that this foot is mine; it is quite impossible to doubt that I have two hands; I *know* that this is my foot; no possible experience could prove the contrary; if someone were to tell me that he doubts having a body, I should consider him half mad; the real question is: why am I so certain that this is my hand? Now it is not through the sight of my hand that I know this.[14] Or as Charles De Koninck put it: "If there is a sense by which we feel ourselves within ourselves and distinct from other things about us, surely it is the sense of touch. I begin down there and end up here. It is by virtue of touch that I feel my hand belongs to me. Of the parts of myself that I could merely see I cannot 'feel' with equal certitude that they belong to me, though I am confident they may be quite essential."[15]

To speak, furthermore, of the human person as if it were forever in act, never knowing sleep, for instance, is weird indeed. Yet if you allow for sound sleep, where no moral deliberation, conscious thinking, or conceiving "of a continuous self" can really take place, you must either claim that the sleeper is, while sleeping, no longer a person, or else claim that he or she is capable of such activities though not actually carrying them out now, which would of course be to acknowledge potentiality as essential to your account of the human experience. If you allow human eyes to shut without making their owner ipso facto blind, you have a similar problem, as Aristotle argued against the Megarians, who could not admit potency; only the actual could exist, they held. Which, as Aristotle points out in his famous refutation, condemned them to remain perpetually sitting, or perpetually standing up—"blind many times a day; and deaf too" (*Metaphysics* 2, 3, 1047a9–10), captives of a magical, superstitious view of everyday life.[16] It would not be difficult, in fact, to argue that most of our existence through time is made up primarily of potentialities.

But Engelhardt's point, "If fetuses are potential persons, it follows clearly that fetuses are not persons," must be commended for going straight to the *res*. The question is: Are fetuses merely "potential persons"?

### AQUINAS ON THE HUMAN PERSON

No one who is familiar with the topic would quarrel with those who, like the authors quoted above, appeal (sometimes inaccurately, as they do) to Thomas Aquinas on the subject of the human person, so luminous and thorough is the latter's handling of it. In the following pages, I shall try to sketch those elements in it that best enable one to answer the points raised. They shed amazing light on many of our most crucial problems.

To Thomas Aquinas the name "person" signifies "what is most perfect in the whole of nature, that is to say a self-subsistent thing of a rational nature" (*persona significat id quod est perfectissimum in tota natura, scilicet subsistens in rationali natura*); for it is best defined, as it was by the great Boethius, as *rationalis naturae individua substantia*, "individual substance of a rational nature." As one can see, the emphasis is on self-subsistent, rather than on self-conscious. And yet it is to their rational or intellectual nature that persons owe their autonomy, since it enables them to act by themselves, to be responsible for their actions (*habent dominium sui actus*).[17] As the prologue to the *Prima Secundae* makes clear, it is indeed according to this latter trait that humankind is in the image of God: insofar as it is principle of its own works, having free will and power over its doings (*secundum quod et ipse est suorum operum principium, quasi liberium arbitrium habens et suorum operum potestatem*).[18]

But the perfection of the human person does not lie in its simplicity as with pure spirits; it lies in the composition of body and soul. Even if it is from its rational nature that the human person derives a dignity not shared by other animals, that dignity belongs to the entire person, body and soul. Already in his Commentary to the *Sentences* of Peter Lombard, Thomas Aquinas is very clear that although the soul's dignity is greater than the body's, the soul remains but a part of the whole human being, which has greater dignity than the soul alone because it is more complete: *quamvis anima sit dignior corpore, tamen unitur ei ut pars totius hominis, quod quodammodo est dignius anima, inquantum est completius*. The notion of person implies a complete whole, and the soul is a part; so the soul alone cannot be said to be a person.[19] No more so, in fact, than a hand could be said to be a person, individual though it is, for it does not exist by itself (*per se*), but as a part of something more perfect, a complete substance.[20] In human nature, "person" means "*this flesh, these bones, and this soul* which are the individuating principles of a human being."[21] In other words, a human person is made up of mind (using "mind" as the equivalent of the "rational" or "intellectual soul": *anima rationalis*, or *intellectiva*, in Thomas's language ) and body; they are both essential parts of this undivided, indivisible entity, this "*individual*" called Mary or Peter. The human person is indeed at the confines of the spiritual and corporeal, benefiting from both.[22] But how mind and body are one, while distinct, in each individual, is again, of course, the question.

For Aquinas as for Aristotle, whom he follows closely in these matters, the relation of mind to body is *not* comparable to that of "sailor to ship" (cf. Aristotle, *De Anima*, II, 1, 413a9) or of body to clothing; for then the soul, or mind, would be all of human nature there is, with the body as an accident. I, soul, would use my body as Socrates uses clothing. The arguments produced by Aquinas against such an understanding are many. One must first go back, he says, to the meaning of the word "soul" as the first principle thanks to which living things have life. But life is spoken of in many ways, and is manifest in a large variety of quite distinct activities at different levels. Hence the soul is the first principle, for example, of nutrition, perception, movement, thought, all of which are evident in ordinary human experience, which reveals that the higher activities invariably presuppose the lower ones (cf. Aristotle, *De Anima*, II, 2 and 3).

Another argument, clearly derived this time from *De Anima*, II, 4, is based on the proposition *vivere viventibus est esse:* (415b13): "for living things existence is life," and the cause and first principle of this is soul. In other words, the soul is what makes the human body exist. Now this, explains Aquinas, is form; this human soul is therefore said to be the form of that body. But if it were in that body in the manner of a sailor in a ship, it could not possibly be its form, with respect to either the parts or the whole. One observes that after death neither the body nor its parts retain their name except equivocally. But on that supposition there could be no such thing as death, because the union of body and soul would be an accidental one. Now this is absurd, for death is a patent fact.[23]

A whole string of further arguments are brought in by Aquinas to underscore the fact that the activities of living and sensing are joint activities of both body and soul. This one for instance: Both man and animal are perceptible, natural entities. But this would not be the case if body and its parts were not of the essence of man and animal, if indeed the full essence of each were soul; for soul is neither perceptible nor material. It is not possible, then, that a man or animal be a soul using a body, rather than a composite of both.[24]

In their essay defending both Aristotle and Aquinas on the mind-body problem, Martha Nussbaum and Hilary Putnam have caught this whole point rather well: "The soul [they write] is not a thing merely housed in the body; its doings are the doings of body."[25]. This is made even clearer from the famous passage in the *De Anima* where, immediately after stating his definition of the soul as "the first actuality of a natural body which has life potentially" (412a27–28), which is tantamount to "the first actuality of a natural body which has organs" (412b5–6), Aristotle goes on to say: "Hence too we should not ask whether the soul and body are one, any more than whether the wax and the impression are one, or in general whether the matter of each thing and that of which it is the matter are one."[26]

"If the eye were an animal, its soul would be the power of sight" (412b18–19) is another helpful analogy offered a few lines later, providing, in addition, another clear illustration for the important distinction between first actuality and secondary actuality implicit in the definition of the soul just quoted: "The waking state is actuality in the same sense as the cutting of the axe [whose form, if it were a natural body, would be its soul] or the seeing of the eye, while the soul is actuality in the same sense as the faculty of the eye for seeing, or of the implement for doing its work."[27]

Actuality clearly has, then, two senses. The sleeping mathematician provides a good example of the necessary distinction between possessing knowledge and exercising that knowledge. The actuality defining the soul is analogous to the possession of knowledge. Whether asleep or awake the mathematician possesses the same knowledge of, say, the theory of numbers. Likewise, "both sleeping and being awake depend on the existence of soul, and being awake is analogous to the exercise of knowledge, whereas sleeping is analogous to having [knowledge] but not exercising it" (412a23–26).[28]

Most striking is thus the ineffable degree of intimacy and unity soul and body enjoy. In *De Anima* II, 1, 412b8–9, Aristotle even states that the paramount sense of being and of one is that of actuality, *entelecheia*, as in the definition of soul. The examples of the wax, of the axe, and of the eye bring out the immediacy of the union of form and matter, carefully established, as Aquinas reminds us, in *Metaphysics I* (VIII). The more so in the case of the soul, in virtue of the above quoted principle: "for living things existence is life" (415b13); for existence (*einai* in the Greek original, *esse* in the Latin translation) "is what belongs more immediately and more intimately than anything to things."²⁹

No treatment of the body-soul relationship is farther removed from Aquinas than the Pythagorean myth of metempsychosis, with its suggestion that any chance body will do. Activities such as perceiving are organically embodied and "require embodiment *to be themselves*." "We think [write Nussbaum and Putnam] that Aquinas is taking this point, and attempting to save God from Pythagorean incoherence. The truly Christian view, says Aquinas, is one that makes God a good philosopher of nature, not a bad one, not one who tries to prize the activities apart from their constitutive matter. This view of embodied form he finds, as we do, in Aristotle."³⁰

This matter of appropriate body, organs, "tools" must give us pause. In *Metaphysics* Z (VII) Aristotle points out that the finger is defined by the whole body, "for a finger is a particular kind of part of a man"; again, "a finger cannot in every state be a part of a living animal, for the dead finger has only the name in common with the living one." And: "Some parts are contemporary with the whole: such as are indispensable and in which the formula [*logos*] and the essence [*ousia*] are primarily present, e.g., the heart or perhaps the brain."³¹

Aquinas also repeatedly quotes Aristotle's remark that "if the old man could recover the proper kind of eye, he would see just as well as the young man."³² Now the heart, the hand, the eye, these and other parts of our bodies are here functionally defined. In other words, a substitute heart or hand, a transplanted cornea *are* my heart, or hand, or cornea once they have become a full-fledged part of me. They make the corresponding activities possible—in the case of the substitute heart, my survival.

"Functionalism" so understood³³ proves once again the special dignity of human bodies. The soul is there entire, whether the organ is deficient or not; hence the old man's recovered vision. In such a view, the soul of the invalid is unaltered and is no less united to the body because the latter is deficient; comatose or not, his face, his hands, his whole body have exactly the same dignity as before; for it is the dignity of the whole, present in it from the moment it came to be. The organized body of which the soul is the first actuality, according to the definition quoted earlier, is made up of a variety of organs; the soul cannot then be said to be the actuality of only one or the other of these, such as of the heart or of the brain, for example, but it must be the actuality of both the whole organized body and of its parts.³⁴

Furthermore, Aristotle had shown in his discussions with his predecessors in *De Anima* I, 5, that while the body is obviously divisible into quantitative parts, it is impossible for the soul to be so divided.[35] His suggestion was that "it is with the whole soul we think, perceive, move ourselves, act or are acted upon." Likewise, Augustine taught that the soul, while simple, was *in unoquoque corpore, et in toto tota est, et in qualibet parte eius tota est:* "in each body, whole in the whole, whole in each part of it."[36]

Since the soul is the first actuality of a natural body possessed of organs, it follows, wrote Aquinas, that the soul cannot exist actually but only potentially in the seed, before the organization of the body (*non est igitur ante organizationem corporis in semine anima actu, sed solum potentia sive virtute*). Quoting in support of Aristotle's remark that "the seed and the fruit are potentially the body of the appropriate kind" (412b27–28), not actually such a body in other words, Thomas believed that because the seed was not an "organized body," it could not therefore be actualized by a "rational soul." For the same reason, he did not believe the early fetus or embryo was already a human being or person; here again he depended on Aristotle, in whose *De Generatione animalium* one finds a theory of the first stages of life which modern, especially contemporary, biology has proven to be quite false.[37]

It is well established by contemporary biology that all life, including human life, begins at the moment of conception.[38] The whole biological development of the human individual is, in admittedly anthropomorphic language, "programmed" from the outset. With such scientific information as we now enjoy, we can see that Aquinas provides the best arguments in favor of what has become the Church's express position—witness the Vatican's statement of doctrine, "Respect for Human Life in Its Origins and on the Dignity of Procreation"—namely that an individual human being is already present in the zygote. (And how, asks the Church, can an individual human being *not* be a human person?) For the zygote, the first cell, is an organized body.

First actuality would mean, then, what it says: not a potential person but an actual person. First actuality, we saw, refers to secondary actualities that may not be realized, as seeing or reasoning when you are asleep or in a coma. So first actuality does not exclude potentiality, it on the contrary implies, notably in the case of human beings, a large number of very different potentialities. Yet surely this is what contemporary biology is telling us: not unlike the full tree from the germ evoked at the beginning of this chapter, but on an infinitely larger scale in the case of humans, these various potentialities do in fact emerge realized from the same initial cell. Would "fetuses, infants, the profoundly mentally retarded, and the hopelessly comatose" be persons too? They must be, since the same particular person is ever individual, i.e., one and indivisible, from the first moment of conception and since its dignity can hardly be confined to the actual *exercise* of higher functions.

CONCLUSION

We saw how easily the exclusion of certain humans from human personhood could be obtained, once again, by dint of abstract definitions set forth in complete defiance of concrete reality. Benjamin Constant's famous formula: *immoler à l'être abstrait les êtres réels* ("to sacrifice to abstract being the real beings"), springs to the mind. Or the Nazi definition of *Mensch* used as a criterion to claim that some humans, such as Slavs, were *Untermenschen* ("subhumans"), others, namely Jews, *Unmenschen* ("nonhumans") pure and simple. In order for the Nazis to be able to proclaim themselves, by definition, the paradigm of humanity, the first prerequisite had to be a peculiar blindness. Goethe said that barbarism consists "in the failure to recognize the excellent." As the twentieth century will have all too amply illustrated, the barbarian is in fact ultimately unable to recognize even his own humanity (let alone to define it). Not the least of the ironies in the creation of the category of "human nonpersons" is the proclamation of *moral standing* as the norm justifying the exclusion. As a prima facie method of approach to ethical issues, abstract definitions disregarding common human experience must be deemed, to say the least, suspect.[39]

From the dawn of civilization, recognition of the dignity of the poor has been foremost: "children, old men, the poor, and the sick, should be considered as the lords of the atmosphere" (*Laws of Manu*, ancient India). Respect even for the dead has been universal, as burial practices illustrate. Why should one, to this day, be moved to assent before the action of the young girl Antigone in Sophocles' great play when she refuses to let the body of her brother, denounced as a traitor, to be left to rot in the sun and be eaten by vultures, at the cost of breaking the law and sacrificing her own life? Her ethical commitment, and the universal echo it provokes, implies that even the dead body of a condemned person deserves sacred rites. These will restore it to the humanity to which it belongs by right. If this be true with regard to the dead, if even the remains of a condemned man deserve such respect, what should one think of a living human body, destitute or defenseless as it may be?[40]

One is reminded today of Emmanuel Levinas's central theme, the human face—naked, poor, out in the open, defenseless, and yet imposing respect. An assassin cannot look his victim in the eye, as if sensing that something sacred is involved. But Sophocles' Antigone goes even deeper, since her brother's face may no longer be recognizable as a human face—not unlike that other face described by Isaiah (52, 14): "so marred was his appearance, beyond human semblance." (Nor, as Dominique Folscheid points out, does the human embryo, which he nevertheless describes as "notre plus-que-prochain" ["our more-than-neighbor"], have a face at all.)[41] What Antigone so forcefully suggests is that, whatever our condition, we all share a common humanity, and thus a common dignity. Unless, of course, the progress of civilization, or of "ethics," should imply the dismissal of such recognitions and age-old practices as ancient mistakes. Neither philosophy nor the marvelous discoveries of science would lend the slightest support to such a conclusion.

### NOTES

1. Cf. Isaiah 66:24; Mark 9:48; Matthew 25:41; Jude 7; Revelation 20:10. Scripture quotations are from *The New Oxford Annotated Bible with the Apocrypha, Revised Standard Version*, edited by Herbert G. May and Bruce M. Metzger (New York: Oxford University Press, 1973).

2. Cf. St. Augustine, *De Civitate Dei*, XXI, 10 (also 7, 8, 9), translation by Henry Bettenson (London: Penguin Books, 1972), p. 986. For the Latin text we use the fourth edition by B. Dombart and A. Kalb published at Leipzig by Teubner in 1928–29, as printed with French translation by G. Combès and notes by G. Bardy in Bibliothèque Augustinienne, 33–37 (Paris, Desclée De Brouwer, 1959–60).

3. *Pensées*, 72 (Brunschvicg); 199 (Lafuma), *in fine*; translated by A. J. Krailsheimer (London, Penguin Books, 1966), p. 94.

4. *De Civitate Dei*, XXI, 8, translation, p. 981. The uniqueness of each individual is corroborated by neuroscience; cf. Gerald Edelman, *Bright Air, Brilliant Fire: On the Matter of the Mind* (London, Penguin Books, 1994).

5. See *Tractatus in Iohannis Evangelium*, VIII,1; Augustine speaks of the "admirable and stupendous works of God in each grain of seed" (*Tractatus*, XXIV, 1); the "infinite power of seeds" (*De utilitate credendi*, 16, 34); cf. *Tractatus*, I, 9; *Epistulae*, 102, 5, *PL*, 33, 372; *Sermo* 247, 2 *PL*, 38, 700. For the *Tractatus in Johannis Evangelium* we use the edition provided in Bibliothèque Augustinienne, 71, printed with French translation and excellent notes by M.-F. Berrouard (Paris: Desclée De Brouwer 1969); for the *De utilitate credendi*, the text provided in Bibliothèque Augustinienne, 8, with French translation and notes by J. Pegon, 1951; second revised edition by G. Madec (Paris: Desclée De Brouwer, 1982); for the *Epistulae* and the *Sermones*, we use *Patrologie latine* (*PL*), ed. J.-P. Migne (Paris, 1841 sq., indicating each time the volume and the page; translations into English are our own. See also G. W. F. Hegel, *Vorlesungen über die Geschichte der Philosophie*, I, Werke 18 (Frankfurt am Main, Suhrkamp Verlag, 1986), pp. 39–47. Finally, we quote from Lewis Wolpert, *The Triumph of the Embryo* (Oxford: Oxford University Press, 1991), p. 5.

6. *Tractatus* (VIII, 1).

7. *Sermo* 242, 1, *PL* 38, 1139; cf. *Tractatus*, IX, 1; XLIX, 1.

8. *De Civitate Dei*, X, 12, translation, p. 390.

9. Michael Tooley, *Abortion and Infanticide* (1972), in Peter Singer, ed., *Applied Ethics* (Oxford, 1986, pp. 57–85; especially 66–67; 69; 76–78; 81–85.

10. H. Tristram Engelhardt Jr., *The Foundations of Bioethics* (Oxford: Oxford University Press, 1986), pp. 107–9. I doubt Kant would espouse Engelhardt's conclusions. However, in *Dignity and Practical Reason in Kant's Moral Theory* (Ithaca: Cornell University Press, 1992), referring to "Kant's principle that humanity in each person must always be treated as an end in itself, never simply as a means" (p. 201), Thomas E. Hill Jr. observes that "the status of infants and the mentally incompetent remains problematic under the principle" (p. 202).

11. Cf. Engelhardt, *Foundations*, pp. 110 ff., 148. Against the appeal to potentiality, cf. Michael Tooley, *Abortion*, p. 74 ff.; Peter Singer, *Practical Ethics* (Cambridge: Cambridge University Press, 1993, pp. 152 ff.; F. M. Kamm, *Creation and Abortion: A Study in Moral and Legal Philosophy* (Oxford: Oxford University Press, 1992), pp. 16 ff.

12. James W. Walters, *What Is a Person? An Ethical Exploration* (Urbana: University of Illinois Press, 1997), pp. 2, 3, 17–20, 24, 26–28, passim.

13. Cf. Fergus Kerr, *Theology after Wittgenstein* (Oxford: Blackwell, 1986); John Locke, *An Essay Concerning Human Understanding*, II, chap. 27: "Of Identity and Diversity," ed. Roger Woolhouse (London: Penguin Books, 1997), pp. 296–313; see also Charles Taylor, *Sources of the Self*, chap. 9, "Locke's Punctual Self," (Cambridge: Cambridge University Press, 1989), pp. 159–76, and notes pp. 542–55. In his letter to Princess Elisabeth of 28 June 1643, Descartes claims we somehow sense the union of body and soul, but do not succeed in conceptualizing it. But as Jean-Luc Marion shows (*Questions cartésiennes* [Paris: Presses Universitaires de France, 1991], pp. 97–98; 100; 103; 105), in the Second Meditation the Cartesian *cogito* thinks itself first in absolute immanence—rather as Aristotle's God; for this latter point see our "L'intellection des indivisibles et l'appréhension des natures simples: Aristote et Descartes," in *Laval Théologique et Philosophique*, 53, 3 (October 1997), 767–83.

14. Cf. Ludwig Wittgenstein, *Über Gewissheit/On Certainty* (Oxford, Blackwell,1974), paragraphs 247; 250; 255; 157; 446; 360; cf. 148; 257; 446; and the remarkable study by Gunter Gebauer, "Hand und Gewissheit," in *Das Schwinden der Sinne*, ed. Dietmar von Kamper und Christoph Wulf (Frankfurt am Main, Suhrkamp, 1984), pp. 234–60.

15. Charles De Koninck, "The Tyranny of Sight," in *Report of Annual Meeting and Proceedings of the Royal College of Physicians and Surgeons of Canada*, September 28 and 29, 1951, p. 3: "Instead of basing ourselves immediately upon the operation which is proper to the highest of our faculties, we rest first of all and with great assurance in the experience of touching, in which we have at the same time an experience of existing. To be sure, this consciousness is not without thought, but the thought implied here is one which depends upon touch and which does not as yet reveal itself as thought." Cf. Gebauer: "Wittgenstein behauptet mit dieser Überlegung, dass fundamentale Gewissheiten des Denkens in der materiellen Struktur des Körpers verankert sind. Die mit Hilfe des Körpers erzeugten Gewissheiten liegen *tiefer* als andere Gewissheiten unseres Weltbildes" ("Hand und Gewissheit," p. 241).

16. On the Megarians, cf. J. Vuillemin, *Nécessité et contingence. L'aporie de Diodore et les systèmes philosophiques* (Paris: Minuit, 1984). On sleep, Engelhardt, *Foundations*, p. 123; Walters, *What Is a Person?* p. 66.

17. *Summa Theologiae, Ia Pars,* q. 29, a. 3, c.; and a. 1, ed. Petri Caramello, cum textu ex recensione Leonina (Taurini: Marietti, 1950); translations of Aquinas into English in this essay are our own. See also Robert Spaemann, *Das Natürliche und das Vernünftige* (Munich: Piper, 1987), quoting with approval Michael Dummett's statement: "man is a self-subsistent thing" (p. 73).

18. *Summa Theologiae, Ia-IIae,* Prologus, ed. Petri Caramello, cum textu ex recensione Leonini (Taurini: Marietti, 1950). Human dignity may be considered at three levels: natural, ethical, supernatural. Thomas Aquinas deals fully with the three, but want of space forces us to limit ourselves here. Cf. Servais Pinckaers, "La dignité de l'homme selon Saint Thomas d'Aquin," in *De Dignitate Hominis* (Freiburg Schweiz, Universitätsverlag, 1987), pp. 89–106.

19. Cf. *Scriptum super libros Sententiarum,* III, d. 5, q. 3, a. 2, *in toto;* cf. a. 3: "persona pars esse non possit"; "hoc est contra rationem personae, quae maximam completionem importat" (ed. Mandonnet and Moos [Paris: Lethielleux, 1933]. Cf. *Super Primam Epistolam ad Corinthios Lectura,* XV, 12–19, lect. 2, n. 924 (ed. Raphaelis Cai [Taurini: Marietti, 1953]: "Anima . . . cum sit pars corporis hominis, non est totus homo, et anima mea non est ego; unde licet anima consequatur salutem in alia vita, non tamen ego vel quilibet homo."

20. Cf. *Summa theologiae, Ia Pars,* q. 75, a. 4, ad 2; *IIIa Pars,* q. 2, a. 2, ad 3 (Taurini: Marietti, 1948).

21. "Persona igitur in quacumque natura significat id quod est distinctum in natura illa; sicut in humana natura significat *has carnes, haec ossa, et hanc animam* quae sunt principia individuantia hominem; quae quidem, licet non sint de significatione personae in communi, sunt tamen de significatione personae humanae" (*Ia Pars,* q. 29, a. 4, c; our italics).

22. "Homo enim est quasi horizon et confinium spiritualis et corporalis naturae, ut quasi medium inter utrasque, utrasque bonitates participet et corporales et spirituales" (*Scriptum super libros Sententiarum,* III, Prologus.) "Et inde est quod anima intellectualis dicitur esse quasi quidem horizon et confinium corporeorum et incorporeorum" (*Summa Contra Gentiles,* II, 68, n. 1453, ed. Ceslai Pera [Taurini: Marietti, 1961]); see also *Q. D. de Anima,* q. un., a. 2, ed. P. P. M. Calcaterra and T. S. Centi, in *Quaestiones Disputatae II* [Taurini: Marietti, 1953].

23. Cf. *Q. D. de Anima,* q. un., a. 1, c.; *Ia Pars,* q. 76, a. 1.

24. Cf. *Summa Contra Gentiles,* II, 57.

25. Martha C. Nussbaum and Hilary Putnam, "Changing Aristotle's Mind," in *Essays on Aristotle's De Anima,* ed. Nussbaum and A. O. Rorty (Oxford: Oxford University Press, 1992, p. 45.

26. Aristotle, *De Anima (On the Soul),* II, 1, 412 b 6 9, translation by D. W. Hamlyn (Oxford: Oxford University Press, 1968); we shall be quoting from other standard translations, however, whenever they seem better; for the Greek text we use *Aristotelis De Anima,* ed. W. D. Ross (Oxford: Oxford University Press, 1956).

27. *De Anima* II, 1, 412 b 27–413 a 3; translation by W. S. Hett, Loeb Library (London and Cambridge Mass.: William Heinemann and Harvard University Press, 1936.

28. Translation by Hippocrates G. Apostle (Grinnell, Iowa: The Peripatetic Press, 1981); cf. *De Anima,* II, 1, 412 a 22–b 1.

29. See *Q. D. de Anima,* q. un., a. 9 and a.10.

30. *De Anima*, I, 3, 407 b 24–27; II, 2, 414 a 22–25; Apostle translation; Nussbaum and Putnam, "Changing Aristotle's Mind," p. 55.

31. Cf. *Metaphysics* Z (VII), 10, 1034 b 20 sq., especially 1035 b 3 sq.; translation by Hugh Tredennick (Loeb Library, London and Cambridge, Mass.: Heinemann and Harvard University Press, 1933); quotes are from 1035 b 10–11; b 24–25; 25–27; cf. *De Partibus Animalium*, I, 1, 640 b 34 sq.

32. *De Anima*, I, 4, 408 b 21–22, translation by J. A. Smith, in *The Complete Works of Aristotle. The Revised Oxford Translation*, ed. by Jonathan Barnes (Princeton: University Press, 1984), vol. 1, p. 651.

33. Nussbaum and Putnam write that "Putnam now dissociates himself from functionalism for reasons that bring him even closer to Aristotle" ("Changing Aristotle's Mind," p. 36).

34. Cf. *Q. D. de Anima*, q. un., a. 2; a.10: "Even the parts of plants are organs, although extremely simple ones, e. g. the leaf is a covering for the pod, and the pod for the fruit; while roots are analogous to the mouth, for both take in food" (*De Anima*, II, 1, 412b1–3: Hamlyn translation).

35. Cf. *De Anima* I, 5, 411 b 6–14.

36. Aristotle, *De Anima*, I, 5, 411b1–3; J. A. Smith translation, p. 655; St Augustine, *De Trinitate*, VI, vi, 8; for the Latin text, we use the edition in Bibliothèque Augustinienne, 15–16, with French translation and notes by M. Mellet and Th. Camelot (Paris: Études Augustiniennes, 1991); translations into English are ours. Cf. Thomas Aquinas, *Ia Pars*, q. 76, a. 8; *Q. D. de Anima*, q. un., a. 10.

37. See especially *Summa Contra Gentiles*, II, c. 89, no. 1737; *Q. D. de Anima*, q. un., a. 11, *Q. D. de Spiritualibus Creaturis*, q. un., a. 3 (ed. PP. M. Calcaterra and T. S. Centi, in *Quaestiones Disputatae II* [Taurini, Marietti, 1953]); *Q. D. de Potentia*, q. 3, a. 9, c., and ad 9. (ed. Pauli M. Pession, in *Quaestiones Disputatae II* [Taurini: Marietti, 1953]).

38. Cf. Gerald Edelman, *Bright Air, Brilliant Fire*, chapter 6, and Lewis Wolpert, *The Triumph of the Embryo*.

39. For further developments on this and related matters, cf. Thomas De Koninck, *De la dignité humaine* (Paris: Presses Universitaires de France, 1995), pp. 1–19; 223–26. Cf. also *Gespräche mit Goethe*, by von Johann Peter Eckermann, ed. Fritz Bergemann (Wiesbaden: Insel-Verlag, 1955), Zweiter Teil, 22 März 1831, p. 455: "Niebuhr was right when he saw the coming of a barbarous age. It is already here, we are already in its midst; for in what does barbarism consist but in the failure to recognize the excellent?" (translation taken from Stanley Rosen, *Nihilism: A Philosophical Essay* [New Haven and London, Yale University Press, 1969], p. 72).

40. For detailed references, cf. T. De Koninck, *De la dignité humaine*; C. S. Lewis, *The Abolition of Man* (Fount Paperbacks, 1978), pp. 49–59.

41. Dominique Folscheid, "L'embryon, ou notre plus-que-prochain," in *Ethique*, no. 4, (1992), pp. 20–43, especially 25; and *Philosophie, éthique et droit de la médecine*, ed. Dominique Folscheid, Brigitte Feuillet-Le Mintier, et Jean-François Mattei (Paris: Presses Universitaires de France, 1997).

# Part II
# Ethics

# 5

# John Case: An Example of Aristotelianism's Self-Subversion?

*Alasdair MacIntyre*

The history of Western thought is punctuated by revivals of Aristotelianism. And often a central part in those revivals is played by some renewed interest in Aristotle's ethics and politics. But such revivals are not lasting and characteristically are the prologue to some anti-Aristotelian mode of thought, so that the history of Western thought is also punctuated by rejections of Aristotelianism. What causes these cycles of revival and rejection? There is certainly no single answer, but sometimes at least it seems to have been the case that moral and political Aristotelianism has been self-subverting, that it has been its protagonists who brought about its downfall. And perhaps this was how it was with some Renaissance Aristotelians.

I

In Philip Sidney's *An Apologie for Poetrie* the claims of the poet to be the preeminent teacher of the virtues are challenged by the moral philosophers and the historians. In this encounter the historians fare worst, but the moral philosophers turn out to be no better than the poets in telling us how we should live, while being a good deal their inferior at motivating us. So Sidney concludes of the poet that "therein, (namely in morrall doctrine, the chief of all knowledges,) hee dooth not merely farre passe the Historian, but for instructing, is well nigh comparable to the Philosopher; and for moving, leaves him behind him. . . . " What philosophers did Sidney have in mind?

At the very beginning of the *Apologie* Sidney provides a mocking portrait of those who compete with the poets for preeminence "among whom as principall challengers step forth the morrall Philosophers, whom me thinketh, I see comming towards me with a sullen gravity, as though they could not abide vice by day light, rudely clothed for to witnes outwardly their contempt of outward things, with bookes in their hands agaynst glory, whereto they sette theyre names, sophistically speaking against subtility, and angry with any man in whom they see the soule fault of anger: these men casting larges as they goe, of Definitions, Divisions, and Distinctions, with a scornefull interogative, doe soberly aske, whether it bee possible to finde any path, so ready to leade a man to vertue, as that which teacheth what vertue is?" Sidney probably wrote these words in late 1581, nine years after he had left Oxford. But he would not have had much, if any, occasion to encounter philosophers during his travels abroad or his time at court, so that it seems reasonable to suppose that it is the teachers of moral philosophy at Oxford whom he still has in mind. And the most notable of these was John Case.

Case was some thirteen years older than Sidney. It was in the same year (1568) that Sidney had entered Christ Church that Case had become a Fellow of St. Johns. Charles B. Schmitt[1] in his splendid account of Case's life and work laid great emphasis both on the knowledge of Sidney's writings exhibited in Case's later work and on Case's acquaintance with some of Sidney's friends and with Sidney's sister. But while Sidney was an undergraduate at Oxford, Case's reputation as a moral philosopher had yet to be made. It was finally made by the publication in 1585, a year before Sidney's death, of his *Speculum quaestionum moralium, in Universam Ethicen Aristotelis*, a detailed exposition of and philosophical commentary upon the *Nicomachean Ethics*, printed by Joseph Barnes on the press recently given to Oxford University by its Chancellor, Robert Devereux Dudley, Earl of Leicester, Sidney's uncle. (So began the long and marvellous history of the Oxford University Press.) And it is to the Earl of Leicester that Case's book is dedicated.

In the same year Sidney published his *Discourse in Defence of the Earl of Leicester* and it seems unlikely that he did not have some knowledge of the publication of Case's book. If he had read it, he might well have felt that its definitions, divisions, and distinctions provided confirmation for his stinging portrait of the moral philosopher. But Case's book is in an important way a reply to Sidney. I do not mean by this to imply that Case had read the *Apologie*, let alone that he had it in mind when writing the *Speculum*. The *Apologie* was not published until 1595 and, even if we entertain the remote possibility that Case had been shown the *Apologie* in manuscript, it is very unlikely that he could have seen it before a large part of the *Speculum* had already been written. What then do I mean when I say that Case's *Speculum* is nonetheless a reply to Sidney's *Apologie?* Just this, that Case's *Speculum* articulates more adequately than any other book (the claim was not peculiar to Case, but is found elsewhere among Renaissance Aristotelians) the thesis that the teaching of moral philosophy, rightly understood, *is* the teaching of the moral virtues, that the moral philosopher is preeminent, not only in affording instruction about the theory of the moral virtues, but in making those whom he instructs virtuous. If Case's arguments are sound, then Sidney's arguments for the preeminence of the poets fail.

The claims made by Case were endorsed in some of the twenty-seven congratulatory Latin poems by his Oxford colleagues which precede the text. "The book," declares the Vice-Chancellor of the university, "teaches all the several virtues by philosophizing." And in the dedicatory epistle Case addresses the students of both English universities as one anxious to instruct them to practical effect. He is not merely engaged in expounding the text of the *Nicomachean Ethics* and in responding to a variety of objections to Aristotle's theses and arguments, but is doing so in order to make his readers, if they are seriously attentive, better human beings in a way that only the teaching of moral philosophy can achieve. So Case's *Speculum* asserts precisely what Sidney's *Apologie* denies. But in so doing Case encounters an obvious initial difficulty.

At the beginning of the *Nicomachean Ethics* Aristotle had argued that the young are not yet capable of learning what the moral philosopher has to teach. Their experience is too limited and they are guided by their as yet disordered passions (1095a 2–6). What they need is the discipline of practical habituation, not theoretical instruction. To act not only in accordance with what virtue requires, but virtuously is first to know what one is doing—that one's action is what justice or courage or generosity requires, secondly to do what one does for its own sake, to do it just because it is the just or courageous or generous thing to do, and thirdly to give expression in so doing to a stable disposition to perform just or courageous or generous actions, whenever they are required. But Aristotle emphasizes that it is not the knowledge that moves us to action (1105a 30–1105b 3). So that it is not only that the young are not the moral philosopher's appropriate audience. It is also that, on Aristotle's view, the kind of moral training that produces virtuous character is a type of practical habituation and not theoretical instruction in moral philosophy.

II

It must seem then that Case would only have been able to answer Sidney if he had been willing to repudiate Aristotle. But this is not at all how Case proceeds. Instead he radically reinterprets Aristotle, without recognizing that he is doing so. Aristotle had remarked that one can grow older without becoming mature and that there are therefore older people who remain in the condition of the young. Case seizes on this as a first step in arguing that "young" is to be understood as referring not so much to age as to *mores*. "Wherefore it is not by being few or many in years, but by inconstancy and levity of *mores* that I define 'young' in these passages" (lib. I, cap. 3). The student, that is to say, must have the habits of a good student, but this habituation is preliminary to the moral education afforded by instruction in the *Ethics*. When we remember the age of the undergraduates whom Case was teaching at Oxford and whom he addressed in his dedicatory epistle, the difference between Case and Aristotle becomes even clearer. (Sidney who, after four years at Shrewsbury School, had become an undergraduate at the age of thirteen was younger than most, but there were many not much older.) The adolescent student whose preliminary education has implanted a desire to excel and a willingness to learn from his teachers is treated by Case as someone who already has all the prior habituation that he needs in order to be moved to the acquisition and exercise of the virtues by philosophical instruction.

Both the scope and the power thus ascribed by Case to moral philosophy make it necessary for him also to revise Aristotle's conception of the virtue of prudence, *phronesis*, although once again Case was plainly unaware that he was engaged in such a revision. For Case in a preface addressed to the students of both universities had ascribed to the study of philosophical ethics great power: "It is the norm of *mores*, the mistress of the virtues, the *gnomon* (the measure on a sundial) of life, the rule of actions." So much so that when he comes to the discussion of prudence, he confronts the problem of distinguishing between moral philosophy and prudence. The problem arises because on his account it seems to be the case that "Moral philosophy is the habit of acting with true reasoning concerning human goods: therefore it is prudence." Case's reply is that "Moral philosophy treats these goods in terms of *genus*, prudence in terms of *species*" (lib. VI, cap. 5). The philosopher supplies a set of moral generalizations; the prudent agent applies them to particular types of circumstance. Prudence is, so to speak, applied moral philosophy and without moral philosophy the agent would not have the requisite stock of generalizations.

How then does Case deal with Aristotle's assertion that knowledge (*scientia* in Case's translation) plays little or no part in virtuous action (*Nicomachean Ethics* 1105b 2–3)? He does so by quoting the passage in question and replying that the knowledge thus referred to is theoretical, contemplative knowledge. The knowledge that is required for virtuous action is what he calls a knowledge of circumstances, by which he means, so it presently becomes clear, the knowledge of what kind of virtuous action is required in whatever circumstances (lib. II, cap. 4). But to this further objections have to be raised. That the *scientia circumstantiarum* that is needed is prudence seems evident from Case's definition of virtue, yet one can be learned without being prudent, so that the knowledge of circumstances—which presumably the learned possess—is not sufficient. Moreover the ignorant and uncultured often possess virtue, but, on this view of prudence, they cannot be prudent.

To this Case's response is that two kinds of prudence must be distinguished. There is on the one hand particular prudence, which is the limited knowledge of how to act virtuously in some range of particular circumstances and this knowledge can be in the less experienced and the less learned. But there is on the other hand "heroic and general" prudence, "which is the knowledge of living well and of acting in accordance with all the virtues in every circumstance, and this is not necessary for everyone." So the ignorant and uncultured can after all be prudent on this or that occasion, but only with an inferior form of prudence. And one can be learned without having the knowledge necessary for heroic and general prudence, a knowledge which is to be provided generally, even if not necessarily always, by moral philosophy. There remains one further objection.

"To obey the precepts of virtue is an act of virtue, but a boy can obey the precepts without prudence: therefore there can be an act of virtue without prudence" (lib. VI, cap. 13). What is noteworthy here is that Case does not reply, as Aristotle presumably would have done, by drawing a distinction between acts that conform to what the virtues require and acts that issue from the settled dispositions of a virtuous human being. Instead Case answers that "As the act of virtue is in the boy inchoately, so is prudence. . . . "

Moral development then is from the inchoate moral virtue and prudence of the very young to the development of virtuous habits over a certain limited range of cases to the heroic virtue, requiring heroic and general prudence, for which an education into the substance of Aristotle's ethics is required. The notion that what Aristotle had provided was primarily a set of general moral precepts which can be taught to the well brought up young, so that they can then learn to apply these to their own particular circumstances, is not of course original to Case. It was this conception of Aristotle's ethics that had led Sir Thomas Elyot in *The Boke named the Governour* (1531) to include the *Nicomachean Ethics* along with Cicero's *De Officiis* in the books of which tutors of young gentlemen were to make use. And when John Wilkinson published the first English translation of the *Nicomachean Ethics* in 1547 (not from the Greek, but from Brunetto Latini's Italian), his title page read: "The Ethiques of Aristotle, that is to saye, precepts of good behavoure and perfighte honestie, now newly translated into English."

Case however brings to the task of expounding Aristotle a kind of learning that is found in none of his English predecessors, but that matches the best of his European contemporaries. He draws upon both scholastic and humanistic sources and methods, making use of a wide range of older and newer commentators, including Aquinas, Buridan, and Burleigh. But his use of commentators is always subordinated to those educational purposes which provide his enterprise with its justification.

His methods of exposition were eclectic. He was, as an Aristotelian, opposed to Ramus's positions and influence and he contributed to the debates between Aristotelian and Ramist dialectic. But he made use of Ramist schemes of division and of Ramist diagrams in setting out his Aristotelian subject-matter, putting these devices to the service of a type of commentary modeled on the scholastic treatment of *Quaestiones Disputatae,* where exposition proceeds through the posing and answering of successive objections, something that I have already illustrated in Case's treatment of prudence.

Not every reader has been charmed by Case's modes of exposition. Nancy S. Struever[2] has called them "technocracy run wild"[3] and "reductive and baroque,"[4] concluding that "the message is virtually submerged under the weight of the organizational modes."[5] And her criticism involves content as well as form, for she takes Case's aim to be "to put forward as many familiar and comfortable moralisms as possible with the least expense of effort of reconciliation."[6] Struever's criticisms however miss the point in two different ways.

First they ignore the excellence of most of Case's expositions of Aristotle. Generally his use of techniques of division clarifies effectively what would otherwise be obscure to the student and his distinctions are just those that the beginning Elizabethan student needs. This is a book that reflects the experience of teaching undergraduates and that speaks to the teaching needs of Case's colleagues as well as to the needs of his and their pupils. The questions put to Aristotle may not be quite the same as either the questions put by their medieval predecessors or their modern successors, but Case's book is well-designed to move the attentive reader from being a naïve questioner of Aristotle to someone who has begun to learn from the text how to question Aristotle in Aristotle's own terms.

Secondly, what Struever says may suggest that Case merely *asserts* what she calls "moralisms." But it is of the first importance that these moralisms are presented by Case as the conclusions of philosophical arguments. And it is on the philosophy that everything turns. It is perhaps because of their recognition of this that the verdict of Copenhaver and Schmitt on Case is very different from Struever's: "More effectively than any other Englishman, he combined traditions of scholastic and humanist Aristotelianism that had been separate in the previous century.... It was Case who brought the new humanist-scholastic Aristotle to Renaissance Oxford, reviving interest in standard philosophical questions."[7] The morality emerges from the philosophy and is so presented that the Aristotelian moral philosopher emerges as a moral teacher. What then is the content of that argumentative teaching?

### III

It is of course for the most part a content that would be recognizable to Aristotelians of any time and place. But as well as those topics on which Case does no more than expound Aristotle, there are topics where he puts to Aristotle questions that are not precisely Aristotle's and topics about which he gives answers that are very certainly not Aristotle's. Let me give an example of each.

On courage Case follows Aristotle closely. And he also affirms Aristotle's view that the good human being is directed towards the achievement of that human being's own good. When therefore it turns out that the supreme exemplification of the exercise of courage is, if necessary, to give up one's life for the sake of the defense of one's city, the question arises of how to act thus can be to act for the sake of one's own good. Surely to act thus is to sacrifice one's own good for the sake of the good of others. The good of one's country and one's own good no longer coincide. Case's response to the objection is both terse and Aristotelian: "He gives his life to his country, as the philosopher teaches, but he preserves his virtue (which is the greatest good) for himself" (lib. IX, cap. 8).

On lying Case is closer to Aquinas than he is to Aristotle. It is not that his conclusions are at variance with Aristotle's. Neither were Aquinas's. But his idiom is Thomistic rather than or as well as Aristotelian. Yet his account is not entirely the same as Aquinas's. Aristotle tells us simply that a lie is in itself bad and culpable (1127a 28–9). Someone with the virtue of truthfulness tells the truth both when nothing else is at stake and, even more scrupulously, when something further is at stake (1127b 3–5). Aquinas sets out the grounds for this condemnation of lying (*Summa Theologiae* IIa-IIae, 110) as Aristotle does not, and in what Case says about lies as perversions of the order of speech and as directing the intellect away from its proper object, truth, he remains close to Aquinas. But where Aquinas had insisted that the essential property of a lie is that it is the intentional utterance of a false statement, Case (lib. IV, cap. 7) makes an intention to deceive, either by word or deed, central to the definition of a lie.

Aquinas treats the intention to deceive as an additional evil of almost all lies (110, 1). Case treats the wrong done to whomsoever is deceived by a lie as an essential part of the wrongness of lying. Yet Case is at one with

Aquinas, not only in his assertion that the prohibition of lying is unqualified and unconditional, but also in his acknowledgment that this prohibition applies even in just wars. Ruses and stratagems by which an enemy may be deceived are permitted. But nothing that involves a violation of good faith is permitted (lib. III, cap. 11).

Consider by contrast an issue in which Case departs from Aristotle's text in such a way as to put himself at odds both with Aristotle and Aquinas and one that is all the more striking because of Aquinas's evident influence on Case's discussion of the relationship between natural law and positive law (lib. V, cap. 7). Both Aristotle and Aquinas had condemned tyranny, but on resistance to tyranny Aquinas seems to have twice changed his mind. In *De Regimine Principum* he had emphasized the dangers involved in attempts to overthrow a tyrant. In the second part of the second part of the *Summa Theologiae* (42, 2), written about half a dozen years later, however, Aquinas, having argued that sedition is always a mortal sin, says bluntly that the overthrow of a tyrannical government is not an act of sedition, except when the disorder that it produces is a greater evil than the tyrant's rule. It is rather the tyrant who is guilty of sedition in harming the community. Since the text makes it clear that violence may be involved in such acts, Aquinas seems finally to have returned to his earliest position on these matters, when he had followed Cicero in holding that on occasion it is praiseworthy to kill a tyrant in order to liberate one's country (*Commentary on the Sentences* II, D. 44, 2, ad 5).

Case's position could not be more sharply opposed. In his discussion of justice he concludes that arms are not to be taken up against any prince, whether good or bad. To do so is madness (*furor*). It is to fail to uphold the dignity of the state (lib. V, cap. 3). In one way this purported version of Aristotelianism that involves a condemnation of *all* rebellion against *any* political authority is very strange, but in another not surprising at all. Pius V's condemnation of Elizabeth in 1570 had legitimized rebellion by her Catholic subjects, and in the two years before the publication of the *Speculum* a variety of conspiracies to overthrow Elizabeth's government had been exposed. Case needed to show that an Aristotelianism such as his, influenced as it was in its interpretation by Aquinas's commentary, nonetheless enjoined unconditional loyalty to the Elizabethan settlement.

IV

Case was in fact not merely a loyal, but an enthusiastic subject of Elizabeth (the seventeenth-century rumor transmitted by Antony à Wood that he was "popishly affected" seems to have no foundation in fact; academic gossip then as now was unreliable). His book on politics, the *Sphaera Civitatis*, published in 1588, the year of the Armada, like the *Speculum*, contains nothing that would have been unacceptable to Elizabeth's government. The Aristotle whom he presents in both books is an Aristotle from whom Elizabeth's regime has nothing to fear. This was in itself a controversial stance, for not all Case's English contemporaries took this view of Aristotle. After Essex's rebellion in 1601 had failed, a plea for clemency was advanced on behalf of one of the rebels, the young Earl of Southampton, on the grounds that he had been corrupted by being made to read Aristotle's *Politics* by his tutor while abroad. And perhaps there is more to be said for this view of Aristotle than for Case's.

Case's enthusiasm for Elizabeth's rule becomes explicit in his unpublished *Apologia academiarum*.[8] Elizabeth is here saluted as the protector of universities, and universities are praised as institutions whose flourishing is necessary for the well-being of both church and state: "Without universities and men educated in letters great empires are nothing other than dens of wolves and tyrants" (quoted by Binns, p. 251). What is the function discharged by universities which might have afforded Case grounds for this extraordinary claim?

It surely can be nothing other than their function as institutions of moral and political education. The responsibility for carrying through the tasks necessary to discharge this function certainly falls in part on the tutors who oversee the living conditions, the studies, the recreations and the discipline of their students—in the *Apologia* Case praises the English universities for their superiority in these respects to their European counterparts—but an essential role has to be that of the teacher of moral philosophy, that is, of Aristotelian moral philosophy and this just because education in moral philosophy is the capstone of moral education. Case's view of the importance of universities becomes fully intelligible only when we remind ourselves of his conception of the moral philosopher as the teacher and inculcator of virtues in those who are going to serve the high purposes of the Elizabethan state.

In making this claim Case had put himself further at odds with Aristotle. I noticed earlier how far he had departed from Aristotle in his view of how the virtues are acquired, at least at the level of heroic and general virtue, and more generally of how philosophical theorizing is related to practice. Now we have to take note of Case's unargued assumption that the Elizabethan state is an Aristotelian polity or, at least, that the Elizabethan state satisfies Aristotelian requirements for an acceptable polity, so that by assimilating his Aristotelianism his students will be well fitted for political and other advancement. And the problem here is not just one of anachronism, of the differences between any fourth-century *polis* and any sixteenth-century kingdom.

Elizabethans were apt to understand the relationship between membership in the nobility, virtue, and the qualities of the upwardly mobile in complex and not wholly coherent ways. Elyot had "identified wisdom, virtue and nobility,"[9] supposing that nobility had first originated in a grant of possessions and dignity by the people "to him at whose virtue they marvelled."[10] But now, Elyot declared, the nobility in order to achieve the virtues need an education informed by Cicero and Aristotle. Noble birth is by itself insufficient for virtue. And later on it became possible to assert that noble birth is not always necessary. Sir John Ferne as a herald in his *Blazon of Gentrie* praised most highly the "mixed noblenes" that combines virtue and noble blood, but also declared, even if contentiously, that he who had achieved the status of gentleman "by industrie of his virtues" was to be preferred before those with ancient lineage, but without virtue.[11]

Elyot, Ferne—and indeed Case—write at different stages in an ongoing Tudor debate about the relationship between nobility of birth, the virtues, and the achievement, by whatever means, of wealth, status and power. The setting for that debate is an intensely competitive social order, one in which the possibility of upward mobility at the expense of others or downward mobility as a result of the rise of others are such that *pleonexia* in the form of ambition and acquisitiveness is a dominant quality. It was only three and a half years after Case's death in 1599 that the fourteen-year-old Thomas Hobbes became an Oxford undergraduate, and his later remark that there is "a generall inclination of all mankind, a perpetuall and restlesse desire of Power after power" (*Leviathan* I, 11) is perhaps more apt as an observation of the later Elizabethan and Jacobean society in which he had grown up than as the generalization about human nature as such which he intended.

V

What I am suggesting then is that Case had set himself and his colleagues the Quixotic task of teaching Aristotle's ethics to a generation of students whose aspirations and ambitions were directed towards success in an increasingly Hobbesian social world and that it should therefore be no surprise that the effect of such teaching, insofar as it had any effect, was often, as with Hobbes himself, to turn the student against Aristotle. The moral and political Aristotelianism of John Case therefore failed in two ways. Its pretension to teach the virtues was bound in the longer run to discredit it, since the inculcation of the virtues into the young cannot be achieved by the teaching of moral philosophy, something that Case should have learned from Aristotle. The *Nicomachean Ethics* is not meant for undergraduates. But in addition Case failed to recognize that the social and political world shared by him and his pupils was one to which Aristotle's ethics and politics were to a significant and increasing degree alien and antagonistic.

The widespread rejection of Aristotle's moral philosophy from the early seventeenth century onwards has been explained by historians of thought in a variety of ways. Teleological modes of explanation were taken to have been discredited by the new science. There were influential theological movements in both the Protestant and Catholic worlds from whose standpoint Aristotle appeared as a pagan antagonist. The types of social, civil, and religious conflict by which seventeenth-century societies found themselves afflicted had rendered Aristotelianism irrelevant. Or so it has been claimed. And perhaps each of these types of explanation has something to be said for it. But reflection on John Case's writings suggests that perhaps something more and other also needs to be said.

For it may be that, even if the scientific, theological, and social climate of Western Europe of the early seventeenth century had not been in these ways inhospitable to Aristotle's moral philosophy, that moral philosophy would still have fallen into disfavor and deservedly so. Why? Because it would have been discredited by the unfounded claims made for it by some of its sixteenth-century teachers. They had advanced large claims for their teaching as a form of practical moral education that it was impossible to sustain. Before they were defeated by others, they had therefore perhaps themselves made their own defeat inevitable. But note that they had done so precisely because they had not learned enough from their reading of Aristotle. Their conception of moral education was inadequate in just those respects in which it rested on a gross misinterpretation of Aristotle's views. And so also did their failure to recognize the extent to which a genuine allegiance to Aristotle's morals and politics would have put them at odds with the political culture of their own society.

To this it may be said that we are not entitled to generalize from one or even from a few examples, that Aristotelian moral philosophy had a number of very different protagonists in the sixteenth century, and that, even where Case himself is concerned, a good deal more reading and a good deal more argument is needed. And this is true. What I have been proposing are therefore questions rather than answers, questions that need to be raised more generally about teaching of Aristotelian moral philosophy in the universities and schools of Western Europe in the sixteenth century. But until we have done this historical work, there can be no fully adequate answer to the question of why in the seventeenth century the protagonists of Aristotle could for the most part no longer make their voices heard in moral debate.

NOTES

1. *John Case and Aristotelianism in Renaissance England* (Kingston and Montreal: McGill-Queen's University Press, 1983).

2. Nancy S. Struever, *Theory or Practice: Ethical Inquiry in the Renaissance* (Chicago: University of Chicago Press, 1992).

3. Ibid., p. 131.
4. Ibid., p. 138.
5. Ibid., p. 139.
6. Ibid., p. 138.

7. Brian P. Copenhaver and Charles B. Schmitt, *Renaissance Philosophy* (Oxford: Oxford University Press, 1992), p. 126.

8. Bodleian Library, Corpus Christi College ms. 321, fols. 1–21; see the account in J. W. Binns "Elizabeth I and the universities" in *New Perspectives in Renaissance Thought*, ed. J. Henry and S. Hutton (London: Duckworth, 1990).

9. Mervyn James, *Society, Politics and Culture: Studies in Early Modern England* (Cambridge: Cambridge University Press, 1986), p. 378.

10. *The Boke named The Governour*, ed. H. H. S. Croft (London: Kegan Paul, Trench, 1883), vol. 2, p. 378.

11. Quoted by James, *Society, Politics and Culture*, p. 382.

# 6

# Keeping Virtue in Its Place: A Critique of Subordinating Strategies

*David Solomon*

In a number of widely read and influential books, Ralph McInerny has developed with both scholastic rigor and Chestertonian panache an account of the kind of natural law ethic which, according to him, is anticipated in Aristotle's ethical and political writings but only brought to completion in the philosophical system of Thomas Aquinas.[1] One of the many remarkable features of the ethics of Aquinas is his attempt to bring together in a grand synthesis the virtue approach to ethics characteristic of most pagan ethical theories in the classical world with a more juridical approach to ethics derived from ancient Stoicism, Roman jurisprudence, and the Hebrew scriptures. Although many philosophers have claimed to find a tension in Aquinas between his emphasis on virtue and his emphasis on law, McInerny thinks the balance is just right. As he puts it in one place, "it is virtuous activity that natural law precepts command."[2]

In modern ethics, of course, an ethics of virtues is regularly contrasted with an ethics of duty, and the recent vigorous revival of "virtue ethics" among anglophone moral philosophers has had as one of its chief aims to supplant the dominant modern ethical theories associated with Kantian deontology and British utilitarianism. The critical response to the new "virtue ethics" on the part of Kantians and consequentialists has been complex. While some have argued that virtue ethics is fundamentally mistaken, others have taken the more irenic course of attempting to accommodate the insights of Aristotelian virtue ethics within the theoretical structures of modern ethical theories. These attempts "to keep virtue in its place" take many forms and pose the most serious obstacles, I believe, to a revived Aristotelianism in ethics. In what follows I attempt a taxonomy of the strategies for "keeping virtue in its place" and I also explore a particular objection that might be brought to certain of these attempts. My intent is to support those who claim that the chasm that separates modern ethical theory from its classical antecedents is deeper than many contemporary irenists suppose. If an ethics of virtue, an ethics of law, and an ethics of ends are to be reconciled, it is unlikely that it will be an Aristotelian doctrine of virtue which will be reconciled with modern accounts of duty and ends. I will conclude with some general remarks about why the contemporary debate between the friends of the virtues and their opponents is frequently so confusing, and I make a plea for taking McInerny's brand of Thomist reconciliationism seriously.

I

The vigorous revival of neo-Aristotelian virtue theory in recent years has been met with an equally vigorous set of criticisms.[3] While a determined minority of moral philosophers continue to advocate a return to some variety of classical virtue theory, the main spokespersons for the modern orthodoxies associated with Kantian deontology and Benthamite consequentialism continue to dominate contemporary discussions. Their criticisms of virtue theory are quite various, and different kinds of criticisms, as always, require different kinds of responses. The criticisms of virtue theory most discussed tend to be relatively direct attacks on the fundamental tenets of any revived Aristotelianism. These criticisms (as well as the standard responses by virtue theorists) are by now quite well-known. They can usefully, I think, be divided into two classes.[4] What I have called *external objections* to virtue theory claim that there are certain objections to virtue theories which are external to ethics itself. The most prominent of these external objections depend either on broadly epistemological or broadly metaphysical considerations. The metaphysical objection usually takes the form of claiming that any viable virtue ethics requires a substantial metaphysical underpinning which is at least rich enough to support a teleological conception of nature—or at least that part of nature which forms the immediate environment for human action. It is further argued that no such metaphysical underpinning is available now that the comprehensive teleology of Aristotelian science has been irreversibly overturned by modern science (and classical theism has become largely irrelevant to the lives of modern men and women). The epistemological objection is frequently deployed in tandem with the metaphysical objection. It claims that even if the metaphysical objection were to fail—i.e., even if we were able to establish a sufficiently rich teleological view of nature—the so-called ends of human nature or human life would be inaccessible to us. It is concluded, then, that either human life has no end or, if it does, we are unable to know what it is.

The internal objections differ from the external ones in that they have their impetus from within ethical reflection itself. These objections claim that there are specifically ethical objections to any strong version of virtue ethics. There is a wide range of such objections, I think, but the three most important ones are what I have called *(1) the action-guiding objection, (2) the self-centeredness objection, and (3) the contingency objection.* The action-guiding objection claims that the resources of a virtue ethics are insufficient to give such a theory genuinely action-guiding power. It is claimed that only a theory giving more prominence to rules and principles will be able to do what any ethical theory is required to do—tell us how to act. The self-centeredness objection argues that since classical virtue theories take their departure from the agent's pursuit of his good, they will be too agent-focused and unable to do justice either to the altruistic elements of ethics or the impartialistic elements. The contingency objection, finally, argues that given the rootedness of virtue in extensive training (and, indeed, in second nature) the agent is unable in the moment of decision to exercise sufficient autonomy in action. The virtuous agent (and even more importantly the vicious agent) cannot really choose to do otherwise.

Both the external and internal objections to an ethics of virtue have been much discussed in recent moral philosophy, and I do not intend to take up these issues again here. Rather, I would like to focus on another kind of consideration that has been used to respond to virtue ethics. This second kind of critical response is distinguished from the direct attacks of the internal and external objections, by having a special indirect character. Instead of arguing that an ethics of virtue is straightforwardly inadequate, it claims instead that the genuine insights of an ethics of virtue can be accommodated within the theoretical framework of modern ethical theories. I will call objections of this indirect sort, *subordinating objections,* and the overall argumentative contexts in which they are imbedded, *subordinating strategies.*

Subordinating strategies are quite various. Some, frequently encountered in and around applied ethics, are, it seems to me, of little theoretical interest. The least interesting of these are what might be called projects of *mere assimilation.* Mere assimilationists argue that there need be no deep conflict between the traditional competing normative theories. Indeed, they claim that the Kantian, the consequentialist, and the neo-Aristotelian are rather developing different aspects of the ethical, and the goal of ethical theory should be to bring these different aspects into a kind of harmony. Sometimes, it is argued that the views are interchangeable in that there is a kind of material equivalence to the views. The question of whether one chooses to put rules, virtues, or consequences at the focal point of one's reflection is to be settled by mere preference. It all comes to the same thing. Other times it is argued that there must be a division of labor among the various theories. Rules do part of the job and virtues another.

Among philosophers who have defended broadly assimilationist strategies are Tom Beauchamp and Edmund Pellegrino. Beauchamp says that "there is no reason to suppose that we need to dispatch or minimize the importance of principles and rules in order to embrace these virtues. The two kinds of theory have different emphases, but they are compatible. A moral philosophy is simply more complete if the virtues are integrated with principles. Again, then *we have grounds to declare virtue theory and principlism partners rather than competitors.*"[5]

Pellegrino, who regards himself as a proponent of virtue ethics, says "what is evident is that full accounts of the moral life, particularly as it regards judgments of accountability and justification, require an integrated assessment of the four elements of a moral event—i.e., the agent, the act, the circumstance, and the consequence—in relation to each other. *Today's challenge is not how to demonstrate the superiority of one normative theory over the other, but rather how to relate each to the other in a matrix that does justice to each and assigns to each its proper normative force.*"[6] And in an attempt to draw back from his assimilationist move, he seems to make things in some respects worse by saying that "I am not suggesting a feeble eclecticism, a cafeteria-style ethics, that would add a spoonful of virtue here, a principle there, and a dash of consequence in another place. Nor do I suggest a formless syncretism based in egregious compromises for the sake of a unity that enervates conflicting theories. Rather, the strength of each theory must be preserved, drawn upon, and placed in dynamic equilibrium with the others in order to accommodate the intricacy, variety, and particularity of human moral acts."[7]

Whether either Beauchamp or Pellegrino is guilty of producing a "feeble eclecticism" or a "formless syncretism," I will not here attempt to determine. What is clear, I think, is that there exists a good deal of unclarity, especially in the introductory materials in applied ethics anthologies, about the relation among normative theories.

In addition to the various forms of mere assimilationism, there are a number of other ways of subordinating virtue which fall into certain regular patterns. These more sophisticated subordinating strategies begin with the plausible thought that any philosophical account of the ethical life will have to find some place for the virtues, or at least for Virtue. If we regard virtues as belonging to a class of dispositions on the part of rational agents to have certain feelings and to be moved to act in particular ways when confronted by particular situations, persons will always have features of character that fall within that class. Since traits of character of this sort are so closely tied to action (since indeed they can't be characterized except by connecting them to motivation to act) and since the ethical life is (among other things) so closely tied to guiding action, it shouldn't be surprising that any account of the ethical life will have something to say about virtue.

Nor should it surprise us when we find classical moral philosophers whose overall orientation is broadly anti-Aristotelian talking much about virtue. If a defense of a broadly Aristotelian approach to ethics requires the claim that only Aristotle and his friends pay attention to virtue, then such a defense is bound to fail. One frequently finds philosophers pointing to lengthy treatments of virtue in Kant (and other Kantians) or in Mill (or contemporary utilitarians like Brandt) with the expectation that successfully so pointing causes some difficulties for the proponent of an ethics of virtue. This seems to me to misidentify the real differences that divide virtue theorists and their opponents. Defenders of a broadly Aristotelian approach to ethics do not, and certainly need not, claim that only Aristotle and his friends give virtue a prominent place in their ethical writings. What they do need to claim, of course, is that only Aristotle and his friends treat virtue correctly, i.e., locate it properly in the overall economy of ethical thought and talk. Virtue theorists sometimes characterize their aim as one of calling attention to the importance of virtue, and such a description might tempt others to suppose that such theorists believe that virtue has been completely ignored by their modern opponents. If they do mean this, of course they are wrong. It is not that modern ethical theory has ignored virtue, but rather that it has distorted it—or so the virtue theorist should claim. This claim deprives the opponent of the easy victory that would be afforded by merely gesturing toward the prominent role that discussion of virtue plays in the views of many modern opponents of an ethics of virtue.

Not only, of course, need Aristotelians not deny that other ethical theorists with whom they deeply disagree can give an account of the virtues, they should be prepared to acknowledge these alternative accounts and make a critical examination of them a part of the defense of their own views. If one regards the major alternatives to an ethics of virtue as consequentialist and Kantian views, then one can discern certain characteristic techniques within these views for locating virtue but displacing it from the center of normative attention. We might call such techniques, *patterns of subordination.* They represent ways in which Kantians and consequentialists attempt to make their ethical worlds safe from virtue—safe, that is, from any tendency on the part of virtue to take ethical center stage.

These patterns of subordination may take two broadly different forms both in consequentialist views and in Kantian views. The first form, which I will call *master subordination,* tends to identify one state of character, specified with reference to the fundamental evaluative orientation of either Kantianism or consequentialism, as the fundamental motivational state to be associated with the theory. This form tends to force such theories toward an emphasis on virtue as opposed to the *virtues.* The central idea in master subordination is that there is a state of character, which we might call the *master virtue,* which is specified by the overall orientation of the ethical theory and which, in some sense to be specified, will be the most important state of character for agents to possess. This form of subordination can be seen in the tendency of some consequentialists to make *benevolence* the central, or perhaps, the only virtue. In a similar manner, Kantians are often accused of (or praised for) giving *conscientiousness* a similar role. This resort to a master virtue involves subordination of virtue because both the content of the virtue and the defense of its motivational centrality are derivative from other, more fundamental, components of the ethical theory.[8]

The second form of subordination is what I will call *distributed subordination.* Here the opponents of an ethics of virtue are inclined to speak of virtues, rather than virtue, and they are prepared frequently to admit a rich and diverse family of states of character that qualifies for this description. Where master subordination singles out a single motivational state that lies at the heart of excellence of character, distributed subordination points rather to a diverse set of ethically valuable dispositions of agents that contribute to the overall ethical well functioning of the agent. Kantians and consequentialist again will distribute subordination in different ways.

Kantians, characteristically, regard virtues as certain relatively determinate states of character that embody motivation to act in accord with certain principles. Thus, corresponding to various principles of right that may lie at the heart of a broadly Kantian theory will be certain states of character that embody dispositions to act in accord with these principles. Honesty, as a virtue, will be a certain disposition to act in accord with those principles for determining honest behavior; the principles, in turn, will be specified within the broader normative theory. In this way, one can expect a one-to-one mapping of principles onto virtues within this scheme of distributed subordination.

This mapping satisfies two aims of a broadly Kantian theory, an aim associated with the notion of right action and an aim associated with the Kantian notion of correct moral motivation. With regard to right action, the mapping insures that what the right action *is* will be determined by some principle of action that is suitably grounded in reason. It is important, if this aim is to be realized, that the action's moral correctness not depend on its origin in a virtuous state of character; rather the virtuousness of the state of character must depend on the content of the principle by which it is guided. In this way, the ordering of the concepts of right action and virtue found in classical virtue theory are inverted and a characteristic form of subordination is realized. The virtue of honesty is subordinated to the principle of honest behavior in that the virtue will be exhaustively characterized as a disposition to act in accord with the principle. This suggests, among other things, that an agent with no motivation to act honestly could nevertheless grasp the relevant principle determining honest behavior and understand its implications for his practice as well as any honest person. Becoming honest and becoming able to discern the honesty of a particular piece of behavior will be distinct in the important sense that the discerning ability can be learned independently of and prior to acquiring any motivational tilt toward honest behavior. The principle for determining which actions constitute honest actions is in no way dependent on identifying honest persons. Indeed, our ability to identify honest persons will be dependent on some prior grasp of *what honest persons will do in typical circumstances.*

There is no doubt, I think, that something like this ordering of the notions of virtue and right action is taken for granted by many contemporary philosophers with a broadly Kantian orientation. Thus, John Rawls in *A Theory of Justice* says that "once the principles of right and justice are on hand, they may be used to define the moral virtues just as in any other theory. The virtues are sentiments, that is, related families of dispositions and propensities regulated by a higher-order desire, in this case *a desire to act from the corresponding moral principles*"[9] (my emphasis). In another place, he characterizes the fundamental virtues as "the strong and normally effective desires to act on the basic principles of right."[10] These passages make clear, first, that Rawls believes that the principles of right can be defined prior to attending to the virtues, and, second, that the virtues are to be defined as dispositions to act for, on or from these principles.

David Richards has similarly characterized the virtues. He says that what will be considered *human* virtues generally depends on "the capacities and desires which are psychologically required for persons to regulate their lives by various principles of action."[11] *Moral* virtues, more narrowly, "involve desires and capacities associated with regulating one's life by some moral principle or some class of moral principles, as the case may be."[12] He goes on to give a number of examples where he believes specific virtues are to be "paired" with principles of morality: the moral virtue of generosity to be paired with the moral principle of beneficence; the moral virtue of justice to be paired with the moral principle(s) of justice; the moral virtue of faithfulness to be paired with the moral principles of "fairness as applied to promise- and contract-keeping" and so on.[13] Richards view does not appear to go as far as Rawls in suggesting that moral virtues can be exhaustively characterized with reference to the principles with which they are paired, but it is clear that he believes that virtues are dependent both for their value and for their determinateness on principles of action associated with them.[14]

Tom Beauchamp (with his penchant for assimilation and not subordination) attempts to stop short of the standard Kantian maneuver that makes virtue dependent, in some sense, on principles of right action. His irenic proposal suggests that duty-based and virtue-based theories can coexist with a suitable division of moral labor. He says:

> No principle-of-duty-based—hereafter simply duty-based—theory need deny the importance of virtues, and any viable theory of principles of duty, in my judgment, will include an account of virtue. If I am right, then we should not set up stereotypes of theories—as do some writers in this volume—such that one must be either a defender of duty-based *or* virtue-based—*or* rights-based—theories. A morality of principles of duty should enthusiastically recommend settled dispositions to act in accordance with that which is morally required, and a proponent of virtue ethics should encourage the development of principles that express how one ought to act. It is a defect in any theory to overlook all of these ways of expressing what is important in the moral life.[15]

The difficulty in Beauchamp's proposal, however, if we read it as an attempt to avoid the question of whether virtue is to be characterized in terms of principles or vice-versa, is that it seems clearly much more acceptable to the opponents of the virtues than to their friends. He suggests that the debate here concerns whether virtue and duty are each to be given a place in an ethical theory. Sensibly enough, he suggests that they both should be given such a place. But, of course, as we have argued above, it is a mistake to suppose that the question here concerns whether virtue is to have any place (or duty, if we look at the debate from the other side). The debate concerns what is to be the place of each of these notions within the developed moral conception. Which is to be, as we might put it, *more fundamental?* But if this is the question, it seems clear that Beauchamp finds himself on the side of duty. His characterizations of virtue as "settled dispositions to act in accordance with that which is morally required," clearly give priority to the notion of the morally required.

The second aim of Kantian theories realized by this mapping is to give an account of moral motivation according to which it involves a disposition to perform morally correct actions because they are morally correct.[16] On this characteristically Kantian view, it is a necessary condition of morally worthy action that it be performed (at least in part) as a result of the agent's belief that it is morally correct. Although Kant is not always clear on this point, something like it is surely what he has in mind when he emphasizes the importance for the moral worth of an agent that he act "for the sake of duty." By regarding distributed virtues as dispositions to act in accord with principles of right, this motivational requirement is surely satisfied. The content of the virtue will be, as we have seen, characterized by the relevant principle of right. To possess a particular virtue is just (ignoring for the moment certain complications) to be disposed to act from certain principles of right. But if this is what virtuous action is, then it seems clear that the agent possessing the virtue is performing the action he performs in acting virtuously because it is right.

This line of reasoning may seem faulty if one supposes that the Kantian takes virtues to be dispositions to act merely *in accord* with principles of right. One could act, of course, in accord with a certain principle, P, without acting from the motive that actions in accord with P are morally right.[17] But the Kantian does not, of course, suppose that virtues should be so characterized. For the Kantian, the virtues in question involve a disposition for one's behavior to be regulated by the principle, and this suggests that the principle has a speaking role and is not confined to a walk-on part.

In general, then, by distributively subordinating the virtues in the way characteristic of Kantian ethical theories, such theories not only domesticate virtue, they also make it serve basic aims of their account of the moral life. First, this account of the virtues gives the notion of morally correct action the prominence within the overall theory that Kantians typically strive for, and, second, it makes action that is virtue-based take on a Kantian motivational shape, i.e., virtue-based action is action done for the sake of duty.

Consequentialist theories, of course, will distributively subordinate virtue in quite a different way. Instead of regarding the individual virtues as so many ways of being disposed to regulate one's behavior by certain ethical principles, consequentialists regard virtues as relatively stable features of an agent's motivational set that tend to bring it about that the agent's actions contribute to the maximal production of whatever intrinsically good things are identified in the larger theory.[18] The strategy involved in this subordination of the virtues is of a piece with the more general tendency of consequentialist accounts of the ethical life to treat the motivational states of agents in a broadly instrumental matter. Generally, for consequentialists, the best motives for an agent to have will be those motives that produce actions which tend to contribute to value maximization. Motives typically do not figure among the things on a consequentialist view that have intrinsic value, and hence they are to be thrown into the instrumental soup.[19]

This attitude toward motives is central to a conception of consequentialism, but many philosophers have thought that it leads to a certain incoherence in the view. The incoherence is alleged to surface when one queries the motivational role of the fundamental principle within a consequentialist view. Consider, for example, certain well-known complications, first explored in detail by Sidgwick, in the motivational implications of the principle of utility.[20]

Sidgwick famously noted that it might well be the case that the principle of utility would enjoin agents to act for reasons not straightforwardly sanctioned by that principle. Consider cases where simple honesty is in question. Sidgwick was well aware that the principle of utility if applied to some concrete practical decisions might yield the action guide that one should in some situations tell a lie. There are certainly many cases in which lying might be more productive of overall human happiness than telling the truth. He was also aware, however, that it might in general be better (i.e., tend to maximize happiness) if every agent had a deep disposition always to tell the truth. If all agents had such dispositions, then confidence among persons would be raised to such a pitch that human benefits unimaginable in a world where persons used discretion with regard to telling the truth would be realized. The benefits of the universal possession of such dispositions obtain even though those persons with such dispositions would be unable (or at least unlikely) to choose particular actions (e.g., lying in the above example) with the greatest expected utility. This kind of tension between what might be required in the way of action by the principle of utility and what might be required in the way of deep dispositions to action and feeling by this same principle is familiar in a number of areas of practical concern.

It is clear that much more needs to be said about the various patterns of subordination and the reasons why so many contemporary moral philosophers have adopted them. I do not propose, however, to pursue these more general questions here. Rather I would like to explore a certain form of "quick and dirty" response to at least some instances of subordinating arguments. This response is possible, I think, because so many subordinating arguments have a similar structure. This general form of argument has five stages. At the first stage, the argument identifies some primary role or position within an ethical theory. For example, it might be argued that the primary task of an ethical theory is to identify the correct action to perform in some particular situation. At the second stage, some argument is given that the virtues cannot fill that role or perform that task. At the third stage a secondary role or task within the theory is identified, e.g., assessing moral worth or providing moral motivation. The sense in which this role is secondary, of course, may differ with different arguments. At the fourth stage of the argument, it is claimed that the virtues can fill the secondary role—and indeed are required in order that it be filled. Finally at the fifth stage of the argument, it is claimed that we can explain the tendency to adopt an ethics of virtue on the grounds that virtue theorists fall into a kind of confusion in which they move from the genuine insight that virtue is required in an ethical theory to the false claim that it is fundamental (or basic or primary) in ethics. Using this style of argument, then, one can explain why we can't do without virtue, but nevertheless why virtue isn't primary, and finally why, through a certain confusion, proponents of an ethics of virtue make the mistakes that they do.

I think that this general style of argument is quite common in contemporary ethics and also that is has been very influential.[21] Instead of surveying the many different ways in which it has been deployed, however, I want to focus on a particular instance—the subordinating argument deployed by William Frankena. I want to show first that Frankena does follow this strategy and then suggest that his argument falls prey to a particular kind of objection. Finally, I will conclude that the tendency of this argument (and other similar ones) to suffer from this defect tells us something of more general interest about this particular subordinating strategy.

The response to Frankena's subordinating argument I will develop is an instance of what I will call a *shallow response* to subordinating arguments. It is not shallow, I hope, in that it is superficial, but rather in that it does not go to the very heart of the issues that divide virtue ethicists from their opponents. Typically, the arguments raised against an ethics of virtue claim that the virtues cannot do something which is regarded as central to an ethical theory—they can't adequately guide action or they can't provide appropriately rigorous moral motivation, for example. A *deep response* to these objections would go to the heart of the issues in that it would claim either that virtue can satisfy the demands placed on an ethical theory by the critics of virtue ethics or that these demands can't be met by any alternative to an ethics of virtue or that meeting them carries with it theoretical or moral costs no reasonable person would want to bear. A shallow response, however, is content with much less. It is directed precisely at strategies that follow the five-stage argument I laid out above and points to a particular difficulty with them. It argues that these strategies fail because the arguments used to displace virtue from the primary place in the theory will also show that virtue can't play the secondary role either. Thus, the arguments which seek to find a role, albeit a secondary role, for virtue in an ethical theory end up making it impossible for virtue to play any significant role. This doesn't of course show that an ethics of virtue is to be preferred to the theories favored by Frankena and others who hold similar views. Indeed, one might conclude that it shows that virtue is in even worse shape than they think. It can't even do the humdrum and secondary chores assigned to it within the overall economy of ethics.

So what is the gain here for those of us who prefer an ethics of virtue? It is the recognition that a certain kind of condescension to virtue is almost surely bound to fail. The attempt to fit virtue into the kind of ethical theory structured by modern concerns and ambitions of the sort that drive broadly Kantian and consequentialist theories is, I think, futile. Either the notion of a virtue will be distorted or the demands of the theory will be stretched beyond what is reasonable. The upshot is, I think, a recognition of the depth of disagreement that exists between broadly Aristotelian accounts of ethics and the main modern alternatives. Only when the depth of this disagreement is fully appreciated can the deep responses to modern ethical theory be fully deployed.

II

Professor Frankena's views on the subordination of the virtues, expressed in his classic textbook *Ethics,* may now seem a bit dated and, for this reason, unworthy of the attention I will give them.[22] But for a number of reasons I think that is mistaken. First, the book, at the time it was published, was enormously influential, and especially influential precisely on the topics of the taxonomy of ethical theories with which we are concerned here. In addition, some of

Professor Frankena's students continue to be influential in these debates, many of them defending subtler versions of the views which he defended in *Ethics*.[23] But, most importantly, many of the views which he defended are still found in contemporary discussions, frequently treated as a kind of uncontroversial ethical common sense. For all these reasons, it is still useful to examine his classical subordinating strategy.

Frankena's views on the place of virtue in a normative theory are expressed in a number of memorable passages from *Ethics*. He expresses his views about the relation between a morality of duty and a morality of virtue as follows:

> I propose therefore that we regard the morality of duty and principles and the morality of virtues or traits of character not as rival kinds of morality between which we must choose, but as two complementary aspects of the same morality. Then, for every principle there will be a morally good trait, often going by the same name, consisting of a disposition or tendency to act according to it; and for every morally good trait there will be a principle defining the kind of action in which it is to express itself. To parody a famous dictum of Kant's, I am inclined to think that principles without traits are impotent and traits without principles are blind.[24]

And he further develops this distinction when he says that

> But the point of acquiring these virtues is not further guidance or instruction; the function of the virtues in an ethics of duty is not to tell us what to do but to ensure that we will do it willingly in whatever situations we may face. In an ethics of virtue, on the other hand, the virtues play a dual role—they must not only move us to do what we do, they must also tell us what to do.[25]

Frankena's view rests on a sharp distinction between the cognitive and motivational elements in moral judgment and action. For successful action, we must both know what we are to do in a particular situation and also be motivated to do it. The moral motivation the agent requires is not merely the motivation to do the required thing, but also the motivation to seek for the right thing to do, to avoid cognitive laziness and inattention.

The second pillar of his view is the claim that only principles or rules can satisfy the cognitive demands of ethical practice and that only virtues can satisfy the motivational demands. Although it is difficult to find arguments in Frankena for this conclusion (other than a kind of ambient Humeanism) it is quite clear that he accepts it. His famous "parody" of Kant, "principles without traits are impotent and traits without principles are blind," surely presupposes this view.[26]

With these element in place then, Frankena's subordination strategy is clear:

1. He distinguishes two elements in an ethical theory—a primary cognitive one and a secondary motivational one.
2. He argues that the virtues are unsuited for the primary one—because they can't determine the right thing to do.
3. He argues that the virtues are required for the secondary task—because principles can't do it, nor can anything else, and it has to be done. (We need to qualify this by adding, "without qualifying the moral," since he admits we might be able to do it with external sanctions, e.g., fear of God or punishment, but this would compromise the ethical.)
4. Therefore, we have to have a "dual-aspect" ethical theory in which the (slightly unequal) partners are each required in the overall economy of the view.

What shall we say about this? There are any number of things that could be said about it at the deep level. One could challenge the sharp distinction between the cognitive and the motivational and, in particular, the sharply noncognitive interpretation of the virtues that accompanies this distinction. But having determined to remain shallow, I would like to avoid these deep (and deeply controversial) matters and focus rather on just the interplay in this view between the arguments that displace virtue from the primary (cognitive) role and place it in the secondary (motivational) role. The question then is this: Do the arguments brought against the possibility of the virtues serving the primary role create problems for the possibility that the virtues might serve the secondary role? Do these arguments indeed, if successful, do so much damage to virtue that any attempt to rehabilitate it is bound to fail? I am inclined to think that they do.

The charge brought against the virtues by Frankena is that they are blind—they are incapable of telling us what to do. Furthermore, they can't be inculcated in some agent without that agent being instructed explicitly by the use of principles. These two points about the virtues go together although there seems to be some tension between them. The first point seems to say that the virtues lack determinate content, (i.e., they are blind) but the second point claims that they can be given content through the teaching of principles. Leaving aside for the moment the clear tension between these points, we can see that Frankena clearly believes that in morally good action we have a kind of cooperation between traits of persons and properties of actions. The agents in question choose the actions that they do both because of their traits and the actions' properties.

Frankena's view here is determined largely by his desire to go between alternatives, each of which he thinks is deeply objectionable. On the one hand there is the specter of action which is merely in accord with duty, but perhaps motivated by mere randomness, or, even worse, by fear of divine punishment or a kind of calculating egoism. On the other hand there is the blundering action of the well-intentioned (indeed virtuous, in some sense) agent who blindly lurches from one well-intentioned disaster to another. Frankena does not want agents to be forced to choose between mere legality or unfocused and perhaps unfocusable good intentions. The solution is to supplement principles with virtues and avoid the first difficulty—and supplement virtues with principles in order to avoid the second. Clear-headed energy replaces muddled impotence.

Any critical response to Frankena's view should begin, I think, by wondering how it is that virtues which are blind can nevertheless motivate us in predictable ways and, as Frankena puts it, "in every situation which we might face." If virtues are going to play the role Frankena wants them to play, they can't give us just any motivation—they have to motivate in a determinately focused way. Indeed, they have to motivate us in a way that is as determinate and focused as the rules or principles that inform them. But how, one might wonder, is such focused motivation possible if the virtues are really blind—just noncognitive forces, as it were? One might think initially that we give the virtues focused motivation by "loading" action-guiding content into them. We fill them up as it were with rules. According to this view, virtues are only blind until they are loaded with content. And one might think of the process of loading as like placing sound on a blank audio tape.

But why should we suppose (if this is the picture) that the virtues can be "filled up" or given explicit content only by some principles of right? If they can be filled up, why couldn't they be filled up by nature or experience? Why couldn't the virtues acquire content for guiding action just by being involved in the business of choosing and deciding for creatures with certain characteristic desires and needs? Why couldn't they be filled up simply by the enormously complicated interaction between human capacities and needs and the environment in which these capacities are exercised and these needs satisfied? But if this is a genuine possibility, then we presumably don't need action-guiding content to be supplied by principles of right. Virtues need not be blind at all. Indeed, Frankena's view about the virtues seems to be not so much a view about their blindness as a view about the only conditions under which they can be brought to see. They can guide action only if they are the subject of some process of explicit training involving explicit principles of right. But if this is his point then he surely can no longer rely on his ambient Humeanism, his simple predilection for a sharp distinction between the cognitive and the motivational to support it. His argument has to be a much more subtle one which provides reason to believe that only under certain conditions can the gap between the motivational and the cognitive be crossed. And it is clear that there is no such argument in Frankena.

In response to this line of criticism I think Frankena would likely respond that I have—perhaps willfully—misunderstood him. He wasn't suggesting, he might say, that the virtues ever lose their blindness. It is wrong to think that they are filled up with content. Rather the correct picture is one of the virtues being "coupled" with principles of right in such a way that the virtues provide the motivational push for the principles. The principles are always there, independent of the virtues, and they aren't incorporated into the virtues. Virtues are, after all, permanently blind. They can merely be paired with—or wedded to—principles which allow them to discern right action. Here we avoid the problem above because if principles can't "write on" virtues, neither can nature or experience. But relief from the first problem seems to me purchased at the expense of a second problem. How is it that the virtues are guided by these principles to which they are wedded or bonded? Mustn't they be able to identify the principles by which they are to be guided? If not, how could the bond between virtue and principle be permanent enough to create moral action-guidingness? But if the virtues have the power to discern which principles to be guided by, why shouldn't they have sufficient power to be guided by the actions (or properties of actions) which fall under the principles? Indeed, if the difference among the principles to which virtues might bond are fairly fine-grained—and surely they should be—won't the power of the discerning capacity of the virtues have to be equally fine-grained? But if the capacity for discernment is this fine-grained, we return to our earlier point—why couldn't these powers of discernment be exercised directly on nature without the mediation of a principle of right?

To put this point in a slightly different way: If we can train the virtues to move us in such a way that our motivation is structured by subtle differences among principles, why couldn't our motivation be structured by subtle differences among our situations or among the properties of the actions open to one? The rule or principle now seems to be an idler wheel. It was put into the machine in order to fix a problem caused by the meager capacities of the virtues. But in order for it actually to engage the virtues, they must have the very capacities the alleged lack of which brought it into existence.

I conclude that if virtues can really ground moral motivation then they can't really be blind—and if they are really blind, they can't really ground moral motivation. The two pictures we might adopt for explaining the motivating power of the virtues—the filling-up picture or the bonding picture—both fail to support Frankena's conception of the sharp divide between the motivational and the cognitive aspects of virtue.

III

This particular problem (if indeed it is a problem) with Frankena does not by itself, of course, show that similar problems will arise with every view that follows the subordinating schema we are examining. It does provide some evidence, however, that the difference between ethical theories that put virtue somewhere near the center of their accounts and those that don't is deeper than many philosophers tend to think. The attempt on the part of Frankena (and others who pursue similar subordinating strategies) to find a place for genuine virtue within their theories is their way of trying to take some of the insights of traditional Aristotelianism seriously. But since they attempt to bring these insights into theoretical contexts which are quite distant from those in which the virtues find their home, these attempts tend to fail—and they tend to fail in a characteristic fashion. The restrictions placed on the virtues by the alien theoretical context make it impossible for the virtues to function even in a subordinate capacity. But nothing I have said here, of course, can be thought to be even an attempt to defend this much broader thesis. Its defense would require a turn from shallow to deep arguments.

Let me conclude with some even more general remarks about the overall project of reviving the virtues in contemporary ethics. One can think of the recent revival of virtue ethics in two quite different ways. On the one hand there is a narrow attempt to find a place for the concept of virtue (or of particular virtues) within a conceptual map of the practical life. This is a relatively focused problem of conceptual analysis. Typically, consequentialists will want to subordinate the virtues to some notion of a "good state of affairs" and deontologists will want to subordinate them to some notion of a right or obligatory action. Virtue ethicists will strive to give the virtues a more foundational role. But in all cases the exercise will be a relatively narrow one of conceptual ordering. The pursuit of this narrow task has occupied much of the time of moral philosophers who have attempted to accommodate virtue.

It is technical, narrowly focused, relatively removed from the larger questions of moral philosophy, and always in danger, I would say, of begging certain larger questions which form both the background for this narrow task as well as its motivation.

These larger questions frame a much more ambitious project which is also associated with the revival of virtue ethics. Here the question is not how to locate the concept of virtue within the local economy of practical life, but how to accommodate certain fundamental commitments of classical ethical theory within the relatively restricted—and restricting—agenda of modern moral philosophy. Those philosophers who are most responsible for bringing virtue theory back into currency—Anscombe, Geach, Foot, MacIntyre, Nussbaum—were not interested primarily in a reordering of the central concepts in practical life. They were concerned with certain larger questions both about the moral life and about the role of general philosophical thinking in that life. They thought that there were certain deep difficulties in modern moral theory connected both to the history of modernity as well as to certain features of modern life. Modern moral philosophy was misleading not only in its answers but also in its questions. It focused our attention on features of our practical life which are not central to the project of successful human living and it encouraged us to have certain ambitions for philosophical reflection or practice almost Promethean in their reach. The modern demands for impartiality and objectivity seemed to these critics excessive and unattainable by creatures like us. But their unattainability was not as serious a problem as the fact that their presence distorted our lives in ways that were inimical both to personal success and to social order.

In this push for virtue theory, the focus was not on relatively technical questions of the ordering of normative and evaluative concepts, but on deeper questions about the nature and ambition of modern ethics and its ability to satisfy our need for reflective guidance. The separability of this broader push for virtue from the narrower argument is confirmed, I think, by the use of these broader attacks on modern moral theory by philosophers like Bernard Williams who have no interest in promoting a virtue theory more narrowly conceived.[27] Indeed, some of these arguments are shared by a number of philosophers who have been called antitheorists because of their reluctance to take any positive view in ethical theory.

We can distinguish, then, a broader agenda for virtue ethics from a narrower one. The former involves, in many cases, a rich and diverse set of objections to the project of modern moral philosophy. It looks to the ancient world for an alternative model for such theory. The latter agenda, however, is more directly involved in the contemporary problematic of analytic—largely English-speaking—ethics. It looks to play the game of contemporary normative theory but to place virtue in the place of privilege in the received theoretical models for the ordering of ethical concepts.

There are, then, two different conflicts going on between so-called virtue ethicists and their contemporary opponents. There is a narrower conflict which is a battle over the ordering of concepts. Here virtue ethicists struggle to plant the concept of virtue at the conceptual heart of ethics—and the opponents develop ingenious arguments and strategies to displace it. This really is a relatively parochial conflict within contemporary analytic ethics. Then there is a much grander conflict between the ambitions and agenda of modern ethics and its classical opponents. Here the debate ranges over much deeper questions about the very nature and status of ethical reflection, and it is probably misleading to speak of a single broader conflict. Rather the battle ranges along a ragged front which separates the classical and the modern. This, too, is misleading as an analogy since one of the most disputed areas of the front involves a battle over the very question of whether there really is a front. Many philosophers, that is, have recently argued that the very idea that there is a divide (or at least a sharp divide) between the classical and the modern is itself a mistake.

Much of the difficulty in knowing what is exactly at stake in the debate over virtue ethics grows out of the interplay between these two different conflicts—and their two different (broader vs. narrower) conceptions of what virtue ethics is. This explains why so many philosophers complain that they are not sure what an ethics of virtue is. It also explains, I think, why so many clashes over the prospects for an ethics of virtue are "unclear." It is precisely because an opponent of the narrow-virtue agenda encounters a proponent of the broader agenda—or vice-versa.

Of course, one must not exaggerate the difference between these two conceptions of virtue ethics. They are clearly connected in a number of different ways. Proponents of the broader agenda will typically also promote the narrower one. But it is certainly not the case that proponents of the narrower agenda will even typically promote the broader agenda. Indeed they occasionally seem a bit embarrassed by it. It seems to me likely that the debates between the friends of the virtues and their opponents will remain untidy and relatively ill-defined until more attention is paid to the interaction between these two quite different agendas.

There can at least be no doubt about where Ralph McInerny's sympathies lie in the contemporary battles within ethical theory. He has been throughout his career a firm supporter of what I have called the broad agenda of the ethics of virtue. Both in his philosophical writings and in his fiction and popular apologetic writing, he works out of a classical Thomistic natural law perspective. His firm commitment to the view that the natural law theory of Thomas Aquinas is the fulfillment of the ethical promise of Aristotle's Nicomachean Ethics could not be clearer. And although McInerny would have no part in contemporary attempts to "subordinate" the virtues to deontic or consequentialist notions, neither would he argue that the virtues have priority over precepts or the natural ends of human action. McInerny's Aquinas finds a place for virtue, law, and human ends within a balanced perspective on human practical life. "The wise man is able with ease and pleasure to act in accord with his principles, because his heart is in the right place, his appetites have been schooled by moral virtues to desire the true good."[28] The task for contemporary Thomists, I think, is to show how Aquinas provides resources for reconciling virtue with law and appetite without falling into the distortions so characteristic of modern theories. Ralph McInerny recognizes that task more clearly, I think, than any other contemporary Thomist, and the clarity and energy with which he has expressed the promise of a comprehensive Thomist view places us all in his debt.

### NOTES

1. His two most important general treatments of Thomist ethical theory are *Ethica Thomistica* (Washington, D.C.: Catholic University Press, 1986) and *Aquinas on Human Action* (Washington, D.C.: Catholic University Press, 1992).

2. McInerny, *Aquinas on Human Action*, p. 122.

3. Alasdair MacIntyre's *After Virtue* (Notre Dame: University of Notre Dame Press, 1981) is the most important contribution to the revival of virtue ethics, but a number of other important works in this revival are collected in *Virtue Ethics* (Oxford: Oxford University Press, 1997). ed. Roger Crisp and Michael Slote.

4. I explore these objections in more detail in my "Internal Objections to Virtue Ethics," *Midwest Studies in Philosophy*, vol. 13 (Notre Dame: University of Notre Dame Press, 1988), ed. Peter French, Theodore E. Uehling, Jr., and Howard K. Wettstein.

5. Tom Beauchamp, "Principlism and Its Alleged Competitors," *Kennedy Institute of Ethics Journal*, September, 1995, vol. 5, no. 3, p. 195.

6. Edmund D. Pellegrino, "Toward a Virtue-Based Normative Ethics," *Kennedy Institute of Ethics Journal*, September, 1995, vol. 5, no. 3, p. 273.

7. Ibid., 273.

8. One might argue, of course, as some have, that on classical virtue theory, the virtues are also subordinated to some other more fundamental value to be specified by the theory. Thus, some have thought that on Aristotle's view the goodness of the virtues is exhaustively explained by their role in promoting some distinct good state, eudaimonia.

Isn't this a form of subordination, too? It would be, of course, if the relation of the virtues to the final good had this broadly instrumental character. It is hardly necessary to argue, however, in light of the sustained criticism of this instrumentalist view by Aristotelian scholars, for the inadequacy of this view.

9. John Rawls, *A Theory of Justice* (Cambridge: Harvard University Press, 1971), p. 192.

10. Ibid., p. 436.

11. David Richards, *A Theory of Reasons for Action*, (Oxford: Clarendon Press, 1971), p. 284.

12. Ibid.

13. Ibid., p. 285.

14. See his comment, for example, that "Virtues are valuable . . . because they involve the desires and capacities required to regulate one's life by the ultimate standards of morality and rationality" (p. 284).

15. Tom Beauchamp, "Principlism," p. 310.

16. We cannot here explore the reasons why Kantians tend to hold this view, but the reasons seem to center on their belief that action motivated by considerations other than the moral correctness of the action will tend to be less stable than action with a moral motive. If one's motivation comes from certain sentiments (say a natural concern for others) it may not be sufficiently "steady" to move one to the correct action in cases where strong countervailing considerations, based in other desires one might happen to have, come up. Kant, of course, also thought, though many of his contemporary followers would not follow him in this, that it was a defect of merely "natural" motivation that it was only contingently based in the character of the agent. While I cannot, that is, "control" the natural motivations I might have, my beliefs about what is morally correct, as well as my ability to act in accord with that belief, are always within my control. One of the many problems with this view, of course, is that in order to sustain it Kant was driven to his metaphysical account of the noumenal self, belief in which is even more difficult to sustain.

17. This is, however, more complicated than I suggest here. Extensionally equivalent principles of action provide most of the problems. If the action description, "morally right action," and the action description, "action commanded by God," are extensionally equivalent, then in acting for the sake of the principle "Always do what is morally right" (and assuming I correctly determine what this principle requires) I am also acting in accord with the principle "Always do what God commands."

18. A particularly good statement of this strategy is in chapter 5 of G. E. Moore's *Principia Ethica* (Cambridge: Cambridge University Press, 1903).

19. Of course, it is possible to hold a consequentialist view that regards motivations, or possibly states of character, as intrinsic goods. Certain forms of perfectionism as defined in recent ethical theory seem to have this character. This strategy is of a piece with the thought that any normative theory can be "consequentialized" if sufficient analytical ingenuity is expended on the effort. I am dubious about this, since it seems to me that the commitments of consequentialism are richer than what might be captured in these bare structural commitments. There is a lively debate in the literature about whether such views are too "gimmicky." I am inclined to think that they are. For further discussion of these matters, see Peter Vallentyne, "Gimmicky Representations of Moral Theories" (*Metaphilosophy*, 19 [1988]), pp. 25–63.

20. These matters are discussed in book 4 of Sidgwick's *The Methods of Ethics* (New York: Dover Press, reprint of 1907 edition).

21. In addition to William Frankena, whom I discuss below, others who employ this strategy include, I think, Peter Railton (see his "How Thinking about Character and Utilitarianism Might Lead to Rethinking the Character of Utilitarianism" (in *Midwest Studies*, volume cited in note 4 above), Robert Audi (in, for example, "Acting from Virtue," in *Mind*, 1996), and R. M. Hare (in *Moral Thinking* [Oxford: Oxford University Press, 1984]).

22. William Frankena, *Ethics* (Englewood Cliffs: Prentice-Hall, 1965).

23. Robert Audi, Robert Louden, and Gregory Trianosky are three of his students who have done important work on the taxonomy of ethical theories.

24. Ibid., p. 65.

25. Ibid., p. 67.

26. Ibid., p. 63.

27. Bernard Williams, *Ethics and the Limits of Philosophy* (Cambridge: Cambridge University Press, 1983).

28. McInerny, *Aquinas on Human Action*, p. 156.

# 7

# Deliberation about Final Ends: Thomistic Considerations

*Daniel McInerny*

Among the orthodoxies of recent interpretation of Aristotle's ethics is the claim that deliberation must include final ends within its scope.[1] Understood in this way, Aristotle's account of deliberation has been thought to diverge from that of Aquinas, who traditionally has been interpreted as limiting the scope of deliberation to the instrumental means to final ends—or, as some have held, to the *one* final end of the Beatific Vision. On this issue at least, Aquinas is in modern eyes a heterodox Aristotelian. Yet the arguments of Aristotle's modern interpreters are compelling ones, and so it is not surprising that they have eventually exerted their influence on readers of Aquinas.[2] Now it is claimed that Aquinas himself holds what I shall be calling the broad, as opposed to the narrow, view of deliberation. The point of this chapter is to evaluate what reasons there are for making this attribution.

The impetus toward the broad view of deliberation among recent commentators on Aristotle was taken in large part from both an appreciation of and a desire to correct the work of D. J. Allan.[3] While Allan was congratulated for dissociating Aristotle from a crude technocratic theory of practical reason, he nevertheless was criticized by David Wiggins for not going far enough in discerning the underlying unity of Aristotle's account as it is presented in Books III, VI, and VII of the *Nicomachean Ethics*. While Allan saw Aristotle torn between the basic means-end account of deliberation and a more nuanced, rule-case account, Wiggins argued for a unified understanding based upon a reinterpretation of the logic of deliberation.[4]

That reinterpretation begins with a disentangling of two "for the sake of" relations which Wiggins thinks Aristotle never sufficiently pauses to distinguish. The first is the relation X bears to Y when X is efficacious in bringing about Y. This is the basic means-end or *instrumental relation* between goods or ends. But there is also the relation X bears to Y when the existence of X, as Wiggins puts it, "will itself help to constitute Y."[5] For Wiggins, this second, *constituent-of-end relation* is masked by the ambiguity of the preposition *pros* in Aristotle's standard description of the subject matter of practical reason: *ton pros to telos* (III.2 1111b27). As with its Latin counterpart, *his quae sunt ad finem*, this phrase has traditionally been rendered as "means" to the end. But whatever Aquinas and other medievals understand by the Latin phrase, Wiggins and those following him have urged a more literal translation of the Greek, one which yields a more flexible sense. What we deliberate about and choose is that which is "*towards* the end," understood to comprise both instrumental means to and constituents of final ends.

Another distinction is often made between the constituents and the *specifications* of an end. Wiggins defines a constituent as that which counts in itself as the partial or total realization of an end.[6] Its simple presence, he argues, need not be logically necessary or logically sufficient for the end. Yet its presence is always "logically relevant" to the end in that, along with other constituents, it helps comprise a final end. In one sense we specify something, if only in part, by naming one of its constituents, and *eudaimonia* as a whole is specified for Aristotle by the range of virtuous activities which constitute it. But in another sense the specification of an end is not so much a "part" of a given end but an embodiment of an indeterminate conception of that end. All agree, Aristotle says, that, whatever else *eudaimonia* is, it is most generally the summation of our desire for the good. Differences arise in how this general conception is specified. Some say it is wealth, others pleasure. Aristotle says it is activity in accord with virtue. Accordingly, it might not be unfair to say that constituents are always (at least partial) specifications, but not all specifications are constituents. In any case, Aristotle's *pros* seems not only to comprise instrumental causes and constituents, but also specifications of ends. But why should we think it comprises these latter two notions at all?

The foremost reason is that, cut off from deliberation about constituents and specifications of final ends, the rationality of our ultimate commitments seems compromised. That is, if practical reason does not include final ends within its scope, then the question arises as to how we are *rationally* to defend the adoption of one final end over another, or one version of happiness over another. All we are able to do, it seems, is argue technically about the most effective ways of achieving certain ends. But this hardly seems a suitable office for the prudent agent, much less the means of distinguishing the virtuous agent from the vicious. And indeed, there are passages in the *Nichomachean Ethics* in which Aristotle apparently recognizes the need for this expanded view of deliberation. In Book II he defines virtuous action properly so-called as that which is choiceworthy for its own sake, not merely for the sake of what might come from it. This suggests that a virtuous action can be directly deliberated over and chosen as a final end. Moreover, in Book III, Aristotle says about choice that it discriminates characters better than actions do. For Wiggins, the only "straightforward way" to interpret this remark is "to suppose choice to be a fairly inclusive notion that relates to different specifications of man's *end*."[7] Finally, also in Book III, Aristotle speaks with notorious ambiguity of the voluntary nature of virtuous action. After repeating that ends are the object of wish and the "means" the object of deliberation and choice, he says "Now the activities of the virtues are concerned with what [promotes the end]; hence virtue is up to us, and so is vice" (III.5 1113b5ff; trans. Irwin). On the face of it Aristotle is saying that virtuous action has to do with "means," with what is "towards" the end. But this statement cannot be squared with the swarm of texts citing moral virtue as concerned with making the end right, or with the text in Book II claiming virtuous action as choiceworthy for its own sake—unless we construe "means" in the broad sense.

Aristotle, however, explicitly states that we do not deliberate about *eudaimonia* (he also mentions health as intrinsically undeliberable: 1111b27). Still, this is no problem if, like Wiggins, we take him to be saying that we do not deliberate about *whether* to pursue happiness or health.[8] Health is not a logically detachable constituent of happiness. And *eudaimonia* just is the whole, considered broadly as "the summation of desire." So in offering us these examples of undeliberable ends, Aristotle is in no way ruling out deliberation about constituents of ends ("Given that I desire to be healthy, what constitutes health for me here and now?") and deliberation about specifications of ends ("What good shall I choose to specify my desire to be happy?").

One of the brightest consequences of these arguments for the modern interpreters of Aristotle is that they keep those final ends, short of the most final end, from being understood as mere means. As these commentators have been insistent in pointing out, *eudaimonia* for Aristotle is an end inclusive of a number of heterogeneous and incommensurable ends. Hence its achievement, even granted the discussion of *theōria* at X.6–9, is not the maximization of any *one* good, but rather the maintenance of a variety of potentially incompatible goods. Such incommensurability precludes conceiving deliberation as exclusively concerned with the means to *eudaimonia*. A second consequence of these arguments is that they jibe with what many take to be the emotivist, historicist nature of the Aristotelian ethical enterprise. Unlike Aquinas, Aristotle, it is claimed, has no notion of a natural, hierarchically arranged order of ends for the human person. At most there are generic ends, e.g. "the summit of desire," "activity in accord with virtue"; but the question of how we specify these generic ends in a determinate conception of the moral life is one that must be left for deliberation.[9]

The foregoing account of Aristotelian deliberation leaves the Thomistic interpreter with at least three ways to go. First, he may simply be convinced by the arguments and uphold that Aquinas, too, is a proponent of the broad view. Hence Scott MacDonald has argued that essential to the Thomistic understanding of practical reason is the inclusion of constituents and specifications in that which is *ad finem*. "Indeed," he writes, "Aquinas's account itself seems to me to show conclusively the deficiency of means-end accounts."[10] A second option is to concede that in interpreting Aristotle on deliberation, as well as in developing his more independent account, Aquinas introduces a critical concept foreign to Aristotle, namely, the idea of a natural, nondeliberative intellectual habit of holding the first principles or ends of practical reason. This was the road paved a few decades back by Harry V. Jaffa,[11] and followed recently by Denis J. M. Bradley.[12] Such a habit, what Aquinas calls *synderesis*, enables Aquinas to restrict practical reason to the consideration of instrumental means while preserving the rationality of our desire for final ends. The downside of this option, obviously, is that it undermines the credibility of Aquinas as Aristotelian commentator. A third option, not necessarily distinct from the second, is to see Aquinas's account of deliberation as fundamentally conflicted. Thus Terence Irwin has accused Aquinas of being a defender of the narrow view in intention and often in expression, but in his understanding of how we "fix" or "determine" an end relying upon the broad view.[13]

The first interpretive option for the Thomist affirms the orthodox view of Aristotle. The second and third expose problems in Aquinas's defense of the narrow view. The second option objects to Aquinas's use of the apparently un-Aristotelian doctrine of *synderesis*—at least as an interpretation of Aristotle, and the third underscores the unreliable nature of this doctrine for explaining our determination of final ends. What I propose to do is to take up a consideration of each of these options in turn, and I shall begin by returning to the reasons given for expanding the Aristotelian account of deliberation to include constituents and specifications.

Wiggins and others have claimed for deliberative inquiry two particular sorts of relation, the relation X bears to Y when X will itself help constitute or specify Y. As we noted, there is for Wiggins a certain "logic" to these relations that is not that of the means-end type. Consider the case of *eudaimonia* in regard to the constituent-of-end relation. A constituent of *eudaimonia*—say good health or a satisfying occupation, to use Wiggins's own examples[14]—

need not be logically necessary or logically sufficient for the end. Yet it is always "logically relevant" to the end; it is a member of a nucleus of constituents which coming together counts as the attainment of the end. We might ask, however, what exactly is meant by the term "logic" in these expressions. In the means-end relation it is clearer what could be meant by such a phrase as X is logically relevant to Y insofar as X is efficacious in bringing Y into being. But in the constituent-of-end relation this is precisely the kind of logic we do not have. For here, X (along with A, B, C, etc.) is not an instrumental means to happiness; this nucleus of final ends *constitutes* happiness. The question is not, then, whether X, A, B, C, etc. are efficacious in bringing Y into being, but of how to bring X, A, B, C, etc. themselves into being so as to realize Y.

So whatever logical relevance holds between the nucleus of constituents and the end they constitute, it is not one which need concern the agent in deliberation. Taken simply *as constituents* of Y, this nucleus of ends is undeliberable. The problem for the deliberating agent is not whether good health or a satisfying occupation will constitute his happiness, but how to obtain these things, and this raises the question of whether deliberation can ever be anything other than of the means-end type.

It will be objected that in fact we do deliberate about whether X, A, B, C, etc. are truly constituents of Y, and this is just to deliberate about whether these are appropriate *specifications* of Y. Aquinas himself appears to endorse this mode of deliberation in distinguishing the different ways in which human positive law can be derived from the natural law (*ST* Ia–IIae, q. 95, a. 2). The first kind of derivation is that of conclusions from principles (*sicut conclusiones ex principiis*), the second is that of a determination of a common principle (*sicut determinationes quaedam aliquorum communium*). For this second kind of derivation Aquinas gives as analogy an artisan deciding to determine the general form of house by constructing this or that style of house, and as example a legislator fixing a specific punishment for a crime.

To employ Wiggins's terminology, the style of house the builder decides upon and the specific punishment the judge hands down are "logically relevant" to their respective ends—the general goods of getting a house built and of punishing a criminal—insofar as they are specifications of them. But again, simply *qua specification* of a more general description of an end, a given item is not of concern to the deliberator. Whether a builder builds a Queen Anne or a classic Victorian is of no consequence unless the question of style is pertinent to the question of efficaciously bringing about that kind of house, or of that house efficaciously bringing about some further end. For example, if one of the styles is more costly than another, and cost is of concern to the builder, then the builder will choose that style which he is able to afford. In choosing the Queen Anne over the Victorian, the builder bases his decision on the availability of the means to construct the Queen Anne. Conversely, he may choose the slim Victorian over the sprawling Queen Anne because it makes better use of a smallish lot, leaving room for a garden and a two-car garage. What about choosing a style simply because we like it? Even here, it is personal aesthetic pleasure which is the further end for the sake of which the style is chosen as an instrumental means.[15]

A builder, therefore, does not deliberate about *whether* the Queen Anne is a specification of "house," nor does the judge deliberate about *whether* a five-year prison sentence is a specification of punishment. This knowledge comes through other kinds of discovery. What the builder and the judge do deliberate about is whether this or that specification is possible or the best given the available instrumental means, or whether it is efficacious in bringing about some further end—or both. Just as constituents are not deliberable *qua* constituents, so specifications are not deliberable simply *qua* specifications.[16]

But while these preliminary distinctions cause us to be suspicious of *deliberation* about constituents and specifications of final ends, we must still face up to some troublesome texts in Aristotle. First of all, what are we to make of Aristotle's pronouncement at *Nichomachean Ethics* II.4 that of the three criteria for virtuous actions properly so-called, the second is that the actions be chosen for their own sake (*proairoumenos di'auta*, 1105a32)? Does this not suggest that we do directly deliberate about and choose a constituent of *eudaimonia*, namely, courage or temperance?

At first glance, Aristotle's *di'auto* qualification of specifically virtuous action, i.e. that specifically virtuous action is chosen "for its own sake," seems vacuous. For if he means that in choosing to do a courageous act for its own sake we choose it because it is a courageous action, we have not said much by way of explanation. In fact, as Bernard Williams has remarked in a recent essay, the claim that a virtuous person chooses virtuous acts *qua* virtuous is, in general, false in a *de dicto* sense.[17] Courageous people rarely choose a courageous act *qua* courageous; they choose it to save the city, or because they see it as their duty, and suchlike. This suggests to Williams, however, that the *di'auto* qualification may be true in a *de re* sense; in other words, that we do choose virtuous acts *qua* virtuous if we understand the qualification to imply that there are certain reasons or considerations which go along with the acts' being virtuous. "The thought of the *phronimos*," Williams writes, "is structurally and materially peculiar; and this is because he thinks of "ends"—we might say, more generally, considerations—that do not occur to other people."[18] Or, if certain considerations are entertained by the nonvirtuous agent, they will not be regarded, as they would be by the *phronimos*, as overriding or relevant.

While dispensing with discussion of Williams's qualms about applying this analysis to the virtues of courage and temperance, we can still profit from his insight that what makes virtuous action properly virtuous is the agent's consideration of certain ends which do not occur or are not seen as relevant or overriding to nonvirtuous agents. Most significantly, the *phronimos* is guided by an end or consideration which he appreciates for its own sake, an end distinct from the external action he performs. This brings us round to Aquinas's comment on our text from *EN* II.4.[19] Here Aquinas notes that the *di'auto* qualification pertains to the appetitive power, meaning that the virtuous agent chooses the act for its own sake when he does not act on the impulse of some passion. At *EN* III.8 Aristotle speaks of a kind of counterfeit courage which is based on fear: some are "brave" insofar as they are compelled by the fear of punishment to be inflicted upon those who desert their posts (1116a29ff.). Aquinas concludes from this that virtuous action must be done from choice in such a way that the choice is the work of virtue and is not for the sake of something else, as when some work of virtue is done for the sake of money or vainglory. This formulation recognizes a distinction between a "work of virtue" (*opus virtutis*) and an end, a remote end, for the sake of which it is done.

Thus the "work of virtue" Aquinas refers to in commenting upon the passage in II.4 is an action which for the virtuous agent would be—at least potentially—sufficient unto itself, but which for the nonvirtuous agent is ordered to some gratification of passion. In the heat of battle I may pull my wounded buddy from the open field back into the foxhole and so perform a "work of virtue." But if my overriding intention is to save my buddy *only* so that I can avoid a court martial for my cowardice, then, Aristotle and Aquinas would agree, my courage is defective. What I should treat as an end in itself, saving my buddy, I treat as a mere means. To summarize, then, in a more Thomistic idiom: the *de re* sense of Aristotle's claim that the virtuous person performs virtuous acts for their own sake implies that virtuous action properly so-called is composite action the exterior act of which is ordered as a means to the object of the interior act, an end regarded as choiceworthy for its own sake. In the case of courage, fighting well for the sake of a just victory *is* the courageous action chosen for its own sake.[20]

Two precisions on these points. First, as Aquinas sees it, the external act chosen by the virtuous agent is always a means *in the instrumental sense* to the end desirable in itself. In aiming at victory, the general chooses some external action—e.g. deploying his troops in *this* position, building a barricade, creating a diversion—which serves as a means to the "production" of victory. This is why Aristotle says in the discussion of deliberation at *EN* III.3 that every action is for the sake of something else (*hai de praxeis allōn heneka*, 1112b33), for in the context of this passage the "actions" referred to are the various alternative external acts being considered as possible means of achieving an end.

This also helps us understand Aristotle's remark that choice discriminates character better than actions do (III.2 1111b5–6). For by "actions" here Aristotle again refers to external acts, which of course include the "works of virtue" Aquinas mentions earlier. As Aquinas comments on this text, a work of virtue might be chosen yet not come to fruition due to some external hindrance. Or again, a virtuous deed might be performed by a nonvirtuous agent "out of fear or some other unbecoming motive."[21] Contrary to Wiggins's reading, therefore, Aristotle's remark that choice discriminates character better than actions do implies *not* that we directly deliberate about and choose final ends as such, but that sometimes the kinds of acts virtuous agents perform are chosen, by nonvirtuous agents, as instruments for ends extrinsic to the concerns of virtuous agents.

Likewise there is no difficulty with Aristotle's apparently anomalous statement that, as Irwin translates it, "the activities of the virtues are concerned with what [promotes the end]; hence virtue is up to us, and so is vice" (III.5 1113b5–7).[22] The point here is not that moral virtue, which in so many texts is correlated with the end of virtuous action, is now being correlated with what "promotes the end" in the sense of constituents and specifications of ends, thus saving the consistency between the passages. Aristotle is simply saying that the activities of the virtues, the actual courageous and temperate choices we make, are manifested in the choices of appropriate means for certain final ends. Aristotle then concludes that moral virtue is voluntary, and this makes sense when we recall that moral virtue is a habit arising from such repeated choices.

The second precision which needs to be made concerns the ordering of the means to the end in virtuous action. The mark against nonvirtuous agents is their failure to act upon what Aquinas calls the *per se* principles of order which hold among ends. To order one end to another in willy-nilly fashion, i.e., *per accidens*, as when a courageous act is performed as a mere means to vainglory, is to disrupt the order of genuine human happiness. While prescinding from a full-scale discussion of the practical syllogism, we can say that, in general, deliberation comes down to the question of how the practical intellect orders one good to another, and so on to a final end. Indeed, having the right conception of order is for Aquinas the key to the entire argument of the *EN*, and that which most separates his reading of this work from so many of its contemporary interpreters. At least a brief sketch, then, of Aquinas's opening to his commentary on the *EN* is vital for a proper understanding of his account of deliberation.

Aquinas begins the proem by distinguishing the twofold order found in things. One is the order of the parts of some whole to each other, as the parts of a house are ordered to one another; the second is the order of things to an end. The second kind of ordering is prior to the first in that the order of the parts of a whole to one another only exists insofar as they are ordered to an end.[23] Now this twofold order in things, Aquinas continues, is related to reason in a fourfold way, the third of which is the order which deliberating reason makes in the operations of the will (*ordo quem ratio considerando facit in operationibus voluntatis*). A human action is a choice imbued with reason's imposition of order, both insofar as reason orders goods to one another and to an end. Reason's imposition of order is not to be understood in any Kantian sense; for the twofold order reason considers, Aquinas has already told us, is an order found originally *in rebus*.[24]

This elaboration upon the theme of order is Aquinas's meditation on Aristotle's terser comments at *EN* I.1 regarding the ordering of goods. There Aristotle cites a basic distinction among ends: some are activities, others are products apart from their activities. Some groups of ends, moreover, fall under a single capacity, as when bridlemaking, horseriding, and strategy fall under the master *technē* of political prudence (*EN* I.2). Aristotle ends this brief opening chapter with the crucial remark that it makes no difference, i.e., when it comes to ordering ends under a single capacity, whether the ends in question are activities or products distinct from the activities which produced them (1094a16–18). Aquinas's example refers to the ordering of gymnastics to medicine. The end of medicine is a product apart from the activity, namely health, but gymnastics, which is subordinated to medicine, is itself an activity.[25]

Neither Aristotle nor Aquinas signals a change in his understanding of order when speaking of ends which just are activities being subordinated to higher ends. The impression left by I.1 is that whenever an end of *any* sort is "for the sake of" another, an efficient causal relationship is set up in which the lower end brings the higher end into being. What follows from this is that the end which serves as the "product" in the causal relationship also serves, *qua* final cause, as the "norm" for the lower activity and its end. Given the relationship of military strategy to the master *technē* of political prudence, military strategy takes its shape under the guidance of a particular conception of virtuous activity. As guided by personal honor Achilles's notion of military strategy becomes a very different thing. This is important in one way because it tells us that *eudaimonia* cannot be, as it is often taken to be, a mere aggregate of intrinsically valuable goods—of pleasure, honor, a collection of Bach cantatas, and virtuous activity. Given that virtuous activity is the ultimate end, lower goods will find their place in the order of happiness insofar as they help bring about and are "normed" by such activity. And even among virtuous activities there will be orderings of some to others, on up to the absolutely final end.[26]

To be clear, Aristotle is not saying that the subordination of one end to another renders the subordinated end *merely* instrumental to the higher end. The concern of Aristotle's contemporary interpreters is that the plurality and incommensurability of final ends can be preserved only by denying them any instrumental relation to other final ends. For Aristotle and Aquinas final ends remain final ends whether or not they are conducive to some more final end beyond themselves (see *ST* Ia–IIae, q. 14, a. 2). Yet activities which are final ends can also bring about a "product" analogously to the way in which mundane *technai* do. Thus courageous activity can be ordered to justice or contemplation without in any way diminishing the intrinsic value of courageous activity.[27]

Successful deliberation, therefore, discerns the best means of producing, in these contingent circumstances, the causal-normative ligatures which hold *per se* among ends. It is given direction by a most final end which is not an aggregate and which "norms" subordinate activities and ends. If more than one means is necessary to achieve the ultimate end, then these means themselves—some of which of course will be final ends in another context—will be ordered to each other according to the same kind of causal-normative relationship.[28] But as we learn from Aquinas's proem to the *Commentary*, the ordering of deliberative items to one another is due to the ordering of them all to the final end.[29]

But then where, on the narrow view, does practical reason come up with its final ends? One answer is that it doesn't. Ends, as Aristotle tells us, are determined by moral virtue, while practical reason, perfected by *phronēsis/prudentia*, concerns itself with the means.[30] Without some further comment this statement would lead us to believe that ends are wholly unavailable to the consideration of reason, and that practical reason is solely concerned with the Humean task of pursuing the means to our desires. But for Aquinas practical reasoning also grasps the end for the sake of which it deliberates about the means, and the first principles or ends of practical reason are held naturally by the intellectual habit of *synderesis* (*ST* Ia, q. 79, a. 12). Without such a habit, Aquinas would say, deliberation would be set the awesome task of determining the constituent ends of human perfection. Human reasoning would no longer be a measured measure, and the rationality of practical reason would therefore be put in jeopardy. The disputed point, however, is whether this natural intellectual habit of holding the first principles of practical reason is also Aristotle's view.

The ascription of *synderesis* to Aristotle occurs by name in the *Sentences* commentary and by strong implication in the *Commentary on De anima*.[31] Terence Irwin, however, has argued that Aquinas backs off from attributing *synderesis* to Aristotle when commenting on the relevant passages of the *EN*.[32] Denis J. M. Bradley has recently claimed that Aquinas imports the doctrine into his commentary, though not by name. For Bradley, there is no solid textual evidence for a doctrine of *synderesis* in the *EN;* it is Aquinas's unwarranted resolution of what for Bradley remains an unresolved tension in Aristotle between the cognitivist and emotivist sources of moral virtue.[33] These writers thus agree with Harry Jaffa's claim that there exists an irrecoverable distance between the pagan understanding of morality and the Christian doctrine of natural law. But whatever differences may exist between Aristotle's understanding of ethical first principles and Aquinas's understanding of natural law, it is a mistake to locate a difference in the doctrine of *synderesis*, and this for the following reason.

What *synderesis* demands is that human agents in their untutored universal apprehension of the good recognize certain things as perfective of their nature. Jaffa agrees that we intuitively recognize certain goods like intelligence, sight, certain pleasures, and honors, as good (*EN* I.6 1096b16–19). Yet he contends that we do not know, not by nature at any rate, how to use such goods for our own *moral* good.[34] But it is precisely this distinction between a basic recognition of good things and specifically moral obligation which is the source of Jaffa's misunderstanding. What he has done is introduce a distinction between moral and pre-moral understanding of the good completely foreign to Aristotelian-Thomistic thought, one which he thinks Aquinas attempts to get around by the doctrine of *synderesis*. For Aquinas as well as for Aristotle, there is no distinction between something's being a fundamental good of human nature, like intelligence or honor, and something's being a *moral* good. A doctrine of natural law does not introduce any special notion of moral obligation at this level; the obligation is there in the perception of good.³⁵ Hence failure to recognize certain goods as genuine perfections of human nature is as basic a failure in *moral* perception as a failure to perceive snow as white is in sense perception. The remedy in the former case is punishment, not argument, while in the latter case the remedy is simply more perception (*Topics* I.11 105a5–7).³⁶

The above is not an argument for the claim that the ordinary Aristotelian agent has a cognitive grasp of what Aquinas understands to be the ontology (or theology) of the natural law. Nothing more is being attributed to this agent in the order of knowing than the basic constituents of the good, e.g., life itself, sexual activity, social relationships, and the pursuit of truth, especially about the highest things.³⁷ But this is enough to allow us to say that the ordinary Aristotelian agent has natural knowledge of himself as measured by extrinsic principles of moral order. There is no need for him to "jump-start" himself into the moral order by deliberating about the basic constituents of his perfection. Interpreters of Aristotle like Jaffa who claim for Aristotle a natural-right as opposed to a natural-law theory have no problem upholding an extrinsic standard of human perfection; what they reject is the natural habit of holding the first principles of this perfection.³⁸ But without this natural knowledge of principles it is impossible to make sense of a natural standard of human perfection. For if the standard is justifiable, there must be knowledge of natural causes. And the discovery of natural causes—if the Meno paradox is to be avoided—must repose upon principles held naturally in the sense of requiring no demonstration.

It is crucial to emphasize that these first principles or ends—what Aquinas more accurately calls precepts—are *extrinsic* to man's power for practical rationality. They are the practical reason's desire for what the speculative intellect perceives to be true about the world. This point is brought out well by Aquinas in his comment on a text in *EN* VI.1. At 1139a11–15 of this chapter, Aristotle distinguishes reason into its "scientific" (*to epistemonikon*) and "calculative" (*to logistikon*) powers, while explicitly equating the calculative power with deliberation (1139a11). Then just a few lines later, at VI.2 1139a26–31, Aristotle distinguishes between the practical intellect, true reasoning by which is so essential to choice (1139a21–26), and the speculative intellect. In commenting upon this latter text Aquinas alerts the reader to a possible confusion. In both pairs of distinction Aristotle seems to speaking about the same powers, yet in the "scientific/calculative" expression Aristotle speaks of distinct powers, whereas the "speculative/practical" expression, as we learn in the *De anima* (III.10 433a15), really only refers to *one* power, the power of the speculative intellect which—as Aquinas elsewhere puts it—"becomes" practical.³⁹

Aquinas clarifies the confusion by stating that practical reason's grasp of its principle in a universal consideration is the same *in subjecto* with the speculative intellect. But because practical reasoning does not stop with this universal consideration—precisely because it is concerned with an action to be performed here and now—practical reason must then enter into its "calculative" mode in which it deliberates about particular options and forms a judgment. And because, as Aristotle says in *De anima*, the universal reason does not move without the particular, the calculative (*ratiocinativum*) is considered a "different part" (*ponitur diversa pars*) than the scientific.[40]

What these texts and arguments are intended to support, once again, is the claim that for both Aristotle and Aquinas practical reasoning, while concerned with efficient causal "means" in its calculative or deliberative mode, also apprehends the first principles of practical reasoning insofar as it is one *in subjecto* with speculative reason. Practical reason in its deliberative mode can thus be exclusively concerned with instrumental means while maintaining a reasoned grasp of final ends.[41] Neither emotivism nor historicism, it is rather the natural ordering of the human good which undergirds for Aristotle, and Aquinas following him, the logic of practical rationality.[42]

In discussing how it is that agents come up with final ends without deliberating over them, we have concentrated on the natural apprehension of the first principles of practical reason, about which there is no inquiry. At this level of generality we are speaking of ends shared by all rational agents. But are we then to conclude that all the rest is deliberation, that given our natural orientation to certain ends the task of practical reason is entirely to go about seeking the instrumental means necessary to achieve them? It would seem, given the generality of these naturally known ends, that a good deal of specification is required in order for practical reason to be effectively action-guiding. My natural desire for justice does me little good in deciding what to do in my particular circumstances. Is the specification I need achieved by means-end reasoning, or is there some other mode of discovery involved? It would be impossible to deal with these questions in all their complexity here, but some initial remarks can be made by way of introduction to the problem.

Surely the place to start in determining Aquinas's response to these questions is the text discussed earlier, *ST* Ia–IIae, q. 95, a. 2. Here, as we noted, Aquinas speaks of two ways in which principles can be derived from the natural law. The first, by *demonstratio*, is like the way in which conclusions in the speculative sciences are derived from first principles, that is, by a syllogistic effort. The second, by *determinatio*, is like the way in which a builder or judge specifies a general design or principle. The second way yields principles which belong exclusively to human positive law, and, as I argued earlier, operates according to means-end reasoning.[43] As an example of *demonstratio* Aquinas refers to the way in which the conclusion "Do not kill," is derived from the more general precept "Do harm to no man." Clearly this inference does not involve means-end reasoning; it is, rather, a species of deduction. And insofar as practical reason busies itself with this kind of reasoning, with discerning the necessary relationships between more general and more specific conceptions of good and evil, we can say that practical reason specifies its ends without resorting to reasoning of the means-end type. So, if it is right to call this kind of practical reasoning deliberation, then it is precisely here where Aquinas holds common ground with so many of Aristotle's contemporary interpreters. Still, Aquinas would part ways with any interpreter who would reject that such *conclusiones* bear a necessary relationship, at least at the very highest level of generality, to naturally known first principles.

It is a question whether means-end reasoning plays any role in helping derive more remote *conclusiones* from the first precepts of the natural law. R. A. Armstrong's study of the relationship between the primary and secondary precepts of the natural law suggests some ways in which it does. Aquinas's argument for monogamy, for example, is based in part upon the relationship between marriage and its remote end, the mutual assistance of the spouses. In regard to the proximate end of marriage, the engendering and education of children, polygamy appears to be a means equally as effective as monogamy. But when it comes to the mutual assistance of the spouses, polygamy is a grossly ineffective means. Thus monogamy is the right determination of the general inclinations to sexual pleasure and life in society.[44]

In general, it would seem that the more practical reasoning descends into the particular, the more it will utilize means-end reasoning in order to act in accord with the natural law. The sphere of *noncontingent* conclusions from first precepts, no matter what sort of reasoning is involved in getting to them, is remarkably constricted. Contingency insists upon its place in the moral life at a very general level, as Socrates tried to explain to Cephalus in challenging his definition of justice as giving back what one owes. As the refrain goes, moral principles for Aristotle and Aquinas hold always or for the most part, and it is these principles and the means to them which most properly comprise the subject matter of deliberation (see *EN* III.3 1112b8–11). Deliberation, then, concerns not so much the discovery that murder is harm, or that honor is due to God or to parents, but rather a consideration of the possible options for the sake of some end, in which reasoning must be of the means-end type.

This sketch of how practical reason derives principles from the natural law is sufficient to reply to a charge of inconsistency raised against Aquinas by Terence Irwin. Irwin writes that for Aquinas virtue "is focused on the right end, not because of prudence, but because of a distinct nondeliberative intellectual state that grasps the right ends, and this is *synderesis*."[45] This creates a problem. At the level of *synderesis* there is as yet no distinction between the virtuous and the vicious agent (*ST* Ia–IIae, q. 94, a. 6; *De Ver.*, q. 16, a. 3, ad 3). Yet Aquinas seems to want *synderesis* to be responsible for establishing the right, that is, the virtuous, orientation to final ends. Irwin puts the conflict this way: "A thick conception of *synderesis* seems to be needed to supply something distinctive of the virtuous person's end. On the other hand, a thick conception seems to conflict with Aquinas's normal view that *synderesis* is present in both the virtuous and the vicious person."[46] Aquinas's mistake, Irwin argues, is his assumption that when Aristotle says that virtue makes the end right, he means that something independent of prudence fixes the end. This mistake could be avoided if we understand prudence according to the broad view of deliberation, thus allowing it a role in fixing the end.[47] Then the difference between the virtuous and the vicious agent would be precisely that deliberation about final ends which the narrow view excludes.

But what we have already said about derivations from the natural law reveals that Irwin is mistaken here in thinking that *synderesis*, and *synderesis* alone, is sufficient to make the end right, at least in the sense which distinguishes the virtuous from the vicious. A key text for his argument is *ST* IIa–IIae, q. 47, a. 6, where Aquinas explicitly states that it does not belong to prudence to fix the ends of the moral virtues, as these are fixed by *synderesis*. But the response's use of the analogy between the first principles of speculative reason and the first principles of practical reason indicates that Aquinas means this statement at a very high level of generality, as though to say what makes moral virtue even possible is the natural orientation to the constituent ends of human perfection shared by all agents.[48]

Irwin in fact misreads other texts in which Aquinas speaks of the end of virtuous action being fixed by nature as texts which speak of virtuous action considered in its proper species, which is to say virtuous action as performed by prudent agents.[49] For example, Aquinas mentions as an end set by nature the natural desire not to divert from the judgment of reason on account of excess fear or confidence (IIa–IIae q. 47, a. 7). This end is not, however, as Irwin takes it to be, exclusively that of the virtuous agent. Our moral assessments diverge according to the way in which different agents pursue this end, i.e., in how they attempt to hit the mean of the virtues to which they are naturally directed. Ideally, prudence will arise in the agent's right decisions about the means necessary to attain the various ends grasped by nature. In the real drama of human action, however, agents will depart from the path of prudence very early, even, if some strong passion is in play, from adherence to the precepts of the Decalogue. But to return to the case of courage, imagine an agent who mistakenly takes the ultimate end to be pleasure, and who reasons that in order to obtain the pleasure he wants he must steal some money from his place of employment. Having never stolen money before, he is initially seized with fear at the thought of getting caught. Yet he knows that if he wants pleasure he must go through with the theft. In order to hit the mean of "courage" his faulty judgment tells him that he must pull off the theft, and his "prudence"—what Aristotle would call cleverness (*deinotes, EN* VI.12 1144a27-28)—goes to work to figure out the means of doing this without giving in either to excessive fear or excessive confidence. The courage of the genuinely courageous agent will hit the same abstract mean, but in a very different way. Thus Aquinas is not inconsistent in claiming that the ends of the moral virtues are fixed by *synderesis* and that *synderesis* is shared by both the virtuous and the vicious agent.[50]

We need not be reminded, in sum, that our moral education begins with *conclusiones,* accurately derived or not, that we simply accept from our parents, family, and political environment. We will have learned from our elders if not by our own lights that we ought to act courageously in the face of fear, yet misunderstand courage as mere bravado on the battlefield. Experience, perhaps a costly one, may show us our mistake. But from Aristotle we learn that there are acts of formal rational inquiry other than deliberation, dialectical, analogical, inferential, not to mention the discernments of the intuitive faculty, by which we are able to discover the structure of the final ends we naturally aim at. The paradigmatic instance of dialectical investigation of final ends is Aristotle's approach to the definition of *eudaimonia* in *EN* I, an approach which combines with analogical reasoning and intuition in the function argument at I.7. Analogical reasoning is also used in the determination of justice in Book V.[51] Aristotle and Aquinas's understanding of rational inquiry is thus sufficiently rich that we need never fear that in restricting deliberation properly so-called to instrumental means we have cut ourselves off from the understanding of final ends.

A complete discussion of these other acts of rational inquiry is no doubt required for a complete understanding of why deliberation is restricted to means to final ends, but such a discussion extends beyond the purview of this essay. My task has been limited to an initial defense of the narrow view of deliberation by way of discussion of three possible Thomistic responses to the view defended by the majority of today's more prominent Aristotelian commentators. First I tried to show that Aquinas has no need to understand Aristotelian deliberation as it is often interpreted today, not least because Aristotle himself did not do so. I argued that insofar as constituents and specifications of ends are regarded *as* constituents and specifications, they have not as yet been entered as items in a deliberative inquiry. Second I indicated some reasons why the attempt to separate Aquinas from Aristotle on the basis of the doctrine of *synderesis* is inadequate, and that only with this doctrine can Aquinas and Aristotle uphold the rationality of practical reasoning. Finally I addressed Terence Irwin's contention that Aquinas's use of *synderesis* is fundamentally conflicted; here I pointed out that Aquinas's employment of this doctrine to explain the nature of moral virtue does not compromise his commitment to the narrow view. The most attractive feature of the Thomistic position I have defended is its appreciation of the best of the current Aristotelian scholarship, i.e. the commitment to a nonreductive, nontechnocratic conception of practical reason. The Thomistic account of deliberation, far from being a threat to that commitment, should rather be seen as the best way of preserving it.

NOTES

1. The short list of prominent contemporary defenders of the broad view would include W. F. R. Hardie, *Aristotle's Ethical Theory* (Oxford University Press, 1968); David Wiggins, "Deliberation and Practical Reason," in Amélie Rorty, ed., *Essays on Aristotle's Ethics* (Los Angeles: University of California Press, 1980). John M. Cooper, *Reason and Human Good in Aristotle* (Cambridge: Harvard University Press, 1975); Martha C. Nussbaum, *Aristotle's De Motu Animalium* (Princeton: Princeton University Press, 1978), esp. essay 4; Norman O. Dahl, *Practical Reason, Aristotle and Weakness of Will* (Minneapolis: University of Minnesota Press, 1984); Nancy Sherman, *The Fabric of Character* (Oxford: Clarendon Press, 1989).

2. Terence Irwin, "The Scope of Deliberation: A Conflict in Aquinas," *Review of Metaphysics* 44 (1990): 21–42; Scott MacDonald, "Ultimate Ends in Practical Reasoning: Aquinas's Aristotelian Moral Psychology and Anscombe's Fallacy," *The Philosophical Review*, vol. 100, n. 1 (January 1991): 31–66.

3. D. J. Allan, *The Philosophy of Aristotle*, rev. ed. (London: Oxford University Press, 1963); "Aristotle's Account of the Origin of Moral Principles," *Proceedings of the XIth International Congress of Philosophy*, vol. 12 (Amsterdam: North Holland Publishing Company, 1953); "The Practical Syllogism," in *Autour d'Aristote*, Bibliothèque philosophique

de Louvain, vol. 16 (Louvain: Publications Universitaires de Louvain, 1955), 325–40. In "Aristotle's Account of the Origin of Moral Principles," Allan locates the modern origin of the question concerning the scope of deliberation in the nineteenth-century debates between Walter, Teichmüller, Trendelenburg, and Zeller.

4. Wiggins, "Deliberation and Practical Reason."
5. Ibid., 224.
6. Ibid.
7. Ibid., 223.
8. Ibid., 227.
9. See Nussbaum, *Aristotle's De Motu Animalium,* esp. essay 4. For a critique of Nussbaum's attempts to mitigate the relativism in her approach to Aristotle, see my article "'Divinity Must Live within Herself': Nussbaum and Aquinas on Transcending the Human," *International Philosophical Quarterly* (March 1997).
10. MacDonald, "Ultimate Ends in Practical Reasoning," 63. MacDonald's claims are limited, however, to his analysis of *ST* Ia–IIae, q. 1.
11. Harry V. Jaffa, *Thomism and Aristotelianism* (Westport: Greenwood Press, 1979), originally published by the University of Chicago Press, 1952.
12. Denis J. M. Bradley, *Aquinas on the Twofold Human Good* (Washington, D.C.: Catholic University of America Press, 1997).
13. Irwin, "The Scope of Deliberation."
14. Wiggins includes as constituents of *eudaimonia* not only its essential constituents (the activities of the various virtues, and especially the virtues of phronēsis and *sophia*), but also its *sine qua non* constituents along with certain specifications of virtuous activity ("a satisfying occupation").
15. The same analysis applies to the specification of a punishment. A judge will evaluate a range of specifications insofar as they are possible means of taking away certain rights and privileges enjoyed by citizens, and thus as a means of squaring the debt to society. Presumably this end could be achieved, in the most unwieldy way, by house arrest. But deliberation asks: what is the most effective means of denying rights and privileges, as well as protecting society from further harm?
16. This seems to be Aquinas's point at *ST* Ia–IIae, q. 14, a. 2, ad 2.
17. Bernard Williams, "Acting as the Virtuous Person Acts," in Robert Heinaman, ed., *Aristotle and Moral Realism* (Boulder: Westview Press, 1995).
18. Ibid., 20.
19. *In X Ethicorum,* II, lect. IV, n. 283.
20. A lucid discussion of the relationship between exterior and interior acts can be found in chapter 4 of Ralph McInerny, *Aquinas on Human Action: A Theory of Practice* (Washington, D.C.: Catholic University of America Press, 1992).
21. *In X Ethicorum,* III, lect. V, n. 433.
22. Aristotle, *Nicomachean Ethics,* translated, with introduction, notes, and glossary by Terence Irwin (Indianapolis: Hackett, 1985). The text at 1113b5–7 reads: "hai de tōn aretōn energeiai peri tauta. eph' hēmin de kai he aretē, homoiōs de kai he kakia." Irwin understands the phrase *peri tauta* to refer to *tōn pros to telos* at 1113b4.
23. *In X Ethicorum,* I, lect. 1, no. 1: "Invenitur autem duplex ordo in rebus. Unus quidem partium alicujus totius seu alicujus multitudinis adinvicem, sicut partes domus adinvicem ordinantur. Alius est ordo rerum in finem. Et hic ordo est principalior, quam

primus. Nam, ut Philosophus dicit in undecimo Metaphysicorum, ordo partium exercitus adinvicem, est propter ordinem totius exercitus ad ducem." The reference is actually to *Metaphysics* XII.10.

24. This point is pursued by Ralph McInerny, *Aquinas on Human Action*, chapter 10.

25. *In X Ethicorum*, I, lect. 1, n. 18.

26. I am much indebted to Richard Kraut's critique of Ackrill's reading of these texts, *Aristotle on the Human Good* (Princeton: Princeton University Press, 1989), 4.6.

27. For an interpretation of *eudaimonia* as an ordered set of virtuous activities, see Ralph McInerny, "Ultimate End in Aristotle," in *Being and Predication* (Washington, D.C.: The Catholic University of America Press, 1986).

28. At *ST* Ia–IIae, q. 1, a. 4, Aquinas speaks of a twofold order of ends in human action. In the order of intention, i.e. the order of interior acts of the will, the first mover is the ultimate end, the unmoved mover. But an "unmoved mover" is necessary in the order of execution as well. This is what deliberation concludes to be the "first means" necessary for the sake of the end (*primum eorum quae sunt ad finem*). What is crucial to note here is that in both orders, in intention and execution, ends are understood by Aquinas as movers, efficient causes, and so we must understand intermediate ends, or means, as being moved by the ultimate end in the order of intention and as movers toward the ultimate end in the order of execution.

29. None of this is to say that deliberation is necessary for an action to occur. On this theme see Daniel Westberg, *Right Practical Reason* (Oxford: Clarendon Press, 1994), chapter 11.

30. For example, *EN* III.3 1112b11ff.; VI.13 1145a2–6.

31. *In III Sent.*, d. 33, q. 2, a. 4, sol. 4, with reference to *EN* VI.2 1138b35–1139a1; and *In De anima* III, lect. XV, n. 826, with reference to *De anima* III.10 433a26.

32. Irwin, "The Scope of Deliberation," 26, n. 9. Irwin thinks Aquinas had his best opportunity to mention *synderesis* in commenting upon Aristotle's discussion of *nous* at VI.11 1143a35-b5 (*In X Ethicorum*, VI, lect. IX, n. 1247)—but passed it up.

33. Bradley, *Aquinas on the Twofold Human Good*, 238.

34. See chapter 8 of *Thomism and Aristotelianism*, esp. 170.

35. I have learned on this point from Alasdair MacIntyre's discussion of the difference between Aquinas and Scotus on the "ought" of practical reason, *Three Rival Versions of Moral Enquiry* (Notre Dame: University of Notre Dame Press, 1990), 154ff. On the Thomistic approach to deriving "ought" from "is," see Ralph McInerny, "Naturalism and Thomistic Ethics" *The Thomist* 60 (April 1976): 222–42, and chapter 3 of *Ethica Thomistica* (Washington, D.C.: Catholic University of America Press, 1982).

36. Cf. Kurt Pritzl, "Ways of Truth and Ways of Opinion in Aristotle," *Proceedings of the American Catholic Philosophical Association* (1993): 241–52.

37. An excellent discussion of the promulgation of the natural law is found in Russell Hittinger, "Natural Law as 'Law': Reflections On the Occasion of *Veritatis Splendor*," *American Journal of Jurisprudence* (1994): 1–32. Hittinger argues (19–20), based upon Aquinas's comments at *In II Rom.*, lectio III, n. 219 (super 2:15) and *ST* Ia–IIae, q. 91, a. 2, that the promulgation of the natural law was sufficiently made to the Gentiles even in their ignorance of the lawgiver, insofar as they knew the basic terms of good and evil. Whether in the order of knowledge these terms were understood *as law* is a further

question. According to Hittinger, Aquinas follows the patristic theologians in claiming that knowledge of the natural law *as law* has become increasingly dim as a punishment for sin. Jaffa affirms the Suarezean view that there cannot be a doctrine of natural law without explicit revelation of the lawgiver to the agent, thus confusing the orders of being and knowing. See Jaffa, *Thomism and Aristotelianism*, esp. 169.

38. To be more precise, Jaffa holds that natural right for Aristotle is a part of political or legal right, in that what is naturally right is modified according to the contingencies of a given community. He does not deny that there is a natural best, a natural standard, which provides the general direction for political decision-making, but this most, if not all, actual polities will fail to attain. See Jaffa, *Thomism and Aristotelianism*, 182ff. Jaffa's central argument for the mutability of natural right is based upon Aristotle's claims at *EN* V.7, esp. 1134b30ff. Aquinas's comment on this text (lectio XII) takes Aristotle to be talking about the mutability of remote *conclusiones* derived from the natural law with *multa consideratio* (*ST* Ia–IIae, q. 100, aa. 1, 3, 11), not the first principles themselves (see n. 1029). On natural justice in Aristotle see Fred D. Miller, Jr., "Aristotle on Natural Law and Justice," in David Keyt and Fred D. Miller, Jr., eds., *A Companion to Aristotle's Politics* (Cambridge: Basil Blackwell, 1991).

39. *ST* Ia, q. 79, a. 11, sed contra. The expression is attributed to Aristotle, *De anima* III.9 433a1, though there is no mention of this particular expression in the appropriate passage of Aquinas's comment on this work. For an excellent discussion of this issue see Josef Pieper, *Reality and the Good*, trans. Stella Lange (Chicago: Henry Regnery, 1967), esp. 47–51. For the analogy between the principles of speculative and practical reason, see *ST* Ia–IIae, q. 57, a. 4; q. 94, a. 2; IIa–IIae, q. 47, a. 6.

40. *In X Ethicorum*, VI, lect. II, n. 1132: "Dicendum est ergo, quod intellectus practicus principium quidem habet in universali consideratione, et secundum hoc est idem subjecto cum speculativo, sed terminatur ejus consideratio in particulari operabili. Unde Philosophus dict in tertio de Anima [III.11 434a16ff.], quod ratio universalis non movet sine particulari. Et secundum hoc, ratiocinativum ponitur diversa pars a scientifico." Cf. *In De anima*, III, lect. XVI, nn. 845–46.

41. *ST* Ia–IIae, q. 66, a. 3, ad 3, does not pose a problem here; for in saying that "prudentia non solum dirigit virtues morales in eligendo ea quae sunt ad finem, sed etiam in praestituendo finem," Aquinas is speaking of "end" in the sense of the "mean" which is hit by prudence's arrangement of the appropriate means.

42. Scott MacDonald argues that Aquinas's notion of ultimate end can make a contribution to the theory of practical rationality even without the baggage of his natural teleology. But this is just to jeopardize the rationality of our ultimate commitments if the constituents of the ultimate end have only human choices as their measure.

43. At *ST* Ia–IIae, q. 100, a. 8, in considering whether any of the precepts of the Decalogue are dispensable, Aquinas argues that if a legislature were to determine a general precept to safeguard the city by ordering men from each ward to guard the city against siege, it could dispense with this particular determination *propter aliquam maiorem utilitatem*, for the sake of some greater utility. See also *ST* Ia–IIae, q. 102, a. 1 and Aquinas's appeal to the two kinds of order in discussing the cause of the ceremonial precepts of the *lex vetus*.

44. *Suppl.*, q. 65, a. 1. See R. A. Armstrong, *Primary and Secondary Precepts in Thomistic Natural Law Reasoning* (The Hague: Martinus Nijhoff, 1966), esp. 60ff.

45. Irwin, "The Scope of Deliberation," 26, citing *ST* IIa–IIae, q. 47, a. 15.

46. Ibid., 40.

47. Irwin (ibid., 41) does not think such determination usurps the role of nature in fixing ends, only that prudent deliberation is required to "discover the character" of these natural ends.

48. At times Aquinas speaks of the natural inclinations as the *seminales* of the virtues, but this is just to emphasize that they are *seminales*, not the virtues themselves. *ST* Ia–IIae, q. 27, a. 3, ad 4; q. 63, a. 1.

49. The distinction Aquinas makes at Ia–IIae, q. 94, a. 3 is especially illuminating in this regard. Here, in considering whether the natural law commands acts of all the virtues, Aquinas argues that in one respect the natural law commands all the acts of all the virtues, insofar as to the natural law belongs everything to which a man is inclined by reason. But in another respect the natural law does not command all virtuous acts considered in themselves, i.e. *qua* virtuous acts, because nature does not immediately incline to this or that temperate act performed as the prudent agent performs it. Action born out of this higher level of understanding and habituation is achieved only through the further inquiry of reason.

50. Cf. Alasdair MacIntyre, "Plain Persons and Moral Philosophy: Rules, Virtues and Goods," *American Catholic Philosophical Association Quarterly*, vol. 66, n. 1 (1992): 3–19.

51. This is discussed by Ralph McInerny in chapter 8 of *Aquinas and Analogy* (Washington, D.C.: The Catholic University of America Press, 1996).

# 8

# Moral Terminology and Proportionalism

*Janet E. Smith*

The furor that surrounded the issuance of *Veritatis Splendor* indicated that greater clarity is needed about certain key terms used by the magisterium in evaluating human action.[1] A lack of clarity about the meaning of certain key terms is one of the primary causes for the conflict between proportionalists and the magisterium.[2] This chapter attempts to make some distinctions not commonly observed in the debates between proportionalists and defenders of the magisterium. (1) First, the need for making carefully enough the distinction between *malum, peccatum,* and *culpa* will be shown. (2) The difference between evaluating acts as kinds (as secondary substances) and evaluating acts as concrete particulars (as primary substances) will be explained. (3) Distinctions will be made between "accidental," "concrete," and "specifying" circumstances."[2] (4) It shall also be shown that the moral prohibitions of the tradition are not merely "formal" or tautological.

### MALUM, PECCATUM AND CULPA

Aquinas makes careful distinctions between what is a *malum,* a *peccatum,* and a *culpa.* In the *De malo,* in response to the question "Whether sin [*peccatum*] consists solely in the will?" he states:

> There was a threefold opinion concerning this question: for some said that no act either interior or exterior in itself is a sin [*peccatum*] but only privation has the nature of sin [*peccatum*] on account of what Augustine says that sin is nothing; but others asserted that sin consists in the interior act of the will alone; still others maintained that sin consists in both the interior act of the will and the exterior act. Although the latter contains more truth, nevertheless all the opinions are in some measure true.
>
> But it must be noted that these three—evil [*malum*], sin [*peccatum*], and fault [*culpa*]—are related to each other as more general and less general. For evil [*malum*] is more general: indeed any privation whatever of form or of order or of due measure either in the subject or in the act, has the nature of evil [*malum*]. But any act lacking due order or form or measure is called

a sin [*peccatum*] (or defect). Hence it can be said that a crooked leg is an evil [*malum*] or bad leg, but it cannot be said that it is a sin [*peccatum*] except perhaps in that manner of speaking in which the effect of sin [*peccatum*] is called a sin [*peccatum*]; but the very limping is called a sin [*peccatum*] or defect: indeed, any disordered act either in nature or in art or in morals can be called a sin [*peccatum*]. But sin [*peccatum*] has the nature of fault [*culpa*] only from the fact that it is voluntary: for no disordered act is imputed to anyone as a fault [*culpa*] except as a consequence of that fact that it is within his power. And so it is clear that sin [*peccatum*] is more general than fault, although according to the common usage among theologians, sin [*peccatum*] and fault [*culpa*] are taken for the same thing.³

Let us extract the pertinent definitions. *Malum* (translated as "evil") is any privation of form or order or due measure either in the subject or in the act; it would be right to speak of this as objective evil. *Peccatum* (translated as "sin"), a subcategory of *malum*, is any *act* lacking due order or form or measure (e.g., limping). And *culpa* (translated as "fault"), a subcategory of *peccatum*, is a *voluntarily* disordered act.

The distinctions are clear enough but finding English equivalents is difficult. Although *malum* is generally translated "evil," most English speakers think that references to evil are always to moral evil. For instance, although Aquinas would speak of a three-legged dog as an instance of evil (*malum*), few English speakers would speak thus. The modern age tends to use the word "evil" to refer only to egregiously bad moral action—such as Hitler's pogrom against Jews. Aquinas clearly means to include in the category of objective evil (*malum*) all kinds of imperfections, large and small, both in the being and in the operation of things.

"Sin" is the common translation of *peccatum*. But, again, speakers of English generally use "sin" to refer only to moral evil, whereas Aquinas, allowing that theologians equate it with *culpa*, states that it refers to any disordered *act*. His reference to limping as a *peccatum* suggests that he includes both acts of man (nonvoluntary actions) and human acts (voluntary actions) in the category of *peccatum*. Certainly, there are defects in human behavior for which one bears no moral responsibility, certainly those resulting from physical defects, which lead to disordered actions, such as "limping" (a *peccatum*). Yet, I believe that *peccatum* includes what has come to be known as "objective" evil in the moral realm; i.e., evil that *if freely chosen* is a *culpa*. Peccatum refers to defective physical acts and also any such disordered acts as "taking another's property" or "causing the death of another" that would be *culpae* if accompanied by a bad intention.

*Culpa*, translated "fault" or more properly "blame," is the word that refers to an act of the will or a human act that is immoral, i.e., it is an act for which the agent is morally culpable, for which an agent is worthy of being blamed and even punished. It is a disordered act—a *peccatum*—that is voluntarily chosen; in the next paragraph of the response Aquinas states: "the exterior deformed act is imputed to man as a fault (*culpa*) because of the will." English speakers generally call such an act a sin.

In order to illustrate Aquinas's terms and to show the disparity between them and common English usage, let us apply his distinctions to four sexual matters. (1) If one were infertile, Aquinas would call this condition a *malum*, since infertility is not the natural or healthy or good condition for an adult person. (2) If one were to undertake an act of sexual intercourse (and here it is irrelevant whether the act is with one's spouse or with one not one's spouse), and were unable to complete the act because of impotence, Aquinas would call this act a *peccatum* (a kind of *malum*), not because the act is blameworthy (assuming it is not) but because it is an act that did not achieve its proper completion or fullness. (3) If one were mistakenly (and not culpable for one's ignorance) to have intercourse with a woman one believed to be one's spouse, this act would also be a *peccatum*, but not a *culpa*. (4) If one deliberately and willingly had sexual intercourse with someone one knew not to be one's spouse, this act would be a *culpa*. (Let us note here a point that will be justified later: agents in instances 3 and 4 would be understood to have committed adultery, an intrinsically evil act, but only the agent in instance 4 would have committed a blameworthy act.)

Now, when the magisterium speaks of acts that ought never to be performed by human beings, of acts that are always intrinsically wrong, it speaks of *intrinsece malum*.[4] From the distinctions made above, one might expect magisterial documents to speak of *intrinsece peccatum* or even of *intrinsece culpa* since they are referring to actions, whereas *malum* is more generic. I believe that the reason for the choice of *intrinsece malum* is that it more clearly than the other terms has reference to the external act, independent of the motive of the agent. As noted above, theologians sometimes use *peccatum* and *culpa* interchangeably and since the magisterium is imputing no moral evil to an agent when it speaks of actions that ought never to be done, the use of *intrinsece malum* may be designed to avoid such confusions. Unfortunately such confusions still exist.

Furthermore, it is important to note that when the magisterium describes an act as intrinsically *malum*, it is speaking about a *kind* (species) of act that can never be the object of a morally good choice; it is speaking about a *kind* of act that a human being ought never to choose to do. Only concrete particular acts can be called *culpae* (or in more modern usage "sins," i.e., blamable actions—hereafter I use "sin" as the translation of *culpa*). One of the points of divergence between the magisterium and proportionalists[5] is that the magisterium, when speaking about intrinsically evil acts, is speaking about acts as kinds (or secondary substances) whereas proportionalists are, for the most part, evaluating concrete particular acts (or, acts as primary substances; more about this later).

It is also important to note that the magisterium is speaking *only* of the object of the act when it speaks of intrinsic evil, not of the act as a whole, which includes the intention (end or motive),[6] object, and what should be identified as accidental circumstances. For instance, a bad intention (motive) may cause an act with an object essentially good in its kind to be a *culpa*. That is, a man because of his evil intention (motive), say, to gain a false reputation as a do-gooder, although doing something intrinsically good (e.g., giving alms), may be sinning. Conversely, of course, the man doing something intrinsically evil, would not be sinning, if, for instance, he is invincibly ignorant of the nature of his deed or if he is being forced to perform the deed. While acts as kinds are intrinsically good or intrinsically evil, no kind of action is intrinsically a *culpa*.

Many are offended by the magisterium's claim that certain acts are intrinsically *malum* because they think that this claim entails a harsh judgment on those who perform such acts. According to the understanding of moral evaluation advanced by the magisterium, however, *no* judgment on the moral status of the agent of an act is possible until it is known that an act was freely and deliberately chosen. We may know, for instance, that a woman has had an abortion. We would know, then, that something intrinsically evil (*malum*) has been done (an objectively evil act has been performed) since abortion is an act that is evil in its species or kind. We would not be able to judge whether she has sinned until we know whether she knew that abortion is the direct taking of an innocent human life. We would not know the severity of her sin, until we know the particulars of the situation. If she was honestly and not negligently mistaken about the ontological status of the fetus, she would not be morally culpable for the objectively evil act that she performed. Again, she would have done evil (*malum*) but not be guilty of a subjective evil, of sin (*culpa*). Again, no action is intrinsically a sin (*culpa*). This distinction needs to be borne in mind throughout discussions on intrinsic evil so that misattributions will not be made to the magisterium.

## METAPHYSICAL CATEGORIES

To understand the debate between the magisterium and the proportionalists, it is also necessary to have in mind that Aquinas is using metaphysical terms—"substance" and "accident," "species," "form" and "matter," for instance—in a metaphorical way to explain ethical realities. When he speaks of placing an act in a "species" he is speaking of an act having a "substance" or "essence" or "nature" that allows us to designate it a certain *kind* of act, one that can be deemed morally good, morally evil, or morally indifferent.[7] Although he does not explicitly state that he is speaking of acts as secondary substances, his reference to acts as "kinds" demonstrates that such is what he is doing. Just as Joe, George, and Bill are primary substances who have the same essence, which is "man," the secondary substance or species to which they belong, a multitude of concrete particular acts, are primary substances and have the same essence. All concrete particular acts of having sexual intercourse with another's spouse are in essence acts of adultery; "adultery" is the secondary substance or species to which all the particulars belong.

Let us elaborate this claim, for it is central to an analysis of the proportionalist understanding of the magisterium. According to the tradition, one could report (or contemplate) a half dozen or so cases of individual concrete particular acts of "having sexual intercourse with another's spouse."[8] "Having sexual intercourse with another's spouse" is the *object* of the half dozen or so particular instances of this act; this is the species of act called "adultery." Again, all these acts of "having sexual intercourse with another's spouse" qualify as the same *kind* of act, they have the same essence; they all belong to the species, "adultery," an act intrinsically lacking order to the human good, an intrinsically evil kind of act. The tradition holds that although each agent has performed an intrinsically evil act, not all the agents of this same kind of act would be equally culpable, because of the different concrete particular intentions (motives), circumstances, and foreseeable consequences. These are the accidents of the act and thus do not impact upon its essence. The essence of an act is to be found in its object; the intention (motive), circumstances, and consequences are accidents (unless these are of the specifying nature; more about this later).

## UNIVERSAL SPECIES VS. CONCRETE PARTICULARS

It is my contention in this section that whereas the magisterium is evaluating acts considered in their species when it speaks of intrinsically evil acts, it seems that proportionalists are often evaluating concrete particular acts. Often they seem to find that the intention (motive) or circumstances of an action render the agent nonculpable, and thus wish to claim that no evil, only "premoral" or "ontic" evil, has been done. Father Edward Vacek, a proportionalist, makes this point clear:

> Contrary to what its critics say, P [proportionalism] is not opposed to the use of the terms "intrinsic evil," "duty," or absolute," but it uses these terms only for concrete acts. One ought not—"absolutely" ought not—do an act that is wrong. Such an act is "intrinsically evil." In the sphere of concrete moral decisions, P often is experientially indistinguishable from classical act-deontology. What P refuses to do is use these terms for norms or for classes of acts viewed independently of the agent or the circumstances. "Absolutes" commonly refer to a class of acts that are always prescribed or proscribed, i.e., in all circumstances, at all times, in all places, and for all persons without exception. For P, the word "absolute" is reserved for a particular contingent deed that is objectively required. Since no behavioral norm can foresee or include all the possible combinations of values involved in a concrete deed, absolute behavioral norms unjustifiably exclude consideration of features of an act that may be relevant.[9]

We must keep in mind that to use the term "intrinsically evil" to refer to acts described in terms of their concrete particulars is simply not to use the term in the same way as the tradition and the magisterium have used it. Again, the magisterium speaks of acts that are intrinsically evil in their *kind* (or species). Vacek contends that proportionalists, when speaking of an intrinsically evil act, are judging some concrete particular act, not a "kind" of act. They deny that it is possible to speak of "kinds" of acts as intrinsically evil (unless speaking "formally"; we will examine this point in some detail below). In their view, no acts are evil "in their kind" because all acts are susceptible to being converted into a good act if a sufficiently good intention (motive), circumstance, or consequence accompanied it. For the magisterium, no further intention (motive), circumstance, or consequence can render an intrinsically evil act good; *that is what it means for an act to be intrinsically evil.*

THE ROLE OF "CIRCUMSTANCES" AND "INTENTIONS" IN DEFINING ACTIONS

Father Richard McCormick, in contrast to Vacek, claims that proportionalists do evaluate actions as kinds. He states: "[A]ll proportionalists would admit this [that some acts are intrinsically evil from their object] *if the object is broadly understood as including all the morally relevant circumstances.*"[10] McCormick claims that the magisterium is inconsistent in the role that it allows circumstances to play in the moral evaluation of actions. He argues that it is inconsistent for the magisterium to allow "killing" in some circumstances—the circumstance, for instance, of "self-defense," but not to allow contraception in any circumstance. In his words:

> [T]he tradition has defined certain actions as morally wrong *ex objecto* because it has included in the object not simply the material happening (object in a very narrow sense) but also elements beyond it which clearly exclude any possible justification. Thus, a theft is not simply "taking another's property", but doing so "against the reasonable will of the owner." This latter addition has two characteristics in the tradition. (1) It is considered as essential to the object. (2) It excludes any possible exceptions. Why? because if a person is in extreme difficulty and needs food, the owner is not reasonably unwilling that his food be taken. Fair enough. Yet, when the same tradition deals with, for example, masturbation or sterilization, it adds little or nothing to the material happening and regards such a materially described act alone as constituting the object. If it were consistent, it would describe the object as "sterilization *against the good of marriage*." This all could accept.[11]

Is the magisterium inconsistent in its use of circumstances in evaluating moral actions?

It is important to keep in mind that the tradition distinguishes different types of circumstances. Since the magisterium and proportionalists are using Thomistic terms to describe actions, we must take a close look at how Aquinas sees circumstances affecting the description of an action. Although Aquinas does not give different names to the different types of circumstances of which he speaks, for the sake of clarity I shall here speak of the two kinds of circumstances identified by Aquinas as (1) "accidental circumstances,"[12] and (2) "specifying (or defining) circumstances."[13] Proportionalists seem to refer to yet a third kind, that which I shall call (3) "concrete particular circumstances." These are the circumstances that accompany some act considered in its very particularity.[14] In Aquinas's analysis, accidental circumstances and concrete particular circumstances play no role in defining an act as to its essence (or object) whereas they do play a role in the evaluation of the whole act. Specifying circumstances do serve to define an act because they, in the words of Aquinas, "enter into the object of the act."

These distinctions seem to have escaped proportionalists. They seem to believe that the magisterium in theory considers all circumstances "accidental" but, in practice, when defining some acts gives them much more weight. In their own analyses of acts, as we shall see, proportionalists seem to define acts ultimately by only one kind of circumstances, concrete particular circumstances.

Let us first get the Thomistic concepts straight.

*Circumstances* are those elements of an action that "surround" what is being defined and that answer such questions as "how, where, when, why, etc."[15]

"*Accidental circumstances*"[16] are those elements answering such questions but not entering into the essence of what is being defined. Like accidents in reference to anything being defined (e.g., the hair color of a human being does not affect his essence), *accidental circumstances* do not affect the species of an act at all; they can only increase or diminish the goodness or evil of acts already so designated in respect to their object or end.[17] Thus to commit an act of adultery in a nice hotel or a seedy one, or with a beautiful partner or an ugly one, or in the evening or midafternoon, does not change the species of the act. Indeed, in reference to the specification of the objective act, even the "why," the "intention" (motive), or the "end" is an "accidental circumstance."[18] Should a man commit an act of adultery out of kindness to a lonely woman, this good intention (motive) does not alter the specification of the objective act; it remains intrinsically evil although less evil than if the motive were sheer selfish pleasure. It often seems that it is these accidental circumstances (as well as concrete particular circumstances, discussed below) that proportionalists wish to give more power and weight to, than does the tradition.

*Specifying circumstances* are not accidental to the act;[19] rather, they "enter into" the object of the act and help determine its moral species (its substance). Indeed, specifying circumstances make the object to be what it is, and the object is what places an act in a moral species. These specifying circumstances share the name "circumstances" because they answer to the questions that accidental circumstances answer to—*but they are not accidental.* For instance, whereas "having sexual intercourse," is morally neutral, should the specifying circumstance "with one's spouse" be added, the act would be specified as an act of conjugal intercourse and thus a good act. To repeat an example used earlier, if another specifying circumstance be added, such as "in a public place," this act would undergo a substantial change and become an act of exhibitionism, an evil act rather than a good one. The inclusion of these specifying circumstances into the substance of the act is not a whimsical inclusion; these "circumstances" have a relation to right reason or nature that determine the object or *species* of an act.

Let me comment on the role of the circumstance identified as the "why." Some are surprised that "why" is one of the circumstances,[20] for "why" seems to correspond to the end of the act, or to what is also known as the intention or the motive of the agent. It must be noted that acts are said to have two ends (at least), the end of the object (the *finis operis*) and the end of the agent (*finis operantis*). The *finis operantis*, or the ultimate end of the whole act, the intention or motive of the agent, is distinguished from the *finis operis* which is often said to be the "proximate intention" or the "intention" of the object of the act (I would like to call this the "specifying intention"). The *finis operis* can be an "accidental circumstance" or a "specifying circumstance"[21] (which it is depends upon how the circumstance relates to right reason).

Let me give an example. "Cutting into a human body in order to remove a vital organ" for the intention (*finis operis*) of organ transplantation would be a moral object and would be called "organ transplantation surgery." The proximate intention, the *finis operis*, the specifying intention, is "organ transplantation." "Cutting into a human body in order to remove a vital organ for the purpose of killing an innocent human being" would be a different object in a different moral species because it has a different proximate intention, a different *finis operis*, a different specifying intention; it belongs in the species of murder. When the whole act is evaluated the intentions (motives), the *finis operantis*, not just the object of the act, would need to be considered. "Organ transplantation surgery" could be done with a bad intention or motive—i.e., not to help the patient but to advance one's medical reputation. Here one has a good object done for a bad end. One could also "cut into a human body to remove a vital organ for the purpose of killing an innocent human being" with a good motive, i.e., to get an inheritance to help the poor. Here one has a bad object, done for a good end. For the tradition the ultimate intention (motive) or *finis operantis* does bear upon the evaluation of the whole act, but it is the specifying intention,[22] the *finis operis* that defines the object.

Proportionalists fail to distinguish "specifying" circumstances from "accidental" and "concrete particular" circumstances and thus wrongly claim that the magisterium is inconsistent in sometimes allowing circumstances to specify an action and sometimes not. Their charge that the magisterium does not give due weight to circumstances and intention (motive) suggests that they do not understand what role the specifying circumstances (including the specifying intention) play in determining the object of the act, and thus in determining the *species* of the act, as well.

The specification given by the specifying circumstances is necessary since every act could be described at a level of generality that makes it a "morally indifferent act" in need of some specifying circumstance to justify placing it within some moral species. "Killing a human being" (always a *malum*, for death destroys the good of life), "having sexual intercourse," "telling a falsehood" are acts that cannot be placed in a moral species because, as described, it is not possible to determine whether or not they are in accord with or in conflict with right reason. Some further information, some specifying circumstance, is needed to determine what moral species such actions belong in.

Again, "specifying circumstances" can be any one of those elements that answer to the questions "when, where, how, why, etc." So acts that belong to the same natural species (such as "having sexual intercourse with one's spouse" and "having sexual intercourse with another's spouse") can be very different acts when specified morally, since they line up very differently with right reason. "Killing a human being" (again, always a *malum*) is, as described, *morally* indifferent; "killing in self-defense" and "killing an innocent human being" are in the same natural species, but because of the "who" (referring to the status of the one who is being killed: innocent or guilty), the first act is morally permissible, the second intrinsically evil. *All* acts that are considered intrinsically evil have some "specifying circumstance" included in their descriptions. Again, let us be clear that "killing an innocent human being," while a *malum* considered as a privation of being, is called intrinsic evil (which is a category that is directed towards an ultimate moral evaluation) whereas "killing in self-defense" is not, because it is the kind of action that ought never to be the object of human choice. Again, "killing an innocent human being," while intrinsically evil, need not necessarily be a *culpa* or sin, since one may perform such an action out of ignorance or involuntarily.

Furthermore, any act described in a very general way can be transformed into an act that is intrinsically evil if a specifying circumstance in violation of right reason is included in its transformed description. For instance, suppose one were trying to categorize instances of "picking up a leaf." If no further information were available, one would have to say that the act is morally indifferent. If a circumstance were specified, we may be able to judge the action. For instance, one could be picking up basil leaves to make pesto; such would, as described, be a good action in respect to its object. Someone else, however, could be picking up a leaf and tormenting his sibling with it; such an action would always be wrong and, should it be a common act needing general condemnation, we might call it "mal-leafing."

*Concrete particular circumstances* are circumstances that accompany a particular act that one has every intention of performing. These are the circumstances that proportionalists think should define a moral action. A classic statement of the proportionalist position is that of Father Joseph Fuchs:

> If the absoluteness of the moral norm signifies objectivity more than universal validity, can moral norms be universal at all, in the sense of being applicable always, everywhere and without exception, so that the action encompassed by them could never be objectively justified? Traditionally we are accustomed to speak of an "intrinsece malum."
>
> Viewed theoretically, there seems to be no possibility of norms of this kind for human action in the inner-worldly realm. The reason is that an action cannot be judged morally at all, considered purely in itself, but only together with all the "circumstances" and the "intention." Consequently, a behavioral norm, universally valid in the full sense, would presuppose that those who arrive at it could know or foresee adequately *all the possible combinations* of the action concerned with circumstances and intentions, with (pre-moral) values and non-values (bona and mala "physica"). A priori, such knowledge is not attainable.[23]

Fuchs makes a distinction between the "theoretical realm" and the "practical realm." By that he means that while some norms may be "virtually exceptionless" when considered in the abstract, in concrete particular reality the circumstances must be taken into account.[24] These circumstances are not the same as the "accidental circumstances" described by Aquinas, for those are the circumstances considered as part of the act considered in the abstract, as part of an act viewed as a kind, as a secondary substance. Nor are they "specifying circumstances" for these define an action considered in the abstract (in Fuchs's terms "theoretically"), not a concrete particular action (in Fuchs's terms "practically"). Yet, for the proportionalist the particularities of the act make all the difference. Proportionalists do not condemn any action antecedently to the concrete particular circumstances. For them, "having sexual intercourse with another's spouse" is morally indifferent until one knows all the morally relevant circumstances of the concrete particular act one is intent upon.[25] Some circumstances might render that action morally good, as in the case of Mrs. Bergmeier, who had sexual intercourse with a prison guard to obtain release from prison.[26] Thus, proportionalists think no circumstances serve to specify an action so definitively that some further circumstances could not alter its specification.[27] This is not the position of the tradition.

## THE "WHOLE" ACT

For the magisterium, once an act is considered evil or *malum* in respect to any of its *per se* elements, it is deemed an intrinsically evil act. No accidental or particular circumstances, intention (motive), or consequences added to such an act can render it good. Let us consider how these "parts" of an act fit together.[28]

One might see the parts of an act as the materials with which one builds a house, with the object equivalent to the foundation of the house, the intention (motive) to the frame, and the accidental circumstances to the trimmings. *The foundation already has its own matter and form before any other elements are added, and, thus, is already good or bad.* The specifying circumstances are some of the materials that go into the foundation; for instance, the concrete foundation of a house may include a set of metal rods giving it further definition. A good foundation (object of the act) is necessary for the house (the whole act) to be good, and if the foundation is bad, nothing added to it can render the house good.[29] A house (the whole act) needs more, though, than just a good foundation (the object of the act) to make it good. The frame of the house, like the intention (motive) of the act, is crucial to the goodness of the whole house. Unless the frame, too, is good, the house as a whole will not be good. If the foundation is bad, however, it matters not at all how good the frame or the other elements of the house are: the house is still defective. The "form" that the foundation has is not absorbed or obliterated by the frame; it retains its own identity and defines the goodness of the house even if the frame is good. Different elements of the house—the windows, the color, the trimmings, the "accidents," as it were—might add or detract from the goodness of the house; they would not affect the fundamental goodness of the house. So even if one considers the object to be the matter of the act, this does not mean that it awaits the addition of any other elements, not even the intention (motive), to render it good or evil.

So now we can see why McCormick is incorrect when he accuses the magisterium of inconsistency in its use of circumstances to define an act. McCormick thinks it right to consider "killing a human being," "using a drug or device to prevent conception," and "permanently negating one's fertility (sterilization)" all to be the morally indifferent "material" for an action to be further specified by circumstances (what kind?), intention (motive), or consequences. As we can see from above, however, not all of these acts are being described at the same level of generality or specificity. The act "killing a human being" as described is morally indifferent because it has no specifying circumstance that serves to make the act in accord with right reason or opposed to right reason. Until one knows whether the individual killed is an innocent human being or a life-threatening aggressor, one cannot know whether to classify the act as an intrinsically evil act of murder or a morally legitimate act of self-defense.

An act such as "contraception," however, does not need to undergo further specification before we know how to categorize it morally. Let us use "the pill" as our paradigm instance. One who uses "the pill" is "taking female hormonal treatments." "A female taking female hormonal treatments," as described, is a morally indifferent act. Different specifying intentions will place the action in different moral categories. Identical hormonal treatments can be taken for therapeutic purposes or for contraceptive purposes (the preventing of an act of sexual intercourse from achieving the natural telos—not its only telos—of procreation). The "specifying intention" specifies the use of such hormones for therapeutic purposes to be a good act (infertility is a tolerable side effect) and specifies the use of such hormones deliberately to render oneself infertile, as the intrinsically evil act of contraception. Equivalently, "removing the uterus to stop the spread of cancer" is morally permissible, whereas "removing the uterus to render one's self permanently infertile" is the intrinsically evil act of sterilization.[30] (No argument is going to be given here for why the preventing of an act of sexual intercourse or the rendering one's self permanently infertile is contrary to right reason; here the intent is simply to show what taxonomy the magisterium uses for specifying acts morally.)[31]

Thus, we can see that the magisterium is not guilty of the inconsistency of allowing "circumstances" to morally specify "killing a human being" and of not allowing them to morally specify "using a drug or device to prevent conception." The magisterium sees the necessity of morally specifying circumstances but maintains that "using a drug or device to prevent conception" already has a morally specifying "circumstance" as part of the description of the act. We can see why the magisterium does not allow, as proportionalists do, that a further intention or accidental circumstance can make an act of which an evil object is a part, a good act. Again, no matter what frame or accouterments are added to a bad foundation, a bad foundation makes for a bad house.

### TAUTOLOGICAL NORMS

The defining of moral terms is all-important to this debate. Here we shall address the claim made by proportionalists that the magisterium describes intrinsically evil acts in "formal terms," i.e., that written into the definition of the terms is an expression of disapproval. This would make the condemnation of actions already described as wrong tautological:[32] one would be saying "Do not do what you ought not to do." In a response to *Veritatis Splendor*, Father Charles Curran stated:

> revisionist moral theologians are willing to accept some intrinsically evil acts when the object of the act is described in formal terms (murder is always wrong, stealing is always wrong) or when the act is described in terms of its significant circumstances (not telling the truth when the neighbor has no right to the truth).
>
> The primary area of disagreement concerns the understanding of the moral object. The encyclical claims that morality is determined by the three sources of morality—the object, the end, and the circumstances—and that some actions are intrinsically evil by reason of their object (n. 71–83). The question is, how does one describe the object? As mentioned above, revisionist theologians would be willing to admit intrinsically evil acts by reason of the object if the object were described in a broad or formal way or with some significant circumstances.[33]

Proportionalists understand the command "do not murder" to mean "do not kill a human being without sufficient justification (that is, for instance, unless in self-defense)." They understand "do not commit adultery" to mean "do not have sexual intercourse with the wrong person." They believe that all absolute prohibitions involve a tautology "Do not kill those whom you ought not to kill"; "don't have sex with those with whom it is wrong to have sex." Here I would like to argue that in the understanding of the magisterium absolute prohibitions are not tautologies. The method of moral analysis utilized in *Veritatis Splendor* operates with descriptive, not evaluative, definitions of moral terms.

Let us first note, however, that for everyday purposes, tautological condemnations of actions denoting the morality of actions are serviceable; precise philosophic, descriptive definitions can be cumbersome. Speaking of theft as "taking property one ought not to take," or "murder" as "killing one who does not deserve to be killed," or lying "as not telling the truth when one ought" are "shorthand" definitions and do seem helpful in guiding the moral behavior of many, but these evaluative definitions are not the descriptive definitions that undergird moral analysis. As we shall see, careful descriptive definitions do not include within them some expression of moral approval or disapproval.

In the understanding of the tradition, murder does not mean "unjust killing"; rather, murder is the "intentional killing of an innocent human being." Although we may have enough information here to immediately evaluate such an action as being wrong, the definition itself is a description of an action, not an evaluation of one. The fact that such an action destroys human goods makes such an action objectionable to us, but, again, the definition is simply descriptive. Some might claim that the word "innocent" is an evaluative term that means "one whose life one ought not to take." Rather, I maintain that it is descriptive; it means, "one who has not deliberately done harm." The evaluation that such a one ought not to be killed is a moral judgment that one makes about what "one who has not deliberately done harm" deserves. One's understanding of justice and one's view of the value of human life determines what one thinks one who has done no harm deserves; mankind seems to agree that justice disallows the intentional killing of one who has not deliberately done harm and thus evaluates an act so described as evil.

"Adultery" does not mean "having sexual intercourse with the wrong person." It simply means "having sexual intercourse with one who is not one's spouse"; the definition expresses no approval or disapproval, although it does, of course, include information on the basis of which one can form a judgment of the action. The evaluation that such an act is intrinsically evil derives from one's understanding of the meaning of marriage: according to the Church's view of marriage, it is never just to have sexual intercourse with someone who is not one's spouse.

"Rape" or the "having sexual intercourse with a person against that person's will" describes an action that immediately offends the moral sensibilities of any decent person, but in itself, the definition is purely descriptive.[34] Certainly, the tradition holds all acts of sexual intercourse which are "against that person's will" to be evil because it understands this act to be against the very nature of sexual intercourse and a violation of human dignity. McCormick seems to understand the phrase "against that person's will" to enter a "formal element" in the definition that makes rape by definition to be wrong.[35] I do not understand how McCormick can be true to his proportionalist principles and maintain this position. That is, if an act "cannot be evaluated apart from the intention, consequences, or circumstances," could not the good of some intention, projected consequences, or circumstances outweigh the evil of "having sex with someone against that person's will"? Proportionalists, however, argue that "intention, consequences, and circumstances" must also be taken into consideration before an act can be evaluated. On occasion they insist that they are not referring to any "total net good" that comes from an action and that "dignity values" may outweigh "welfare values."[36] If they hold that "sexual intercourse against an individual's will" is a "dignity value" that cannot be outweighed by any other dignity value or welfare value, then it does seem that they believe in intrinsic evil.[37]

Theft is not (as McCormick states) "taking property against the reasonable will of the owner." Such a definition serves for the most part, and is often given in the manuals, but does not give a precise description of theft. A precise description is cumbersome, but could be stated in the following fashion: "taking another's material goods when the agent taking them has no needs that surpass those of the owner and has failed to obtain such goods otherwise." The phrase "having no needs surpassing those of the owner" is not synonymous with "when one ought not to take goods" or with "against the reasonable will of the owner." The status of the will of the owner does not determine when an act is theft for not. Rather a judgment about the nature of property and ownership and the nature of human community, determine one's moral judgment of taking what belongs to another.

"Lying" is not "telling a falsehood when it is not just to do so." It is also cumbersome to devise a descriptive definition of lying but it would be something on the order of "telling a falsehood to someone with whom one has a relationship in which trust is a key element." One's understanding of which relationships require trust (most do) determines when it is moral or immoral to tell a falsehood. (Those who think all human relationships have trust as a key element would hold all telling of falsehoods to be intrinsically evil.)

As we can see, actions considered by the magisterium to be intrinsically evil include within them no terms expressing moral approval or disapproval, although, they do, of course, include concepts, "specifying circumstances and intentions", that will determine one's moral evaluation. The magisterium judges these actions to be intrinsically evil because they violate some intrinsic good. It is essential to note that the magisterium holds that no intention (motive) and no circumstance and no projected consequences could make "intentionally killing an innocent human being" or "having sexual intercourse with another's spouse" or "lying," for instance, to be morally good. The foundation has already been laid for such actions; the "specifying intentions and circumstances" already define the action as evil, and the evil cannot be undone by adding some further good. (Still, we must remember that if one were to do these actions unwillingly or unknowingly one would have done evil, but one would not have sinned.)

The terminology surrounding the analysis of moral action is clearly tangled. Much of the dispute between proportionalists and the magisterium is characterized by different understandings of key terms. When the magisterium speaks of *malum*, I suspect proportionalists understand *culpa;* whereas the magisterium evaluates actions as kinds, proportionalists evaluate them as concrete particulars; whereas the magisterium allows "specifying circumstances" to "enter into" the object of an action and allows "concrete particular circumstances" no role in *defining* an action, proportionalists insist that actions cannot be defined without reference to "concrete particulars"; and whereas proportionalists understand various moral prohibitions of the magisterium to be tautologies, the magisterium considers them to be descriptive. Until these differences are kept in mind, conversations between proportionalists and the magisterium will remain confusing and frustrating.

NOTES

I would like to acknowledge the assistance in the writing of this essay given to me by Lance Simmons, Ronald K. Tacelli, S.J., and especially Mark Lowery and several members of his class on moral theology.

1. Proportionalists generally argued that *Veritatis Splendor* misrepresented their views. See Richard McCormick, S.J., "Some Early Reactions to *Veritatis Splendor*," *Theological Studies* 55 (1994), 481–506, for a sampling of such responses.

2. Professor Mark Lowery and I have for years been discussing and refining many of the distinctions made here. His explanation of some of them are laid out in "A New Proposal for the Traditionalist/ Proportionalist Discussion" forthcoming in *Irish Theological Studies*. To him I owe the useful term "specifying circumstances." Brian Mullady in *The Meaning of the Term "Moral" in St. Thomas Aquinas* (Pontificia Accademia de S. Tommaso: Libreria Editrice Vaticana, 1986), p. 115, uses the same term for the same concept.

3. This translation of *De malo*, Q. 2 art. 2, res., is from *On Evil*, trans. Jean Oesterle (Notre Dame: University of Notre Dame Press, 1995), 49–50. I have inserted the Latin words.

4. When speaking of the evil of contraception, *Humanae Vitae* makes reference to it as an act that is *intrinsece inhonestum (HV* 14).

5. I believe that the distinction between *malum* and *culpa* may also be a factor in my disagreements with Germain Grisez, John Finnis, and William May on how to evaluate human acts; they insist that human acts must involve a choice. That is true when evaluating acts in the particular. When Aquinas and magisterial documents speak of intrinsically evil acts, however, they are speaking of *kinds* of acts, evaluated *prior* to an individual choice.

6. The word "intention" is problematic. In a following section of this chapter I will distinguish the intention of the agent or motive, the *finis operantis*, from the *finis operis* or "specifying circumstantial intention," which is the end or intention of the object (I shall define this term more fully later in the chapter). Throughout, when I am using "intention" to refer to the ultimate end or intention of the agent, I will insert "motive" in parentheses after "intention."

7. *Summa Theologica*, Q. 18, art. 8, resp.: "As we have said [articles 2 and 5], every act takes its species from its object; and human action, which is called moral, takes its species from the object as referred to the principle of human acts, which is reason. Hence if the object of the act involves something which is in accord with the order of reason, it will be a good act according to its species, for example, to give alms to the poor. But if the object involves something opposed to the order of reason, it will be a bad act according to its species, for example to steal, which is to take what belongs to another. However, the object of an action may not involve anything as relevant to the order of reason, for example, to pick up a leaf from the ground...." (This translation is from *Treatise on Happiness*, translated by John Oesterle [Notre Dame: University of Notre Dame Press, 1983], p. 171).

8. I am using this phrase "having sexual intercourse with another's spouse" as shorthand for the more precise but more cumbersome definition of adultery as "a married individual's having sexual intercourse with one who is not one's spouse." Note that my definition does not require that the agent know or intend that he or she is having sexual intercourse with another's spouse. Note also that adultery is not being defined as "a married individual's having sexual intercourse with one who is not one's spouse *unjustifiably*." The importance of precise definition of moral terms will be made clear later in the chapter.

9. Edward V. Vacek, "Proportionalism: One View of the Debate," *Theological Studies* 46 (1985), p. 294. See also Brian Thomas Mullady, O.P., *The Meaning of the Term "Moral" in St. Thomas Aquinas* (Pontificia Accademia de S. Tommaso: Libreria Editrice Vaticana, 1986); Mullady claims that proportionalism (which he calls "moderate teleology") grew out of a response to Karl Rahner's call for an existentialist ethics that provides individual norms for concrete particular actions.

10. Richard McCormick, S.J., published essentially the same article three different places: "Document begs many legitimate moral questions," *National Catholic Reporter* (October 15, 1993) p. 17; "*Veritatis Splendor* and Moral Theology," *America* (October 30, 1993), p. 8–11, and "*Veritatis Splendor* in Focus: Killing the Patient," in *The Tablet* (October 30, 1993) pp. 1410–11.

11. *America*, October 30, 1993, p. 10.

12. *ST*, I–II, Q. 18, art 3, ad 1: "Circumstances are external to an action in the sense that they are not of the essence of an action, but they are in the action as accidents of it. So also accidents in natural substances are outside the essence."

13. *ST*, 1-II, Q. 18, art. 5, ad.4: "A circumstance is sometimes taken as an essential difference of the object in reference to reason, and then it can constitute a moral act as to its species. This would be the case whenever a circumstance changes an act from good to evil, for a circumstance would not make an act evil unless it were opposed to reason." See also Q. 18, art. 10, ad. 1 and 2, and Q. 7, art. 3.

14. Aquinas seems to speak of these sorts of circumstances in *ST* I–II, Q. 20, art 4, resp., and Q. 20, art. 5, resp., but in his view they are of interest morally only insofar as they complete an act; they do nothing to define an act unless they are a *per se* part of the act. They can increase or mitigate the evil of an action, evaluated retrospectively, but not evaluated as a kind of action. He also seems to consider consequences to be circumstances in Q. 7, art. 3, reply to 3.

15. *ST* I–II, Q. 8, art. 1 and 3.

16. *ST* I–II, Q. 7, art. 1 and 3.

17. *ST* I–II, Q. 7, art. 1 and Q. 18, art. 11, resp.
18. *ST* I–II, Q. 7, art. 3, ad. 3. and Q. 7, art. 4.
19. Aquinas speaks of these as "adjoined circumstances" in *ST* I–II, Q. 7, art. 3, reply to 3.
20. *ST* I–II, Q. 7, art. 3.
21. Aquinas speaks of the end being both a circumstance that exists outside the substance of an act and one which is an "adjoined end" in *ST* I–II, Q. 7, art. 3.
22. Aquinas speaks of the end as a "circumstance" that defines an action in *ST* I–II, Q. 7, art. 3, reply to 3.
23. Joseph Fuchs, S.J., "The Absoluteness of Moral Terms," in *Readings in Moral Theology No. 1* ed. by Charles E. Curran and Richard A. McCormick, S.J. (New York: Paulist Press, 1979), 24. One tends to think that *Veritatis Splendor* had such a passage in mind when it claimed: "teleological and proportionalist theories . . . *hold that it is impossible to qualify as morally evil according to its species—its 'object'—the deliberate choice of certain kinds of behaviour or specific acts, apart from a consideration of the intention for which the choice is made or the totality of the foreseeable consequences of that act for all persons concerned*" (sec. 79).
24. Whereas in this passage, Fuchs speaks of "all" the circumstances, in recent writings, proportionalists have been careful to speak of "the morally relevant circumstance." On occasion they insist that they are not referring to any "total net good" that comes from an action and that "dignity values" may outweigh "welfare values" (in Richard McCormick, *Notes on Moral Theology: 1965–1980* [Lanham, Md.: University Press of America, 1981], p. 717; hereafter *NMT*.
25. See Richard McCormick: "the question is not whether adultery is justified by a good intent. It is rather how the circumstances and intent must be weighed before an action is called adultery (or theft, or blasphemy)" (*NMT*, p. 581).
26. McCormick cites Fuchs and others as approving of Mrs. Bergmeier's action in *NMT*, p. 512 and p. 536. In my forthcoming article, "Tangled Web, Part II," I analyze Mrs. Bergmeier's case in greater detail.
27. Proportionalists may be backing off from this, but then it seems they are no longer proportionalists as they define themselves. James Gaffney, for instance, says "Most ethicists of even the most quibbling kind could, if pressed, come up with *some* description of *some* kind of behavior that they could not in *any* circumstances imagine being justifiable" ("The Pope on Proportionalism" in *Veritatis Splendor: American Responses*, edited by Michael E. Allsopp and John J. O'Keefe (Kansas City, Mo.: Sheed & Ward, 1995), p. 63). To some of us, this concession is not indicative of a commitment to intrinsic evil, but of an impoverishment of imagination: the question imaginatively needs always to be asked: What if hundreds of people could be saved, if one performed an action considered heinously evil? What if hundreds of women could be saved from rape, if one rape were committed?
28. See *ST* I–II, Q. 18 for identification of these parts of an action and their role in the evaluation of an action.
29. See *ST* I–II, Q. 20, 1, resp.
30. The use of female hormonal treatments for therapeutic purposes also renders one infertile (temporarily) as does the removal of the uterus as cancer therapy (perma-

nently). These conditions are tolerated as side effects of the treatment under the principle of double effect; they are not the *finis operis* of the act chosen. When infertility is the *finis operis* of the act, it is the primary and specifying *finis* of the act.

31. For such arguments, see my book *Humanae Vitae: A Generation Later* (Washington, D.C.: Catholic University of America Press, 1991).

32. This point is made repeatedly by proportionalists. For instance Father Richard McCormick states: "When something is described as 'adultery' or 'genocide', nothing can justify it; for the very terms are morally qualifying terms meaning unjustified killing, intercourse with the wrong person, etc. That is they are tautological" (*NMT*, p. 700).

33. Charles Curran, "*Veritatis Splendor:* A Revisionist Perspective," in *Veritatis Splendor: American Responses,* 238. Several of the essays in this volume typify the proportionalist response to *Veritatis Splendor.*

34. The fact that our moral responses or judgments to some actions only descriptively presented are so immediate and strong, supports the natural law contention that our moral judgments follow our inclinations. Indeed, this is so to the point that some precepts are self-evident to us. The definition of rape is not a precept, but we are so immediately moved to condemn rape that we respond to it as precept—we have an immediate reaction "that ought not to be done."

35. McCormick cites an accusation that I make against proportionalists as paradigmatic of false understandings of proportionalism. In response to my claim that *Veritatis Splendor* "carefully discusses the claim that such acts as 'having sexual intercourse with someone against that person's will' is considered a premoral or ontic evil in the view of dissenters," he objects that "Of course, no one says that. As soon as one adds 'against that person's will,' a qualifier has been added that makes the described action morally wrong, much as does 'against the reasonable will of the owner' in the definition of theft" ("Some Early Reactions," p. 486). Occasionally, McCormick speaks of a "formal element" that enters into a definition that makes it tautological and thus irrefutably true. Thus he understands my description to mean "Do not have sexual intercourse with someone when it is wrong to have sexual intercourse with her (i.e., when it is against her will)."

I do not understand the definition of rape that I gave to be formal in that way—as stated in the body of this chapter I understand my definition to be descriptive. I believe that humans are equipped by nature to spontaneously find such an action to be morally objectionable, but I do not believe the term includes within it a moral judgment.

36. *NMT,* p. 717.

37. *NMT,* pp. 717 and 723.

# 9

# The Gospels, Natural Law, and the American Founding

*Michael Novak*

### MCINERNY'S EXPOSITION OF MARITAIN

Ralph McInerny became the director of the Jacques Maritain Center at the University of Notre Dame in 1979, and wrote an extremely helpful introduction to the thought of Jacques Maritain, under the title of *Art and Prudence*,[1] in 1988. There he gives a short and clear account of Maritain's arguments concerning both the American founding and the United Nations Universal Declaration of Human Rights; the two arguments are closely related. In McInerny's honor and following his lead, I would here like to offer supporting evidence from early American sources solely in regard to Maritain's reading of the American founding.

Most of the interpretation of America's founding, particularly since the generation of World War II, but even reaching back to Parrington and Beard, has been in the hands of nonbelievers. By this I mean historians or political philosophers who were neither Christians nor Jews but atheists or agnostics; and even those who were agnostics were, perhaps, rather less skeptical of atheism than of Christian faith. Such interpreters have tended to fall in one of two schools. Most have taken their cues from the nonbelieving side of the Enlightenment. The other significant school, following Leo Strauss, has added to the Enlightenment a good deal of wisdom from the ancients.

Both of these schools agree in minimizing the role of Christianity in the American founding. Both stress, almost to the exclusion of biblical faith, the role of the unbelieving side of the Enlightenment, citing especially Thomas Hobbes and a particular interpretation of John Locke. This interpretation leaches the Christian faith out of Locke, and presents his true meaning as both atheistic and directly subversive of a Christian view of humankind. The American founding, in both views, is a child of the Enlightenment, built upon the ejection of biblical faith from public institutions and its confinement

147

to private quarters. It should be added that not a few Christian theologians today, especially far right Catholic theologians, hold an analogous view.[2]

As late as his fifty-fourth year, Maritain held a not entirely dissimilar view of America. In *Integral Humanism* (1936), he held capitalism responsible for much that is worst in the world, and the United States was by then the leader of world capitalism. In addition, he had, as he later confessed, the typical Continental disdain for America's form of "bourgeois democracy."[3]

As the shadows of Hitler over Europe grew darker and darker, Maritain's visits to the United States increased in frequency and in length. He finally took refuge here early in 1940 for the duration of the war years. During these years Maritain gained a fresh and "contextual" understanding of the American way of life. He could now discern with his own eyes and ears that American life as it was actually lived was not, in fact, what it had earlier seemed to him from afar. McInerny empathizes with Maritain's fresh reading of daily experience—especially in the American midwest—and with his judgment about the inadequacy of conventional theories. In its daily practice, the United States is neither a child of the unbelieving Enlightenment nor materialistic, atomistically individualistic, self-enclosed, and walled off from the transcendent. So, at least, it seemed in the 1940s and 1950s. No one, Maritain wrote, can walk among the American people and observe how they live, how they speak, and what they hope for, and then force such theses upon the facts.

By this time, Maritain had thought more deeply about several themes crucial both to philosophy and to political philosophy than any one in the preceding centuries of the tradition of the *philosophia perennis*. Since these themes include such concepts as person and liberty, they are crucial to Christian philosophy (a species that Maritain was one of the first to identify with adequate precision). On these points, of course, Maritain had teachers, Thomas Aquinas foremost among them. But, on the one hand, Thomas Aquinas had not faced the same kinds of concrete questions as arose from the social and political experiments of the last two hundred years (especially those between, say, 1745 and 1945). On the other hand, very few scholars who knew the thought of Aquinas had had the complicating experience of life under "the new science of politics" in this "new world."

New distinctions cried out to be made, and Maritain made them. New terms cried out to be invented to give old principles new applications, or applications in unprecedented contexts, and Maritain invented them. In these achievements, it would be difficult to show that Maritain strayed from the Catholic tradition. On the contrary, he advanced that tradition in a living, vital, and even lifegiving manner.

In the larger world, his efforts helped to bring to life the Universal Declaration of Human Rights, to which later popes have paid homage. In that effort, Maritain proposed a sophisticated and profound extension of the reasoning of St. Thomas on two points: on practical reason and on the often-denied but never-failing workings of the first principles of natural law.[4]

In the same vein, Maritain extended the reach of the *philosophia perennis* in regard to democracy, religious liberty, and pluralism. He extended this perennial tradition into the realm of new social arrangements and new human experiences, and no one shows how he did so better and more succinctly than McInerny. McInerny's account is clearer than Maritain's, and I draw on it here.

FOUR REQUIREMENTS OF A GOOD SOCIETY

Maritain holds that four foundational ideas must be clearly understood and well institutionalized in a society worthy of humankind. Such a society must be *personalist, communitarian, pluralist,* and *theist*. Each of these receives a brief comment from McInerny. First, such a society must respect the dignity of the human person. Then it must nourish the many ways, natural and voluntary, by which the person thrives in communion with others. Third, it must give to Caesar the things that are Caesar's, and to God the things that are God's, respecting, in particular, freedom of conscience in private *and* in public. Finally, it must either manifest in its public life due respect to the Source of human rights and the Supreme Judge of consciences (as the U.S. Congress did with respect to Thanksgiving Day in 1789), or at least be effectively *open* to the transcendent, permitting to its citizens free expression of homage thereto.

Maritain holds that these four concepts have been given temporal shape—both in theory and in practice—in the institutions of American democracy. In this context, "democracy" does not mean rule by a majority in direct plebiscite; on the contrary, it means both representative government and limited government bound by the rule of law (i.e., a constitutional democratic republic). Such a government, furthermore, operates through the separation of legislative, judicial, and executive powers; under due process; and with ample safeguards both for the rights of individuals and minorities and for averting tyranny by a majority. These distinctive elements in the American practice of democracy have been added by trial and error down the centuries, and in English-speaking countries in particular under the sway of the common law and common sense. (An excellent supplement to Maritain's work, although conceived on other lines, is Russell Kirk's *The Roots of American Order*.)[5]

In English-speaking countries down the centuries (as those of us who are immigrants from non-English-speaking lands have noted with admiration), many religious persons were champions of liberty; and religion and liberty have often been allies. This good fortune was seldom matched on the Continent, where proponents of liberty often felt thrown into rebellion against the forces of tradition and power, the *ancien régime* in which church was united with state.

In Britain and America, therefore, common sense still carries with it a tacit religious sensibility and understanding. Further, what the Scots described as "moral sentiments" usually carried with them an implicit religious significance. Adam Smith's appeal to "sympathy," for instance, was defined in terms appropriate to a Christian sentiment.[6] In America, too, one did not have to choose between liberty and faith. On the contrary, it was quite often religious faith that nourished the most ardent appeals for independence from Britain, in the three hundred or so local declarations that predated the congressional one of July 4, 1776.[7]

Coming from France, which had already experienced several great declarations and many constitutions, and in which unbelievers who favored secular goals often fought pitched battles in the street against traditionalists and believers, Maritain read the Declaration of Independence and the Constitution of the United States not only with admiration but with a willingness to be instructed. He did not esteem the achievement of Paris in 1789 as he did that of Philadelphia in 1787. Of the latter he wrote:

> Peerless is the significance, for political philosophy, of the establishment of the American Constitution at the end of the 18th century. This Constitution can be described as an outstanding lay Christian document, tinged with the philosophy of the day. The spirit and inspiration of this great political Christian document is basically repugnant to the idea of making human society stand aloof from God and from any religious faith. Thanksgiving and public prayer, the invocation of the name of God at the occasion of any major official gathering, are, in the practical behavior of the nation, a token of this very same spirit and inspiration.[8]

Maritain further insisted:

> The concept of natural law played, as is well known, a basic part in the thought of the founding fathers. In insisting . . . that they were men of government rather than metaphysicians and that they used the concept for practical rather than philosophical purpose, in a more or less vague, even in a "utilitarianist," sense (as if any concern for the common good and the

implementing of the ends of life were to be labeled utilitarianism!), one makes only more manifest the impossibility of tearing natural law away from the moral tenets upon which this country was founded.[9]

There is no doubt about the high regard in which Maritain held the Constitution for its evangelical inspiration and expression of the natural law. The American system embodies the four characteristics of the good society.

(1) *Person.* Maritain held that the concept of the person is a philosophical concept, accessible to human reason, but thrust into the consciousness of philosophers by theologians. Such theologians were seeking precise ways to express what it is in the Man-God, Jesus Christ, that remains the same when we say that He possesses both a divine and a human nature. In that context, a notion of "person" is needed that is different from the notion of "individual."[10] A difficulty here arises, since individuals are individuated by their material conditions, not their form. But that cannot be true of God, who is beyond material conditions. Luckily, however, "person" is an available term, denoting a subsistent capable of insight, judgment, choice, and love, that is, the essential capacities of spirit; and spirit that may be either immaterial or embodied (or both). Thus, in human beings the concept "person" designates an independent subject, capable of understanding, loving, and deciding; a subsistent agent who is unique, incommunicable, creative, responsible, and inimitable.

(2) *Community.* Similarly, Aristotle noted that human beings are communitarian in essence, that is, social and political animals whose natural habitat is a *polis*. Biblical faith has drawn the attention of philosophers to the universality of the human community as children of the one God, whose concern is especially for the weakest. Today, philosophers who describe themselves as atheists, such as Bertrand Russell and Richard Rorty, freely acknowledge that they have borrowed such central concepts as compassion and solidarity from the moral teachings of Jesus (even though they regard him as a merely human teacher like Socrates or Goethe). In their philosophical thinking, our "progressives" have gone well beyond the vision of human unity in the reason of Stoicism and universals of Kant; they pay special attention to the poor and the weak, in almost Christian tones.

The preamble to the U.S. Constitution begins "We the people." It is the ordering document of a political *community*, composed of free persons. It represents, further, a *covenant* among ratifying states, uniting several free political communities in one nation; it is the states, rather than the national government, that are expected to be the character-forming entities (the Constitution assigns no such function to the national government). While the Constitution is not an "atomizing" document, it is not morally perfect. Among other things, it temporized with the evil institution of slavery, for the very good communitarian reason that in no other way could a union be formed whose future expansion would with high probability guarantee the abolition of slavery.[11]

The Constitution's communitarian nature is further shown in its implicit confidence in a joint and united future. It was designed to protect the U.S. from the perpetual self-fragmentation of Europe. In the Declaration of Independence, further, the signers from the different states had pledged *to each other* (in a communitarian bond) their lives, their fortunes, and their sacred honor. The Declaration was a compact, a covenant, the act of an entire community. Each individual who joined this community placed himself in peril of punishment for high treason. (As the war proceeded, of the 56 signers 9 fought and died, 12 had their homes looted and burned, 17 lost their fortunes, 2 lost sons.) The United States was not founded by or for lone rangers, individual atoms, mere rugged individualists. It was founded for union.

(3) *Pluralism (The Realm of Conscience)*. Further, even the idea of the secular state, as well as the idea of pluralism, is of Christian inspiration. This claim seems contrary to the historical evidence, which shows so many examples of the union of church and crown. During a thousand-year stretch from Charlemagne to Napoleon, 800–1800 A.D., for example, the pope of Rome laid the imperial crown upon the brow of the Holy Roman Emperor, regent of all Europe. Nonetheless, Maritain holds that the teaching of Jesus about what belongs to Caesar and what belongs to God (Matt. 22:21) has finally worked its way out in social history, so that Christians, above all, ought to accept it. This ideal, different from the ideal of its historical predecessor, "Christendom," inspires the formation of states that are *not* sacral but respectful of diversity of conscience (respectful, too, of religion, not aggressively secularistic). Further, in philosophy and conscience and fealty, such states should be pluralistic, not monistic. Finally, they should be respectful of both the nonestablishment and the free exercise of religion. (In the U.S., the Constitution forbids establishment at the national level, in part to respect establishment at the state level.) No system, Maritain argues, represents at once a higher and a more practical working out of the gospels in history.

No doubt, such a system bears within it its own perils. Every system in history does, and certainly the systems that went before it did. To take but one random example (well known to many Americans who studied in Innsbruck): the deeply Catholic culture of Austria, directed for centuries by the Habsburgs. The almost sacral culture of Austria did not prevent the widespread popular embrace of National Socialism in 1938, which led to abominations still painful to plumb. Those who worry about dangers to Christianity in American culture, while hankering for something akin to the sacral practices of life in Austria, need to recall that the gospel is always in peril.

The Maritain who in *The Peasant of the Garonne*[12] turned his full wrath upon the corruptions introduced by interpreters of the Second Vatican Council—a council which his own work had been widely recognized as preparing—would be equally unsparing about the corruptions that have polluted America since he wrote lovingly of her in the 1950s. Of that we can be sure.

(4) *Theism (Natural Theology)*. Finally, Maritain held that a good society, worthy of the human being, while it need not be Christian, must at least be theist. Here, he stood on common ground with the American founders. Text after text from the founding period asserts that institutions of democracy of the American type can only work among a theistic and moral people. James Madison, for instance:

> The belief in a God All Powerful, wise and good, is so essential to the moral order of the world and to the happiness of man, that arguments which enforce it cannot be drawn from too many sources nor adapted with too much solicitude to the different characters and capacities to be impressed with it.[13]

Thomas Jefferson:

> And can the liberties of a nation be thought secure when we have removed their only firm basis, a conviction in the minds of the people that these liberties are of the gift of God? That they are not to be violated but with his wrath? I tremble for my country when I reflect that God is just: that his justice cannot sleep forever.[14]

George Washington asserted in his "Farewell Address" of September 17, 1796, that the probability of human beings continuing to be moral while not believing in God is virtually nil. No doubt, the thing can be done, but not by a great many people at once and not for a long time:

> ... let us with caution indulge the supposition that morality can be maintained without religion. Whatever may be conceded to the influence of refined education on minds of peculiar structure, reason and experience both forbid us to expect that national morality can prevail in exclusion of religious principle.[15]

Others in the founding generation argued that in those situations when no one else can observe one's conduct, self-love is overwhelmed with reasons to bend the moral law to one's own purpose. *Nemo judex in causa sua.* Thus, the same reason that impelled nineteenth-century Americans to insist upon checks and balances in matters of public self-government led them to insist upon checks and balances in private self-governance. In their eyes, the decisive check upon self-love is the undeceivable Supreme Judge of all consciences, to whom in signing the Declaration of Independence they appealed for judgment upon their own motives. They insisted that in every court of law, truthfulness should be witnessed by oaths in his name.

Whereas Americans today dread seeming to be judgmental, the founders of our country positively demanded the constant judgment of others upon their thoughts and deeds. They knew full well that every thought and deed is susceptible of being evil or good. To be judged and held responsible, the early generations of Americans held, is the very essence of liberty. And this is the radical, the founding impulse behind the project of republican government. Thus, as Tocqueville notes, from the very beginning John Winthrop distinguished between the liberty proper to animals and the liberty worthy of humans:

> Concerning liberty, I observe a great mistake in the country about that. There is a twofold liberty, natural (I mean as our nature is now corrupt) and civil or federal. The first is common to man with beasts and other creatures. By this, man, as he stands in relation to man simply, hath liberty to do what he lists; it is a liberty to evil as well as to good. This liberty is incompatible and inconsistent with authority, and cannot endure the least restraint of the most just authority. The exercise and maintaining of this liberty makes men grow more evil, and in time to be worse than brute beasts: *omnes sumus licentiā deteriores.* This is that great enemy of truth and peace, that wild beast, which all the ordinances of God are bent against, to restrain and subdue it. The other kind of liberty I call civil or federal; it may also be termed moral, in reference to the covenant between God and man, in the moral law, and the politic covenants and constitutions, among men themselves. This liberty is the proper end and object of authority, and cannot subsist without it; and it is a liberty to that only which is good, just, and honest. This liberty you are to stand for, with the hazard not only of your goods, but of your lives, if need be.[16]

Such texts as these indicate the range of the evidence to which Maritain's analysis appeals.

MARITAIN'S ARGUMENT FOR PLURALISM

In his work on the Universal Declaration of Human Rights (UDHR), Maritain sharpened further his demand that a good society be theistic.[17] By 1945, the regime of Adolf Hitler had deepened the world's understanding of the depth of evil. New depths, never before seen, had been explored and evoked almost universal revulsion. Events in our own time, such as the Gulag Archipelago, the Cambodian holocaust, and other huge massacres, as in Rwanda, have shown, of course, that not all peoples learned revulsion; some, alas, learned imitation. But in the aftermath of 1945, there seemed to be a will to start afresh, on a worldwide stage, in a framework larger than the sphere of the Western or Christian horizon. A great representative of the Arab world (Charles Malik), and another of the Asian Third World (Carlos Romulo, president of the Philippines) played especially prominent roles in the drafting and the passage of the UDHR.[18] However reluctantly, representatives of the officially atheistic world such as the leaders of the Soviet Union—since the days of Lenin and Stalin stained with blood themselves—were willing to take part; they did not want to be seen as outside the civilized world.

The United States, as we have seen, faced the necessity of forming a union without first abolishing slavery. In an analogous way, Maritain and his colleagues sought a way to draft a Universal Declaration of Human Rights that might establish the principles leading to at least the first three of the above-mentioned conditions for the good society. The drafters of the declaration faced a great dilemma: How can a pluralistic world, locked in a vast ideological-moral struggle, come to any agreement on fundamental principles? Here the reflections of St. Thomas on the first principles of natural law and the workings of practical reason gave Maritain an idea for a way through the roadblock.

Maritain's first move was to get everybody to see that agreement on principles of *theory* was not possible. Among representatives of different faiths, worldviews, philosophies, ideologies, there was no one theory that all of them shared. On the other hand, Maritain knew from St. Thomas that practice and theory are·activities of two different habits, and operate under different constraints and laws. This point is worth a brief excursus, in which I am going beyond McInerny in support of his point.

Sometimes, people do quite well in practice what they cannot explain in theory. Sometimes people who are excellent in the theory fail in practice. Again, theory is curiously impersonal; anyone, from any point of view, should be able to examine a theory, and to falsify or verify it in an objective way. But practice is incurably personal; the batting grip that works for one hitter in baseball does not work for another. In practice, coaches, not theoreticians, are of maximal help. (Theory may be highly useful to coaches, but it is not enough.) Moreover, three or four persons often engage in the same practice, even though each has a very different reason for doing so, and even though each has a very different theory and/or life-plan underlying his practice. This last is the clue Maritain was looking for.[19]

How much agreement can a world body reach regarding *practices*, even while remaining incurably divided regarding the underlying theory for such practices? This is how Maritain rearranged the earlier question. Maritain's answer was to raise two further practical questions: Are there not some things so terrible in practice that no one will publicly approve of them? Are there not some things so good in practice, that no one will want to seem opposed to them? This relatively simple and yet often overlooked distinction between agreement in theory and agreement in practice broke the logjam.

One feature of this solution is especially important. Such a distinction allows people to stand firm on all points of principle. In this way, it avoids the trap of moral indifferentism or moral relativism. It does not require a Christian to surrender one iota of Christian faith. It did not oblige a communist to abandon communist theory. It faced its signers with one question only: Do you agree that support of *this practice* and prohibition of *that other practice* is a worthy criterion for the world community? Do you agree to declare that your nation will live under this code of practices? In the event, the Soviet Union did not veto the action of putting the declaration forward, but then did not sign it.

There were obvious dangers to this course of action. Like the U.S. Constitution, the UN declaration is susceptible to behavior that can break through such legal threads like a whale through a fisherman's net. On the other hand, after 1975, with the publication of an extension of the declaration in the Helsinki Accords, the Universal Declaration proved of inestimable importance to human rights activists behind the Iron Curtain. Indeed, these "mere words" were credited with being one of the most useful of all tools in the final discrediting and dismantling of the Soviet Union. The failure of that state to live up to this simple and elementary code of practice played a decisive role in delegitimating it, even in the eyes of serious communists of the generation of 1989–91. It worked much as Maritain had hoped it would.

For Maritain, *whether* it would work was in a sense a testable hypothesis. Even people who deny the existence of the natural law cannot help exemplifying it, he knew, because they are human beings who use practical reason every time they act. Maritain had learned from Aquinas that "natural law" is only the name for the actual working principles of practical reason. (Natural law presents no concrete ordinances, but does make principled demands regarding methods of practical inquiry.)

These reflections on the reasoning behind Maritain's support for the Universal Declaration of Human Rights also help to illuminate why he held such high esteem for the principles implicit in the founding of the American Republic, and particularly in the Constitution and the Declaration of Independence. The principles of natural law, he noted, are evident in the effort of the Americans to submit the principles of the Constitution to popular understanding, judgment, and ratification—the whole exercise was, explicitly, an exercise in "reflection and choice," that is, an exercise of the practical reason. Thus, the very opening of *The Federalist:*

> It has been frequently remarked that it seems to have been reserved to the people of this country, by their conduct and example, to decide the important question, whether societies of men are really capable or not of establishing good government *from reflection and choice,* or whether they are forever destined to depend for their political constitutions on accident and force [emphasis added].[20]

More than that, the founders were explicit about their care and reverence for the natural law, whose authority they invited in judgment upon their work. They did their best to uncover the laws proper to human liberty, and to conform themselves to these. Further still, they believed that Christian faith ratifies the workings of natural law. They claimed two witnesses to their own sincerity of purpose: natural reason and faith.

#### FURTHER EVIDENCE FROM THE FOUNDING

Among the eighteenth-century designers of the American Declaration and Constitution, both reason and revelation (Jewish and Christian revelation) were frequently called upon to vindicate their appeal to "the laws of nature and nature's God." A good witness to this twofold appeal is Samuel Cooper, one of the prerevolutionary preachers of independence whose words were rescued for our use by the invaluable collection of Ellis Sandoz:

> We want not, indeed, a special revelation from heaven to teach us that men are born equal and free; that no man has a natural claim of dominion over his neighbours, nor one nation any such claim upon another; and that as government is only the administration of the affairs of a number

of men combined for their own security and happiness, such a society have a right freely to determine by whom and in what manner their own affairs shall be administered. These are the plain dictates of that reason and common sense with which the common parent of men has informed the human bosom. It is, however, a satisfaction to observe such everlasting maxims of equity confirmed, and impressed upon the consciences of men, by the instructions, precepts, and examples given us in the sacred oracles; one internal mark of their divine original, and that they come from him "who hath made of one blood all nations to dwell upon the face of the earth," whose authority sanctifies only those governments that instead of oppressing any part of his family, vindicate the oppressed, and restrain and punish the oppressor.[21]

The American founders held that the Creator and Redeemer of humankind wrote his law in the human heart and wove its lessons into the tapestry of nature and history, to instruct us through contemplation both of nature and of the workings of his Providence in events. Even of Thomas Jefferson, one of the founders whose faith was least Christian,[22] his biographer and sympathetic student of his religious life writes: "Jefferson assumed an ordered, theocentric world; chaos was not king. He also affirmed that ours was and is a moral universe; unrestrained libertinism did not, must not, rule."[23]

To attempt to do justice to the religious views of all those preachers, teachers, magistrates, and yeoman who did so much to put their necks at risk in joining the rebellion against the legitimate monarch, George III, and then placed their fates, with due reflection, under the rule of their new Constitution, would be a very large task. The religious life of the founding generation is not a field in which secular historians of the last fifty years have accomplished much work, but new beginnings have at last become evident.[24] Permit me, therefore, to conclude these remarks with but two citations from the nation's second president, John Adams of Massachusetts. The first is as follows:

> Statesmen may plan and speculate for liberty, but it is religion and morality alone which can establish principles upon which freedom can securely stand.[25]

The second text is a communication from Adams to the "Officers of the First Brigade of the Third Division of the Militia of Massachusetts, October 11, 1798":

> We have no government armed with power capable of contending with human passions unbridled by morality and religion. Avarice, ambition, revenge, or gallantry, would break the strongest cords of our Constitution as

a whale goes through a net. Our Constitution was made only for a moral and religious people. It is wholly inadequate to the government of any other.[26]

Maritain, I submit, got it right. The Constitution *is* a work inspired by evangelical sentiments and due respect for the natural moral law.

POSTSCRIPT

While McInerny's account of Maritain's thought is unusually clear and helpful, it does suggest a range of problems that have arisen since Maritain's death. Maritain's account of the founders, while never carried through with scholarly detail, seems more correct than that of many scholars who overlook the religious sources of the founding almost entirely. The political principles of the founding do not *require* moral indifference or an aggressive antireligious secularism. Still, it may be asked whether among the aggressive few and the inattentive many they in time *generate* such negative developments. In the United States from about 1946 onwards, an aggressive attack upon the public religiousness of the American people has certainly arisen.

An accurate diagnosis of *why* this is so, and what might be done to correct it, remains to be persuasively presented. My own suspicion is that those who care about the practice of religion both in nonpublic and in public settings would make a great mistake if they regard the United States as ill-founded, jettison the founders as seriously misled, and call for a new Constitution. Not only are they not likely, in our time or the foreseeable future, to get a Constitution that is closer to the gospels and to Christian philosophy; worse still, they would be depriving themselves of the prestige, acuity, and peerless historical accomplishment of the founders, who are much closer to the Catholic tradition (evangelical and medieval), than to the dry and lifeless relativism of the aggressive secularizers.

The founders were theocentric, convinced that the Creator from all eternity shaped nature, nature's laws, and the grand drama of history by His gracious Providence. These are for us a precious heritage, which it would be worse than ungrateful to throw away. It would be, to reach for a medieval term, *stultus;* indeed, self-stultifying.

NOTES

1. Ralph McInerny, *Art and Prudence: Studies in the Thought of Jacques Maritain* (Notre Dame: University of Notre Dame Press, 1988).

2. See, e.g., David Schindler, *Heart of the World, Center of the Church* (Grand Rapids: Eerdmans, 1997).

3. See Jacques Maritain, *Reflections on America* (New York: Charles Scribner's Sons, 1958), pp. 19, 22–25.

4. See McInerny, *Art and Prudence*, pp. 123–136.

5. Russell Kirk, *The Roots of American Order* (Chicago: Regnery, 1992).

6. An example from Smith: "And hence it is, that to feel much for others and little for ourselves, that to restrain our selfish, and to indulge our benevolent affections, constitutes the perfection of human nature; and can alone produce among mankind that harmony of sentiments and passions in which consists their whole grace and propriety. As to love our neighbour as we love ourselves is the great law of Christianity, so it is the great precept of nature to love ourselves only as we love our neighbour, or what comes to the same thing, as our neighbour is capable of loving us" (Adam Smith, *Theory of the Moral Sentiments* [Indianapolis: Liberty Fund, 1976], I,i,5,5, pp. 71–72). For a fuller discussion, see Nicholas Phillipson, "Adam Smith as Civic Moralist," in Istvan Hont and Michael Ignatieff, eds., *Wealth and Virtue: The Shaping of Political Economy in the Scottish Enlightenment* (Cambridge: Cambridge University Press, 1983), pp. 179–202.

7. Pauline Maier, *American Scripture: Making the Declaration of Independence* (New York: Knopf, 1997), e.g., pp. 48, 53, 87, and 89.

8. Maritain began the passage cited in this way: "Far beyond the influences received either from Locke or the XVIIIth Century Enlightenment, the Constitution of this country is deep-rooted in the age-old heritage of Christian thought and civilization. Paradoxically enough, and by virtue of the serious religious feelings of the Founding Fathers, it appeared, at a moment of unstable equilibrium (as all moments in time are) in the history of ideas, as a lay—even, to some extent, rationalist—fruit of the perennial Christian life-force, which despite three centuries of tragic vicissitudes and spiritual division was able to produce this momentous temporal achievement at the dawn of the American nation." (*Man and the State* [Chicago: University of Chicago, 1951], pp. 183–84.

9. Ibid., p. 95, note 12.

10. Maritain makes this distinction sharply in *The Person and the Common Good* (Notre Dame: University of Notre Dame Press, 1972). For other references, see my *Free Persons and the Common Good* (Lanham, Md.: Madison Books, 1989).

11. See Robert A. Goldwin, *Why Blacks, Women and Jews Are Not Mentioned in the Constitution, and Other Unorthodox Views* (Washington, D.C.: The AEI Press, 1990), esp. chap. 2.

12. Jacques Maritain, *The Peasant of the Garonne*, trans. Michael Cuddihy and Elizabeth Hughes (Toronto: Macmillan, 1969).

13. Edwin S. Gaustad, *Faith of Our Fathers* (San Francisco: Harper and Row, 1987), p. 96.

14. *Thomas Jefferson, Writings* (New York: The Library of America, 1984), p. 289.

15. In W. B. Allen, ed., *George Washington: A Collection* (Indianapolis: Liberty Classics, 1988), p. 512.

16. Alexis de Tocqueville, *Democracy in America*, vol. 1, 5–110 (New York: Alfred A. Knopf, Inc., 1945), pp. 44–45. Tocqueville cites this account from Cotton Mather, *Magnalia Christi Americana*, 1820 Hartford ed., vol. 2, p. 13.

17. Besides his discussion in Chapter 9 of *Art and Prudence*, McInerny has also published a long article in *The Journal of Jurisprudence*, "Natural Law and Human Rights" (vol. 36), pp. 1–14, setting forth his own position with respect to writings on this theme

by such central figures as Michel Villey, John Finnis, Alasdair MacIntyre, and others. McInerny wishes to accept "natural rights," as Finnis and Maritain do, and gives tentative arguments in their support. The actual *record* of the United Nations gives him pause, as well as serious misuses of the term "rights."

18. For a brief account of the background to the declaration, see Mary Ann Glendon's "Reflections on the UDHR," *First Things* (April 1998). See also her essay "Knowing the Universal Declaration of Human Rights," *Notre Dame Law Review* 73 (July 1998), pp. 1153–1190.

19. See Maritain's speech in Mexico City, November 6, 1947, cited by him in *Man and the State*, pp. 77–79.

20. "Federalist No. 1," *The Federalist Papers*, Isaac Kramnick, ed. (New York: Penguin Books, 1987), p. 87.

21. Samuel Cooper, *A Sermon on the Day of the Commencement of the Constitution*, from *Political Sermons of the American Founding*, ed. Ellis Sandoz (Indianapolis: Liberty Press, 1991), p. 637.

22. Jefferson hoped finally that all Americans would in time become Unitarians, rejecting a religion of miracles and holding fast to a religion of reason. See Edwin S. Gaustad, *Sworn on the Altar of God: A Religious Biography of Thomas Jefferson* (Grand Rapids: William B. Eerdmans, 1996), p. 138.

23. Ibid., p. 228.

24. The Library of Congress launched a major exhibit on the Religion of the Founding Generation in June 1998; the author of the accompanying handbook is James H. Hutson, *Religion and the Founding of the American Republic* (Washington, D.C.: Library of Congress, 1998).

25. G. Hunt, ed., *The Writings of James Madison* (New York: Putnam's Sons, 1900–10), vol. 9, p. 230.

26. Quoted by William Bennett in *Our Sacred Honor* (New York: Simon & Schuster, 1997), p. 370.

# 10

# McInerny Did It, or Should a Pacifist Read Murder Mysteries?

*Stanley Hauerwas*

### READING MYSTERIES

I am not supposed to begin this way. At least I am not supposed to begin this way if Ronald Knox is right about the first law of detective stories in his "A Detective Story Decalogue." Knox decrees the first commandment for writing detective stories is, "The criminal must be someone mentioned in the early part of the story, but must not be anyone whose thoughts the reader has been allowed to follow."[1] Yet as my title indicates, I want you to know the perpetrator from the beginning. Ralph McInerny did it. He made me hopelessly addicted to murder mysteries.

It happened this way. I was just another member of the Notre Dame faculty that inhabited the basement of the library. The one advantage of the basement of the library was that faculty from diverse disciplines actually had to talk to one another. Usually such conversations were about the latest game or comparing notes about our families, but after we grew tired of those subjects we might even say something like this: "What are you currently working on now? I see, very interesting. Have you read X's or Y's recent book on that subject? I think you would find it very interesting. And so on and so on." I never expected that in one of these exchanges I would be blindsided by Ralph McInerny.

I had always had some problem in putting McInerny together. As a Texas Protestant I had no idea that someone like Ralph McInerny existed or could exist. Possible world metaphysics did not prepare me to believe it was possible to combine in one person philosophical astuteness, conservative Catholicism, and cultural urbanity. But McInerny was all of these and more. Indeed, for me, he was Notre Dame just to the extent he signaled that this was an intellectually serious place. So I was completely unprepared when Ralph, without embarrassment, told me he was writing a murder mystery. I had never heard an academic admit to reading a murder mystery, much less writing one. Yet Ralph McInerny, the representative of all that was good at Notre Dame, acknowledged he not only reads mysteries but writes them. What could I possibly make of this counterfactual?

I did what any self-respecting academic would do. I started reading murder mysteries, some of them written by Ralph, to try to understand Ralph's fascination with mysteries. I soon lost interest in understanding Ralph's interest in mysteries because I became such an avid reader of mysteries that the problem was now understanding *my* fascination with mysteries. So it is McInerny's fault that I now use this occasion to try to understand why I love to read about murders and murderers. If the reader of this essay feels compelled to discover the dark figure behind this exercise please remember: McInerny did it!

### JUSTIFYING MYSTERIES, OR WHY READING ABOUT MURDER IS GOOD FOR YOU

Of course one of the problems for people who like to think they are "serious thinkers" is they are inclined to provide more reasons than is necessary to justify *anything* they do but, in particular, for reading work that is not by definition serious. Mysteries are not considered serious by most academics. No one knows why mysteries are not considered to be literature, but at least one of the reasons is due to their popularity. It is assumed, by many intellectuals, that if a book or genre is popular then it cannot deal with the eternal verities of the human condition. Chesterton observed this has led some "modern critics" to falsely infer that not only may a masterpiece be unpopular, but unless it is unpopular it cannot be a masterpiece.[2]

Of course writers of detective fiction are aware of these "put downs." They realize there is no way to defeat those who dismiss murder mysteries as "entertainment" other than to write well about matters that matter. For example, Arthur Upfield in his mystery *An Author Bites the Dust* makes the discovery of the murderer of a "modern critic" (of the kind Chesterton described, above) turn on whether the distinction between commercial fiction and literature could be maintained. Upfield's detective, Napoleon Bonaparte, half aboriginal and half white, usually solves murders in the Australian outback by combining aboriginal and modern police skills. Confronted by the murder of Mervyn Blake, a critic intent on the development of an Australian literature, Bony went to his friend and popular author, Clarence Bagshott, to help him understand the difference between literature and popular fiction. In response to Bony's question whether Blake ever criticized Bagshott's work he was told:

"Mine! Lord, no! I don't produce literature."
"Then what do you produce?"
"Commercial fiction."
"There is a distinction?"
"Terrific."
"Will you define it, please."
"I'll try to," Bagshott said slowly. "In this country literature is a piece of writing executed in schoolmasterly fashion and yet so lacking in entertainment values that the general public won't buy it. Commercial fiction—and this is a term employed by the highbrows—is imaginative writing that easily satisfies publishers and editors because the public will buy it."[3]

I do not want to keep the reader in suspense—it turns out that Blake was killed by his wife who, in order to make a living for them, had written popular fiction under a pseudonym. Her husband's novels sold only when she helped him with them, but when he tried to write on his own, he could not get his work published. This led him to treat her so badly she finally killed him—I might add, in a quite ingenious way. Bony was able to discover she had been the killer learning that (at least in this case) the only difference between literature and popular fiction was between what was written poorly and what was written well. Which is but a reminder, as Chesterton remarks, that there is as much difference between a good and bad detective story as that between a good epic and a bad one.[4]

That murder mysteries can be not only entertaining but good literature does not, however, explain how the crime novel became only recently such a distinctive as well as such a popular genre. I have no great insight about the rise of the mystery novel from a historical and cultural standpoint (though I will make some suggestions about that below), but I confess I cannot resist speculating about their moral significance. I am after all, like McInerny, something of a "moralist." Accordingly I cannot help but think that there is something morally important about murder mysteries.

Chesterton thought the essential value of the detective story consisted in its ability as a form of popular literature to express what he called "the poetry of modern life." According to Chesterton the detective story helps us see at once the chaos and beauty of the city, so that "even under the fantastic form of the minutiae of Sherlock Holmes, to assert this romance of detail in civilization, to emphasize this unfathomably human character in flints and tiles, is a good thing. It is good that the average man should fall into the habit of looking imaginatively at ten men in the street even if it is only on the chance that the eleventh might be a notorious thief."[5]

Chesterton's observation does not entail that murder mysteries are a peculiarly urban phenomenon. The English village is obviously one of the prime sites for murder, as is the Australian outback, or the American south.[6] Chesterton's point, I believe, is rather that murder mysteries depend on the development of rich detail of place and character which turns out to be a training in practical reasoning. Practical reason deals, at least according to Aristotle, with those matters that can be other. But the "other" is constituted by the rich detail displayed through storied description. Murder mysteries are about the testing and retesting of stories by which the subtle interrelation of character and circumstance is discovered and displayed.[7] What better training in practical reason could one wish? To learn the complexities involved in distinguishing good from bad writing in order to discover "who did it" is at least analogous to learning to distinguish between honesty and bluntness.

Of course such skills are not peculiar to murder mysteries. Novels, plays, poetry, conversations are equally good schools for developing practical reason and, in particular, how such reasoning involves narrative display. Chesterton, however, argues that detective stories involve another good work that is peculiar to the genre. He identifies that work as nothing less than resistance to the tendency of the Old Adam to rebel against so "universal and automatic [a] thing" as civilization. In Chesterton's words:

> The romance of police activity keeps in some sense before the mind the fact that civilization itself is the most sensational of departures and the most romantic of rebellions. By dealing with the unsleeping sentinels who guard the outposts of society, it tends to remind us that we live in an armed camp, making war with a chaotic world, and that the criminals, the children of chaos, are nothing but the traitors within our gates. The romance of the police force is thus the whole romance of man. It is based on the fact that morality is the most dark and daring of conspiracies. It reminds us that the whole of noiseless and unnoticeable police management by which we are ruled and protected is only a successful knight-errantry.[8]

If Chesterton is right—that morality is this "dark and daring conspiracy"—then it can be asked why it took so long to develop the peculiar genre we currently identify as murder mysteries. For surely morality so understood has always been present confronting the chaos of immorality and crime.[9] Dorothy Sayers argues that the reason detective fiction is a rather recent development is because the detective cannot flourish until the public has some idea of what constitutes proof, which requires that there be in place common criminal procedures such as arrest, confession, and punishment. In short, the detective story could not flourish until "public sympathy had veered round to the side of law and order."[10]

Somewhat more speculatively Sayers also suggests that the development of detective fiction is the result of the end of the age of exploration. In place of the adventurer and the knight errant,

> popular imagination hailed the doctor, the scientist, and the policeman as saviours and protectors. But if one could no longer hunt the manticora, one could still hunt the murderer; if the armed escort had grown less necessary, yet one still needed the analyst to frustrate the wiles of the poisoner; from this point of view, the detective steps into his right place as the protector of the weak—the latest of the popular heroes, the true successor of Roland and Lancelot.[11]

Sayers' most eloquent account of the moral significance of detective fiction occurs in the last Peter Wimsey/Harriet Vane mystery, *Thrones, Dominations*, left unpublished at her death.[12] Newly married Wimsey asks Harriet if she thinks his detective work a frivolous pose—a rich man's game:

> "No; I think it is very serious. A matter of life and death, after all. What I haven't got clear is how this connects with the war. I think it does, in some subterranean fashion."
>
> "When you have seen people die," he said, "when you have seen at what abominable and appalling cost the peace and safety of England was secured, and then you see the peace squalidly broken, you see killing that has been perpetrated for vile and selfish motives. . . . "
>
> "Oh, yes, I can see that," she said. "Beloved, I do see."
>
> "Justice is a terrible thing," he said, "but injustice is worse."
>
> He came suddenly towards her, and knelt in front of her chair, putting his arms around her knees, and laying his head in her lap. When he spoke again his voice was muffled in the folds of her dress. "Dearest, do you want me to discuss this case with you? Or would you rather not?"
>
> "I'd rather you did, if you can bear to."
>
> "It's what you can bear that I was thinking of. I would spare you distressing topics, if I could."
>
> "Nothing you could tell me would be as bad as the thought that there was some subject we couldn't talk over together. That would be really hateful."

"It is to be the marriage of true minds we try for," he said, looking up at her.

"I thought it was; yes."

"Then so it shall be. We'll bear it out even to the edge of doom—Yes, Meredith, what is it?"

"Dinner is served, my lord."

"Later," said Peter, getting up and extending her his hand. "I will tell you all later."[13]

"Telling all later" is what the mystery writer does and, in particular, what Sayers did. Later in the novel Wimsey and Harriet have an exchange that is impossible not to read as Sayers' justification for her work. Harriet observes that she knows writing detective stories is not great art. "You read them and write them for fun." Wimsey objects to this description of her work, noting that she takes great pride in her craft. Harriet acknowledges the point but notes that a craft may be admirable yet nonetheless frivolous. She observes, for example, that it is simply a given that detective stories are not of the same quality as *Paradise Lost* or *Crime and Punishment* or real detection that deals with real crimes. Wimsey responds:

> "You seem not to appreciate the importance of your special form. Detective stories contain a dream of justice. They project a vision of a world in which wrongs are righted, and villains are betrayed by clues that they did not know they were leaving. A world in which murderers are caught and hanged, and innocent victims are avenged, and future murder is deterred."

"But it is just a vision, Peter. The world we live in is not like that."

"It sometimes is," he said. "Besides, hasn't it occurred to you that to be beneficent, a vision does not have to be true?"

"What benefits could be conferred by falsehood?" she asked.

"Not falsehood, Harriet; idealism. Detective stories keep alive a view of the world which ought to be true. Of course people read them for fun, for diversion, as they do crossword puzzles. But underneath they feed a hunger for justice, and heaven help us if ordinary people cease to feel that."

"You have rather an exalted view of it, Peter."

"I suppose very clever people can get their visions of justice from Dostoyevski," he said. "But there aren't enough of them to make a climate of opinion. Ordinary people in great numbers read what you write."

"But not for enlightenment. They are the slackest. They only want a good story with a few thrills and reversals along the way."

"You get under their guard," he said. "If they thought they were being preached at they would stop their ears. If they thought you were bent on improving their minds, they would probably never pick up the book. But you offer to divert them, and you show them by stealth the orderly world in which we should all try to be living."

"But are you serious?" she asked.

"Nevermore so, Domina. Your vocation seems no more frivolous to me than mine does to you. We are each, it seems, more weighty in each other's eyes than in our own. It's probably rather a good formula: self-respect without vanity."

"Frivolity for ever?"

"For as long as possible," he said, suddenly sombre. "I rather wish the Germans were addicted to your kind of light reading."[14]

As I suggested at the beginning of this section, the reader may suspect that all this is a very elaborate and largely unnecessary justification for the pleasure we get from reading murder mysteries. Yet I think Chesterton and Sayers are right to think that detective fiction involves an extraordinary metaphysical draft on the way things are. That draft is nothing less than the presumption that justice is deeper than injustice. Accordingly detective fiction can be profoundly Christian just to the extent evil is bounded by a greater good. Such a presumption does not entail that justice will always be done, that the murderer will always be caught, or even that we will not be sometimes more sympathetic with the murderer than the victim. Rather it means that we are not irrational to hope that justice will be done.

P. D. James observes that the crime novel reassures us that we live in a morally comprehensible universe and accordingly we have an obligation to try to put things right.[15] But she notes that though it may appear you get justice at the end of the modern detective story, all you in fact get is the fallible justice of men;

> You don't get divine justice, you can't achieve that. It is very reassuring to have a form of fiction which says that every form of human life is sacred, and if it is taken away, then the law, society, will address itself to finding out who did it. The attitude is not, "Well, one more chap's got murdered—hard luck." Infinite pains and money are spent trying to find out who did it because we still have the belief that the individual human life is sacred; we all have a right to live out our lives to the last moment.[16]

Moreover, if this account of the moral presuppositions of the murder mystery is right, and I think it is, it makes it particularly important for those of us who think about as well as teach ethics to be students as well as readers of novels about crime. For one of the temptations for those of us who "do ethics" is to assume that ethics is about the more subtle aspects of our lives. As a result we forget that few things are more important for the sustaining of our lives than the conviction that murder is wrong. As Chesterton suggested above, to lose our hold on that fundamental conviction would mean to lose our hold on the very possibility of living humane, to say nothing of Godly, lives. Just to the extent that the reading of murder mysteries reminds us that we were not created to kill one another we are made better.

### BUT CAN A PACIFIST READ MURDER MYSTERIES WITH PLEASURE?

So runs my justification for reading murder mysteries. But have I "justified" myself into a contradiction. I am, after all, a declared proponent of Christian nonviolence. McInerny is a well-known proponent of just war. Was tempting me to read murder mysteries a clever way to undermine my nonviolence?[17] If I believe murderers should be caught and punished, have I not in effect accepted the fundamental practice that justifies the restrained use of violence by public authorities?[18] To answer this challenge would require an extended discussion of how Christian nonviolence should be understood as well as the complexities of just-war thinking.[19] I have no intention of imposing either on readers who have read this essay because they thought it was about murder mysteries.

Besides, I have a witness in defense of why pacifists not only do not contradict themselves when they read murder mysteries, but why reading murder mysteries may be further training in a nonviolent way of life.[20] That witness is Ralph McInerny. McInerny observes most readers are content to use rather superficial criteria to distinguish Catholic mysteries from those that are not Catholic—e.g., Catholic mysteries require the presence of a priest or a nun. Yet commenting on his own work, which obviously accepts the convention of having a priest or nun as the detective, McInerny notes "I wanted a priest to represent the contrast of sin and forgiveness and a cop, Captain Keegan, to represent that between crime and punishment."[21]

I may well be overreading McInerny's comment, but sin and forgiveness name the realities that make the Christian commitment to peace intelligible. Crime is ontologically a subset of sin which means, for Christians, forgiveness is a more determinative reality than punishment. Christians rightly believe that sin is punishment healed through reconciliation with God, ourselves, and our wronged neighbor. Such reconciliation creates the space that allows the narration of our lives, individually and collectively, through which our sins can be acknowledged without deception. The "realism" of the crime novel is but the realism required by the acknowledgment of sin and made possible through reconciliation.

Such realism is at the heart of the Christian commitment to nonviolence. Christians are not committed to nonviolence because we believe nonviolence is an effective strategy to free the world of war. Rather we are nonviolent because we know we live in a world at war yet believe that the forgiveness wrought on the cross of Christ makes it possible for us to live nonviolently in a world at war. In like manner we know we do not live in a world free of murder. Indeed, like advocates of just war, we know how important it is to distinguish between murder and other ways life is taken. Yet we also know that God's forgiveness is not only for those who are the victims of murder but for murderers.[22] Indeed we know part of the process such forgiveness names is the discovery of those that have unjustly killed. For without discovery, they have no way to be made part of the process of judgement, penance, and reconciliation.

To be a murderer is to be condemned to absolute aloneness. To kill another human being is to be enveloped in secrecy, even if others know of it, that makes our lives incapable of being shared. To be discovered is, therefore, a kind of redemption. Indeed one of the remarkable aspects of most murder mysteries is they end with discovery. What happens after discovery is anticlimatic because what matters is that the murderer is known not just by us but by himself. Such knowing is the beginning of the process which redemption names. The name Christians have been taught to call that process is peace.

I should like to end with these enigmatic remarks pretending I have given adequate justification for pacifists to read murder mysteries. Yet there is a challenge I cannot avoid. It is wonderfully put by Sayers and Walsh at the end of *Thrones, Dominations*. Harriet tells Peter she is pregnant and asks if he is "pleased." "Pleased?" he responded, "*Pleased?* That's no sort of word for it—my blood rejoices in my veins! I can feel the eternal stage-hands shift the scenery around us as we stand." Continuing, he turned somber observing that "The future opens up before us real and urgent." Which elicits from Harriet, knowing the threat of war, the question "Do we do right to bring a child into the present time?" Peter responds,

> "There's what we can do for any child of ours," he said, "and there's what no one can do for any child at all."

"They make their own way, you mean?"

"They claim or renounce their inheritance in their own time, and make or break the time accordingly. We shall lavish every gift we can on ours, but we cannot give it safety."

"You know, until this happened I would have said that I no longer cared a fig for the fate of the world as long as you and I were together."

"Let Rome in Tiber melt, and the wide arc of the ranged empire fall? No, Domina, that's not our style. If there's another war we shall have to face it, and we shall have to win it," said Peter.[23]

This, I take it, is Sayers' final answer to the earlier question of the relation between detective work and war.[24] Her answer is profound, but, I believe for Christians, a wrong answer. It is wrong just to the extent we know we cannot make our children safe. At least we cannot make them safe if it means we must use violence to insure their safety. Rather we believe we have been given better work to do in a world at war. We have been made part of a company of people who would not have our lives or our children's lives protected through further killing. It is a dangerous way to live, but then the alternative, as we learn from murder mysteries, is that lives lived safely are not worth living.

### NOTES

1. Ronald Knox, "A Detective Story Decalogue," in *The Art of the Mystery Story*, edited with a commentary by Howard Haycraft (New York: Carroll and Graf Publishers, 1992), p. 194.

2. G. K. Chesterton, "A Defence of Detective Stories," in *The Art of the Mystery Story*, p. 4.

3. Arthur Upfield, *An Author Bites the Dust* (New York: Collier Books, 1948), p. 73.

4. Chesterton, "A Defence," p. 4.

5. Ibid., p. 5.

6. My wife, Paula Gilbert, who is a much more accomplished reader of detective fiction than I can claim to be, discovered that one of the best ways to prepare to go to a new place is by reading murder mysteries. That is how we became readers of Arthur Upfield as no one provides a better introduction to Australia than Upfield. Of course detective fiction is not only an introduction to countries but also cultures and institutions. Oxford always seems different after I have read a new Colin Dexter.

7. Laura Yordy pointed out to me that good detectives are right (more often than not) not because they "reason" perfectly but because they astutely understand the fallibility of practical reason. It is interesting, for example, how good detectives depend on the work of others. Watson is no longer "dumb" but the detective requires others to help her or him

see the obvious. I am grateful to Laura Yordy, a theologian who reads mysteries, for her criticism of this paper.

8. Chesterton, "A Defence," pp. 5–6. That Chesterton uses the language of "conspiracy" to describe how "law and order" may embody our deepest moral convictions is a reminder how "order" may also be a form of violence. Thus the "detective" often acts "outside the law" exactly because the law has become disorder. More on this below.

9. This observation might well seem to commit me to a view of natural law closer to McInerny's account than my more determined arguments about the distinctiveness of the Christian ethic. My views on these matters have, I fear, been often misunderstood as I have never denied that all people are anything less than God's good creation thus gifted with God's law sufficient to live well. My argument against advocates of natural law has been against those who think, in the interest of showing that Christians can be good democratic citizens, that Christians as Christians cannot have anything morally distinct to say about the way we should live. That is to put the matter too simply, but nonetheless suggests the heart of the matter. The fundamental questions, of course, are Christological.

10. Dorothy Sayers, "The Omnibus of Crime," in *The Art of the Mystery Story*, p. 74. Sayers duly acknowledges her indebtedness to E. M. Wrong's essay, "Crime and Detection," as the influence behind her account. Wrong's essay can also be found in *The Art of the Mystery Story*, pp. 18–32. One of the reasons, I suspect, that writers of detective mysteries often try, and often quite successfully, to return to the past as a setting is to show that in fact the "discovery" that the crime novel suggests is anything but new. Indeed the success of these endeavors can be used to justify a kind of natural law account of morality. Eco's *The Name of the Rose* is obviously one of the most exemplary forms of the re-narration of the past using the form of mystery. I suspect it is not accidental that his mystery depended on the forms of life shaped by monasticism—i.e., it takes monastics to exemplify the law that should shape life outside the monastery. In other words, monasticism is the institutional form of Aquinas' claim that charity is the form of all the virtues.

11. Sayers, "Omnibus of Crime," p. 76.

12. Dorothy L. Sayers and Jill Paton Walsh, *Thrones, Dominations* (New York: St. Martin's Press, 1998) was recently published through the good efforts of Jill Paton Walsh acting as a co-author of the unfinished manuscript. This, of course, presents the problem of whether in fact the book represents Sayers' views or those of Walsh. I think any reader of Sayers, however, will find the following quotes quite characteristic of her perspective.

13. Ibid., p. 131.

14. Ibid., pp. 151–52. The rise of Germany under Hitler and the outbreak of WWII hovers in the background of *Thrones, Dominations*.

15. McInerny makes much the same point commenting on what makes Chesterton's Father Brown mysteries Catholic—classified "perhaps generically as Christian, maybe even as religious (and, if you are Socrates or Plato, as philosophical). *The consequences of action reach beyond time and the span of earthly life.* This enhances the importance of fleeting deeds; it puts an enormous premium on what we do here and now. Religion was once dismissed as pie in the sky, but the pie, or its withholding, is the just desert of what one does on earth. The moral dimension of human action is included in the religious, but not vice versa, and that is why the first mark is, as Flannery O'Connor suggests, universal to imaginative literature" ("Saints Preserve Us: The Catholic Mystery," in *The Fine Art*

of *Murder: The Mystery Reader's Indispensable Companion*, edited by Ed Gorman, Martin Greenberg, Larry Segriff, with Jon Breen [New York: Carroll and Graf Publishers, 1993], p. 149).

16. P. D. James, "The Baroness in the Crime Lab: Interview by Martin Wroe," *Books and Culture*, IV, 2 (March/April, 1998), p. 15. James, in the same interview, observes rightly, I think, that the classical detective story is not primarily concerned with violence. "It is concerned with bringing order out of disorder, with exploring human nature under the impact of this unique crime" (p. 14). In *Thrones, Dominations* Harriet explains to Peter that "murder is the only crime for a detective story. It has true glamour. Anything less is liable to strike the reader as Perrier to champagne" (p. 222). Raymond Chandler comes as close as anyone to explaining why murder is the singular crime of mysteries when he observes that "murder, which is a frustration of the individual and hence a frustration of the race, may, and in fact has, a good deal of sociological implications" ("The Art of Simple Murder," in *The Art of the Mystery Story*, p. 223). "A good deal of sociological implications" is, to say the least, an understatement.

17. Of course when I was first tempted by McInerny to read mysteries I was not a pacifist. That was the result of another Notre Dame colleague—John Howard Yoder. I suspect that Yoder was not a reader of mysteries.

18. This was the argument of Paul Ramsey, who insisted that just war not only provided a casuistry for thinking about war but was also a theory of statecraft. See, for example, his *Speak Up for Just War or Pacifism* (University Park, Pa.: Pennsylvania State Press, 1988) with an Epilogue by Stanley Hauerwas.

19. As a pacifist I am quite committed to trying to think what is necessary to allow a Christian committed to nonviolence to consider performing police functions. I refuse to accept the presumption that the police function must be understood as controlled violence. Rather I assume most of what police officers do is nonviolent response to violence. After all police officers are called peace officers. Indeed I think one of the most interesting challenges before pacifists and just-warriors is to think together what would be required to have a society in which the police would not be required as part of their task to use lethal weapons.

20. Some pacifists do write murder mysteries—Irene Allen and Chuck Fager are Friends that have done so. I confess I know of no Mennonite who has written a murder mystery. I particularly commend Allen's *Quaker Silence* (New York: Villard Books, 1992).

21. McInerny, p. 149. Crime does not equal that which is immoral and/or sin, which is why Aquinas maintained an immoral law cannot and should not be obeyed. The difficulty, given the contingent character of law (and morality), is discovering when a law is immoral. For example, a law may be moral in one context and become something less in changing social contexts. I am thinking in particular of laws that structure economic relations. Perhaps one of the reasons that murder is *the* crime in mysteries is that the law against murder is less open to injustice.

22. Sarah Freedman pointed out to me that in this way the great Dostoyevski does go beyond the mystery genre (beyond crime and punishment!) by exploring how such redemption is possible.

23. Sayers and Walsh, *Thrones, Dominations*, pp. 302-3.

24. One of the issues I have not addressed in this essay is whether murder mysteries are inherently conservative literature to the extent that detection of crime always favors the

status quo. There is, of course, some truth to that generalization, but interestingly enough murder mysteries often provide ways to explore in what ways such a generalization is wrong. They do so not only by helping us understand the desperation and loneliness of those who murder, but also by positioning the "detective" on the edges of established society. The work of Anne Perry is particularly interesting in this respect just to the extent that the class nature of Victorian England is at once reinforced and challenged by her accounts.

An even more powerful objection to mysteries as a genre than their conservative bias has been raised by Oliver O'Donovan in a letter to me (of 7-30-98) responding to this essay. Oliver observes that while the detective story trades upon and reinforces our sense of justice, "but does its modernity not lie precisely in the isolation of criminal justice from relational justice, in which we are all involved not just as witnesses but as perpetrators? The essential modernity of the genre, as I see it, lies in its identification of the justice-moment as the *exceptional moment,* and its location of the justice-act in the *exceptional individual,* i.e., the detective who alone construes the world and its testimonies coherently. The detective is certainly a hero. But making justice the prerogative of heroes reflects a curiously *gesellschaftlich* view of social relations. The knight in armour in the Arthurian romance contributed a certain skill (i.e., at arms) to the performance of justice in which other people were in other ways, by their commonplace virtues, involved. But the detective works in a moral vacuum—and must do so, for one rule of the detective mystery which you have not articulated is the sceptical canon: *All must be suspect!* There is no place in a detective story for a character who is simply too good to have committed a murder."

I wish I had a good response to O'Donovan's point, but I do not. I can say that I think the murder mystery genre just to the extent that it is often so contextually located at least suggests that the justice being enacted is—to use O'Donovan's description—"relational."

# Part III
# Metaphysics

# 11

# Religious Pluralism and Natural Theology

## Laura Garcia

In a recent issue of the journal of the Society of Christian Philosophers, *Faith and Philosophy*, John Hick opines, "We do not yet have any adequate response from conservative Christian philosophers to the problem of religious diversity."[1] Several authors in the same issue seek to correct Hick on this point, to defend both religious exclusivism and the epistemic innocence of its adherents. These critics address two of Hick's major theses: (a) Kantian agnosticism about the ultimate ground of being (or the Real) is the only defensible position, and (b) religious exclusivism is unwarranted either by natural theology (Kant again) or by religious experiences of the sort featured in so-called "Reformed epistemologies." Though I side with Hick's critics on the falsehood of (a), I believe it has been adequately treated by others.[2] As for (b), I sympathize with Hick's concern that epistemologies that rely heavily on private religious experience to provide warrant for Christian beliefs can be undermined by the phenomenon of religious pluralism. Against Hick, I hold that natural theology and apologetics can provide a remedy for this situation.

In defense of these claims, I first briefly describe a virtue-based epistemology, drawing heavily on the work of Linda Zagzebski[3] and Jorge Garcia, to clarify what I take to be our epistemic goals and the typical means for achieving them. The next section addresses the evidentialist's challenge to religious believers, and I argue that the firmness of believers' assent to articles of faith rightly exceeds the evidence they have for them. Finally, I discuss the claim central to most versions of Reformed epistemology, that some religious beliefs are properly basic, conceding that this may be true, but suggesting (along with Hick) that it does not give a fully satisfactory answer to the challenge of religious pluralism. I argue that such an answer depends on a bright future for natural theology and apologetics, and that for many believers, while there may be a Reformed objection to natural theology, there is no viable alternative to it. One of the main concerns of Ralph McInerny's philosophical work has been to defend the capacity of human reason to arrive at a genuine, if partial, grasp of moral and religious truths.[4] In what follows, I suggest that this should be a concern of all of us.

### VIRTUES, MORAL AND INTELLECTUAL

Here I wish to sketch in very brief fashion some suggestions for a virtue-based epistemological theory. Zagzebski has given a much fuller account in her recent book, and although I part from that theory at some points, the debts to her work will be obvious. Virtue theories in ethics normally define the moral virtues as traits of an individual person, settled dispositions to act in certain ways or to respond (volitionally and affectively) in certain ways. Moral virtues, for Aristotle, are those traits that enable one to achieve human happiness, or perhaps that are themselves constitutive of happiness or flourishing (depending on the interpretation of Aristotle). Developing a theory of virtues requires the existence of a significant set of properties that are common to all human beings (a shared nature) and an account of why some traits are conducive to this end and others (and the actions inspired by them) are detrimental to it. More recent virtue theories abandon this account of the source of the virtues, deriving them either by a kind of intuition (its being self-evident, say, that courage is intrinsically good) or grounding them in the social roles and relationships in which we stand vis-à-vis God, others, and ourselves.[5]

All virtues theories acknowledge a hierarchy among the virtues, with some taking precedence over others either on a constant basis or on a given occasion. Typically it is held that the virtue of phronesis or practical wisdom (or some equivalent) enables one to decide which virtues to pursue and which actions are permissible, forbidden, obligatory, and the like in a context of choice. In most virtue theories, vicious acts (motivated at least in part by vicious dispositional states—desires, attitudes, etc.) are morally wrong without exception. To the extent to which they are within the control of the agent, they are also blameworthy. Zagzebski develops at length the sense in which the moral virtues are said to be within one's control, even though they are also rightly called habits.[6]

Disputes arise among virtue theorists over the basis of moral obligations, however. Aristotle (and Aquinas following him) seems to ground all moral obligations in the will's natural (and inevitable) desire for happiness, i.e., for the agent's own good. Jorge Garcia contends that moral obligations should be grounded instead in the natural claim that others have on our love simply in virtue of their relationships to us (as mother, friend, colleague, fellow human being, and so on). Aristotle's theory can seem overly intellectualist in focusing on the realization of the individual's highest capacities (e.g., in contemplation) and overly self-absorbed in treating the well-being of others as merely instrumental to one's own flourishing. This latter feature clashes with a strong moral intuition that we ought to care for others *for their own sake*. However it may be for Aristotle, Thomists usually endorse this moral intuition, urging that loving others *as intrinsically valuable* is just what will lead to one's own flourishing, so the two duties (to seek happiness and to love others for their own sake) are really one. Something similar is proposed in Karol Wotyla's personalist ethics, as he claims that persons can only fully realize themselves by loving others in a genuine and selfless way.[7]

It's not obvious that there is a major difference between the Thomistic and the personalist approach to this question. St. Thomas says that to be a good person is to perfect one's own nature, but perhaps perfecting one's own nature as a social being requires that one become a good friend, spouse, colleague, etc. This may involve a shift from Aristotle's emphasis on *intellectual* goods, since the person is seen as made for love more than for knowledge (or for knowledge at the service of love). But the objectionable ego-centeredness of the theory vanishes, I think, if one fulfills oneself by seeking the good of others (in Wotyla's phrase, making a sincere gift of oneself to another).

I believe that a virtue theory of this Thomistic/personalist sort indicates some fruitful directions for epistemology, including religious epistemology. Assume for the moment that the most fundamental moral virtue is love—benevolence, wishing well, goodwill—in that other virtues can be seen as species of benevolence or at the service of benevolence. What is the most fundamental intellectual virtue? How should we govern our acts of assent (and related acts—of inquiry, reflection, etc.)? In order to realize the most basic end (love of God, others, and self) we must acquire some *knowledge* of these. Further, love of God requires that we seek to realize God's plan for ourselves, which presumably includes the development of our rational faculties. Such development may also be a duty to ourselves (a desire to see oneself mature and flourish) or to others (who depend on our honest and well-informed efforts to assist them). Nonetheless, acting so as to acquire *knowledge* cannot be the most basic intellectual obligation, since as St. Paul famously says, not all things are profitable. The goal of the life of the mind has to be integrated into the goal of life generally. Perhaps the most basic virtue in this area could be called *wisdom;* it includes an appreciation of which things are worth knowing and an ability to discern what knowledge one ought to seek, how and when to seek it, and when to set aside fact-gathering for other legitimate and worthy goals.[8]

Epistemology has suffered from too narrow an understanding of the end of intellectual inquiry. Some have thought this end could be summarized in the two-part maxim: seek truth and avoid error. But this is too simple. The goal is to live well as a human being, and this may or may not mean acquiring lots of truths and perfecting one's skill in weeding out falsehoods. There are truths not worth knowing (how many M & M's are in each package, whether Jerry Springer's guest will marry her boyfriend after discovering that he's been having an affair with her best friend), and there are errors too trivial or too obscure to bother with (being off by a day about one's last oil change). Just as the goal of the moral life is to act from love, not to succeed in benefiting others (since this is largely outside of one's control), so the goal of the intellectual life is to develop and exercise something like *wisdom,* not to attain knowledge (justified *true* beliefs). Or, as McInerny succinctly puts it, "For an act of thinking to be true is for it to be good in one sense, but not in the moral sense."[9]

Some epistemic virtue theories see *knowledge* as the premier epistemic value, and so build success into the notion of an intellectual virtue. Zagzebski makes this move explicitly, and even defines intellectual or cognitive virtues as "traits persons who desire the truth would want to have."[10] The difficulty is that achieving knowledge (cognitive contact with reality) is at least partly outside the control of the individual, and these externalist considerations have a way of trumping all other epistemic values. If the goal is knowledge, then reliability in the belief-forming processes will be the paramount concern, and virtues are important only insofar as they are instances of such mechanisms. Indeed, some virtue-epistemologies turn to a focus on the features of the beliefs themselves, rather than on features of the believers, treating the truth of a belief as one of its virtues or excellences.[11] By contrast, the theory I am proposing treats virtues as intrinsically valuable and their development and exercise as the primary goal of human activity. Certainly a loving person will seek to benefit others and a wise person will seek to have true beliefs, but one must take as one's *goal* what is accessible to one's will, and whether one's well-intended actions *in fact* benefit others or whether one's properly motivated assents turn out to match reality is not accessible in this way.

## EVIDENTIALISM

The virtue-epistemology outlined briefly above may seem to underdetermine one's epistemic duties, just as an ethical virtue theory seems to underdetermine one's moral duties. But one practical consequence of a virtue theory is that while there are many ways of living virtuously, any act that stems from a moral vice is wrong (without exception). Many epistemic virtues track moral virtues, and I believe (along with Zagzebski) they just are moral virtues exercised in our intellectual pursuits. Seeking wisdom will either include or require many other virtues—prudence, docility, perseverance, courage, humility, diligence, and so on. One can be morally criticized, therefore, for acting from opposite motives or failing to possess the courage, diligence, etc. required in the context of belief. Though the ethics of belief seems to require that our beliefs are immediately within our control, this does not follow. One can be morally criticized for past failures or for a pattern of sloppiness, even if these issue in an act (or belief) that is not *presently* within one's control.

The extent to which we are permitted to acquiesce in the beliefs we already possess, and when it is incumbent on us to reexamine or discard them, is to be dictated by prudence. Such duties cannot be summed up in simple slogans, such as "proportion the strength of your belief to the strength of the evidence you have for that belief." John Henry Newman suggests a strategy of "innocent until proven guilty" with respect to our currently held beliefs—a kind of optimism about the reliability of the normally functioning mind and the testimony of others—but even this advice needs elaboration. We have duties to seek knowledge of some things (in order to care for our children or to do our jobs well) and we have a duty of avoid knowledge of others (in order to respect another's privacy or to safeguard other virtues). Further, duties to seek knowledge or to consider evidence for beliefs must often yield to the other duties of daily life, so that they are largely context-sensitive. W. K. Clifford's infamous ship captain who fails to check out the seaworthiness of his vessel has violated a moral duty, not just an epistemic one. But as Van Harvey points out, the passengers who later perished on this account cannot be similarly blamed for failing to substantiate *their* belief in the ship's condition.[12]

Evidentialists are famously definite about our epistemic duties and about what sorts of assent are vicious without exception. But these views suffer from similar problems of oversimplification and a lingering vagueness. There is Clifford's oft-quoted dictum that "It is wrong always, everywhere, and for any one, to believe anything upon insufficient evidence."[13] For a similar view, Newman quotes John Locke on the love of truth: "There is this one unerring mark of it, viz. *the not entertaining any proposition with greater assurance than the proofs it is built on will warrant*. Whoever goes beyond this measure of assent, it is plain, receives not truth in the love of it, loves not truth for truth-sake, but for some other by-end. . . . *All that surplussage of assurance* is owing to some other affection and not to the love of truth."[14] The difficulty with these very plausible maxims is that, if they are taken too strictly, they require a kind of fastidiousness of belief that is neither desirable nor attainable, while if they are taken more broadly, they tell us very little about how to govern our lives. Everything depends on how much evidence is "sufficient evidence" and how much proof is needed for justified belief, and these will vary according to the type and context of belief. Too strict an interpretation of these maxims may be in fact unwise, and may even interfere with the narrower goal of loving the truth. Even in the so-called hard sciences, it is rare that a scientist immediately abandons a well-tested theory in the face of anomalies, since that may lead her away from the truth instead of closer to it. William James and others have described many other contexts in which belief strictly proportioned to the objective evidence is counterproductive for achieving either truth or happiness.

One of Newman's great contributions to this discussion, I believe, is his suggestion of how the wise person proceeds in matters of belief and reflection. Evidentialists operate on the assumption that we can determine both what evidence (or grounds) our current stock of beliefs rests on and whether these are reliable or not, but Newman shows that with respect to the vast majority of our beliefs neither of these is the case. Since we cannot do without our natural cognitive faculties, says Newman, we may as well assume their general trustworthiness and focus on acquiring the virtues that will help to perfect and strengthen these faculties. The virtuous person, he claims, will gradually see which of his initial beliefs need to be discarded. "Error having always some portion of truth in it, and the truth having a reality which error has not, we may expect that, when there is *an honest purpose and fair talents*, we shall somehow make our way forward, the error falling off from the mind, and the truth developing and occupying it."[15] Further, in many concrete matters of fact, we give our assent based on what he calls the illative sense, the operations of which are not usually recoverable by the average person. "It is the cumulation of probabilities, independent of each other, arising out of the nature and circumstances of the particular case which is under review; probabilities too fine to avail separately, too subtle and circuitous to be converted into syllogisms, too numerous and variable for such conversion, even were they convertible."[16] Nevertheless, Newman argues that reasoning of this kind can lead to moral certitude, in which "the mind feels as if the matter was strictly proved."[17]

Since Newman leaves so much to the operation of a faculty which admits of few universal rules, it may seem that no one could ever be rightly criticized for his or her beliefs. This would be mistaken, since there are surely instances of intellectual laziness or carelessness that result in assent based on insufficient evidence or an insufficiently careful assessment of the evidence.

But due caution should be exercised when accusing someone of cognitive sins, since they may have justifying grounds of which we are unaware, and of which even they may be only dimly aware, if at all. There are many intellectual gifts, and we must respect the fact that others may possess greater facility than we do in a given field of inquiry. Thus the illative sense is not so much a faculty of the mind as a family of faculties, and with respect to each area we consider, says Newman, "our duty is to strengthen and perfect the faculty which is its living rule, and in every case as it comes to do our best."[18]

This brings us to the heart of the dispute between the evidentialists and their critics: whether religious believers' certitude about the articles of faith is morally licit. According to the evidentialists, this depends on whether there is sufficient evidence for these articles of faith, and most evidentialists add various constraints as to what qualifies as evidence. Clifford and others hold that the evidence for God's existence is insufficient to render it even a reasonable belief, and that certitude with respect to this claim (and to any further claims entailing it) is thus illicit and blameworthy. Locke, himself an evidentialist, claims that evidence of the right sort can be found for God's existence and for the divine origin of Scripture, so that certitude with respect to these is justified (for those who possess the relevant evidence).

One way of interpreting Newman is to see him as promoting another version of Locke's position, accepting the evidentialists' call for sufficient evidence, but broadening the definition of evidence to include deliverances of the illative sense. This interpretation should be resisted, I think, for two reasons: (1) Newman's critics complained that the illative sense was an instance of the kind of "overbelief" that they were concerned to eliminate,[19] and (2) the illative sense issues in certitude but not in certainty. The cumulative effect of the considerations favoring a certain conclusion may approach demonstrative force, but there will always be at least a possibility of doubt, so that assent based on the illative sense is voluntary in a way that assent to logical truths or demonstrated propositions is not (generally speaking).

What is the contribution of the will in assent to religious beliefs, in cases where these are not demonstrated? This is an area of great controversy, since the voluntary element in faith seems closely connected to talk about the merit of faith and the sin of unbelief. While theologians and philosophers in the Reformed tradition are generally suspicious about such voluntary elements, lest it seem that salvation depends in some way on creatures rather than wholly on God, Catholic thinkers generally include a voluntarist element. No doubt there are many possible strategies here, but I will briefly discuss two recent proposals concerning how to locate the contribution of the will to religious belief, and then offer a third alternative that I think avoids some of the problems associated with the first two.

In some recent essays, Thomas Sullivan has developed an account of faith that is inspired by Newman's work on assent and certitude.[20] According to this model, the intellect first gathers a certain amount of evidence in favor of the religious belief in question, in this case, in favor of (C) *Catholicism is true*. Then, assuming that one recognizes a moral obligation to seek union with God, evidence for (C) will also be evidence for (O) *I ought to believe firmly in (C)*, that is, believe with as much certitude as I can muster, where this level of certitude exceeds the evidence one has for (C), either of an internal or external kind. The moral principles Sullivan invokes are the following: (M1) *Acts indispensable to an obligatory end are themselves obligatory*, and (M2) *If S believes there is a better case for than against (a) an end E being obligatory and (b) an act A being indispensable for achieving E, then A is obligatory for S*.[21]

This account leaves some unanswered questions with respect to the role of the will. There is first the matter of recognizing that one has an obligation to seek union with God. Aristotle claims that everyone by nature seeks happiness and that therefore we cannot help directing our actions toward this end. Indeed, the moral life consists in directing our actions in ways that will promote happiness, flourishing, eudaimonia, etc. When later Christian thinkers adopted the Aristotelian ethic, they argued that genuine happiness for humans could only be found in the knowledge, love, and service of God. Perhaps if one sees that this is one's true end, then one has an obligation to seek it, but the will might enter in to prevent one from seeing that this is one's obligation or from pursuing the good once it is seen. Sullivan's account, that is, so far seems to presuppose that one has evidence for the existence of God, at least, and perhaps for some further truths about God's will. If one hasn't much evidence for these, then it would seem that one's obligation to believe firmly in (C) is greatly reduced.

On the other hand, for someone who sees that union with God is her chief end and who has sufficient evidence for (C), firm belief would be a duty for her, but it's not clear that it is an epistemic duty, or that it confers any epistemic advantage on her. More needs to be said about the connections between God's existence, God's revealing himself to us, and our assent to what is revealed. Otherwise the believer is open to the charge that firm belief is *prudentially* wise (as necessary for some great good), but that it might not take one in the direction of truth. This is especially troubling if in order to recognize that one has an obligation to assent firmly, one has first to accept many other claims that need independent backing. Sullivan says, "It may seem (highly) probable to someone (properly disposed to hear the evidence) that God has revealed that a certain end is an obligatory end (union with himself) and an action indispensable (absolute adherence to his teachings)."[22] But if it doesn't seem highly probable that God has revealed this, then perhaps a weaker assent would be appropriate. A final difficulty for this account is that if someone really does find the relevant theological claims highly probable, then any failure to believe (and believe firmly) would seem to indicate a serious level of either irrationality or perversity.

James Ross offers a second proposal as to the will's contribution to the act of faith and to its certitude.[23] He claims to be explicating St. Thomas's view of the matter, though I will not here venture an opinion as to the accuracy of the interpretation. On Ross's view, the intellect may provide some evidence for (C) (the truth of Catholicism), but this evidence cannot be in itself compelling, given that much of the content of (C) is not accessible to natural reason and can only be believed on the basis of authority. But (C) is at least possibly true, and may even be more probable than not with respect to the evidence I do have and consider. Further, it's necessary that (H) *I want happiness—the end of the moral life (eternal happiness if possible)*. This is the Aristotelian and Thomistic claim discussed above. Ross's argument seems to be, then: Probably (C); If (C) then, if (H) then (O); (H); Therefore, (O). Here the conclusion, that I ought to believe very firmly in the truth of (C), follows largely from my desire for happiness, so the "ought" involved seems to be a prudential ought, not primarily a moral ought. It is one of the peculiarities of the kind of moral theory attributed to Aristotle and Aquinas here that the moral ought is ultimately to be understood as a prudential ought.

But producing beliefs (or beliefs of a certain strength) in order to help one realize a goal other than truth seems at least a little suspect. There is a prima facie moral dilemma in such cases, it seems, since "believing for profit" (as Ross titles his essay) can indicate a disregard for the truth of one's beliefs and a kind of crass utilitarian approach to our cognitive activities. If this sort of mercenary attitude is not in general acceptable, why is it permitted (or even obligatory) in this case? Even if there is no other way to attain one's supernatural end, it would seem that Ross's theory asks one to adopt an irrational means to a good end, and it's not clear that this can be a virtuous act, either from a moral or from a more narrowly epistemic point of view. Ross suggests that we should trust that the finality of our cognitive faculties is truth, so confidence in them can rightly go beyond the evidence we have for their reliability. Even if this is correct, however, it does not help us decide when a particular exercise of these faculties is to be trusted or relied upon.

The account I wish to propose here of the role of the will in faith attempts to accommodate the following intuitions: (a) that faith is not knowledge; (b) that the will plays a significant role in faith; (c) that faith should be a kind of certitude (firm assent); and (d) that faith is meritorious. Focusing for the moment on faith in (C), it seems that although faith is not knowledge, nevertheless faith is (even if psychologically possible) morally impermissible in the absence of any evidence whatsoever for what is believed. Let's assume then, that the believer has some evidence for the truth of (C)—this evidence may be internal or external, and it may be acquired through natural cognitive mechanisms or received from God in some supernatural way.[24] This evidence cannot amount to a demonstration of every part of (C). It is de fide for Catholics, however, that some parts of (C) can be known with certainty by the ordinary use of reason; if one does come to know these truths, they can add to the case for (C) taken in its totality. Knowing (let's say) that there is a God is a reason for thinking that we have a more than natural end, and this is also reason to think that God will reveal some things to us about how to attain that end.

What is important for the question of degrees of certitude, I think, is the following principle: (R) *If a divine revelation has been given to us, then we ought to believe as firmly as possible in the content of this revelation, and we ought to live in conformity with it so far as we are able.* I believe the obligation to firm belief in this instance is principally a moral ought, though it is also a prudential and a cognitive ought. The moral obligation stems from the relationship we stand in to God, since as his creatures we should offer the obedience of our minds to what he tells us.[25] But since any revelation from God would be one that cannot be false and any directions from God would be ones that lead us to our good, this commitment of our minds will also lead to forming true beliefs and to attaining eternal happiness. To the extent that I ought to seek both the truth and my own happiness, I ought to believe what God reveals with as much certitude as possible. The role of the will, then, is to move the intellect to assent to revealed truths. The will is necessary here because, as Thomas says, the evidence for (C) is not sufficient to compel the intellect to assent. Faith is not knowledge. Much of (C) must be accepted on authority, not just because we have not had time to investigate it for ourselves, but because natural reason could not in principle come to know these truths (what Thomas calls the "mysteries of faith"). This by itself means that one can be tempted to doubt (C), and so to miss the reward of faith (which includes missing out on some important truths). Hence the advice to hold fast to the faith, even in the face of objections that one does not know how to answer, since it will always be easier for the mind to stay with what it can find out for itself rather than take the risk, as it were, of assenting to what is beyond its competence. This is not to say that no amount of contrary evidence should move one to give up one's faith, but that trimming the strength of one's belief to the present state of one's evidence may lead one away from the truth rather than toward it. Further, evidence against some item of faith is also evidence against the entirety of it, so the interaction between evidence and belief is much more complicated than the simple proportionality principle would suggest. Our beliefs don't stand in atomistic isolation from one another, and the evidences supporting them are often partly inaccessible to us and impossible to enumerate.[26]

The duty of obedience to a divine revelation involves one's heart and actions as well as one's mind, and this provides a further reason for the injunction against entertaining doubts to one's faith. It may well be that the life of faith involves sacrifices and hardships of various kinds, so that one will always be tempted to seek one's short-term comfort or happiness at the expense of one's true or long-term good. Within (C), this is not just a failure to attain a good for oneself, but a failure to correspond to the unimaginable generosity and grace of God, that is, a failure of love and trust. Just as we are tempted to stay with what our minds can ascertain, so we are tempted to find our good in ourselves, rather than in the love of God and others. Atheistic philosophers are fond of warning religious believers of the dangers of accepting a claim as true just because it corresponds to one's hopes or wishes, but a similar danger accompanies the rejection of a claim just because its acceptance would require some difficult changes or sacrifices in one's life.

Since the will is thus involved in the act of faith (and in perseverance in the faith), faith can be meritorious. This is consistent with the Catholic view that divine grace aids the will in the act of faith, though I believe it is inconsistent with a stronger Calvinist view that the grace involved here is irresistible. By the same token, unbelief can be a sin, but the determination as to whether a given person is guilty of this sin cannot plausibly be made by anyone other than God (except, perhaps, the person concerned). This is because only God would know what grounds are available to that person for accepting (C), or for accepting various parts of (C), and to what extent that person is guilty of moral vices in approaching the evidence.

One defect of current theories of epistemic justification is that they treat belief in isolation from the other aspects of a person's life and character. As Newman asks, "For is not this the error, the common and fatal error, of the world, to think itself a judge of Religious Truth without preparation of the heart? . . . Every one is considered on a level with his neighbour; or rather the powers of the intellect, acuteness, sagacity, subtlety, and depth, are thought the guides into Truth. Men consider that they have as full a right to discuss religious subjects, as if they were themselves religious."[27] This point is directed mainly toward religious skeptics, but a similar point can be made for believers as well. To the extent that one's life (especially one's interior life) fails to correspond to one's beliefs, it is likely that this will have a negative effect on one's ability to perceive the truth. McInerny takes this to be a central claim within the Catholic tradition. "Unless the intellectual life is seen as a vocation, as a special way of leading the Christian life, it will become a lily that festers and smells worse than weeds. . . . This is the dark side of the picture. The bright and attractive side is this. The great heroes of the Catholic intellectual life have always been holy men and women, saints, mystics."[28]

### RELIGIOUS BELIEF AND PROPER BASICALITY

The discussion so far has left open just what sorts of evidence one has for one's religious beliefs. More specifically, must one be able to provide propositional evidence in support of such beliefs in order to be epistemically responsible? Within the kind of virtue epistemology sketched above, this depends on our view about how a wise person will conduct his or her intellectual activities. It does seem that a general reliance on our cognitive faculties is appropriate, since any wholesale skepticism would render rational action impossible. There is no need to prove that they are reliable, just as there is no need to prove that our acting to benefit others actually promotes their welfare. It's enough that we are striving for this end. So even if an evil demon from Alpha Centauri has put our brains in a vat and produced warped certitudes in us, our moral and epistemic requirements remain the same. It seems to follow, then, that we are permitted to accept (or continue holding) those beliefs that arise in us from the testimony of our senses and from memory. These can be called into question, of course, if we have an overriding reason to doubt them, or reason to doubt that our faculties were working properly in the environment in which they were intended to function.[29] But these natural faculties produce beliefs that are prima facie justified, other things being equal. Assent to self-evident propositions (including propositions about one's own mental states) seems equally innocent.

A large part of the reason for thinking such assents innocent is that they are largely involuntary and so cannot be properly subject to blame. Naturally there will be exceptions (when one should have looked more carefully or reflected less hastily). If Plantinga and other foundationalists are right in claiming that beliefs in the past and in other minds are similarly involuntary and spontaneous, then they will share the same status as perceptual and memory beliefs—innocent until "proven" guilty.[30] Further, if these beliefs are not normally accepted on the basis of propositional evidence, then it will be morally and epistemically permissible to accept them without such evidence. That is, I see no objection within a virtue theory to treating such beliefs as properly basic.

However, divisions arise even within the Christian philosophical community over whether *religious* beliefs can be properly basic. Objections to this claim tend to fall into two groups: (I) Religious beliefs, though grounded in certain private experiences, as are other basic beliefs, lack some of the features of the other less controversial categories of basic beliefs. These features are either a necessary condition for proper basicality or are such that their absence casts doubt on any claim to proper basicality. (II) Religious beliefs cannot truly be basic, since they involve at least an element of interpretation that is not itself basic.[31] Either (I) or (II), if accepted, would require that responsible religious believers must attempt to find other kinds of justification for their religious beliefs. But Christian philosophers in the Catholic as well as the Reformed traditions have endorsed the proper basicality of at least some religious beliefs (not necessarily in those terms, of course), and many spiritual writers in both traditions seem enthusiastic, so to speak, about the epistemic excellence of beliefs arising from certain vivid religious experiences. The Catholic theologian Romano Guardini, to take just one example, writes: "Doubtless the 'purest' manner of communication would be the simple stirring of the inner man by God, without word or image. There are people who are intensely conscious of his presence in and about them, who know themselves in his protection, under his guidance—all without the least image or 'voice' and yet with perfect clarity."[32] While a philosophical case can be made for (I) and (II), Plantinga, Alston, and others make a strong case for their denials, and have on their side the phenomenological data which suggest that for some (many?) believers, certain of their religious beliefs arise in them in much the same way as perceptual or memory beliefs arise (i.e., they are involuntary and are not accepted on the basis of propositional evidence). If these phenomenological facts are correct, then given the innocent until proven guilty strategy endorsed above, one ought to conclude that such beliefs are properly basic and are prima facie justified (acceptable).

Natural theology, then, is not required in order to see to it that each believer is epistemically blameless. It will still be true, however, that for anyone whose religious beliefs are not basic, natural theology and apologetics will assume a crucial role. Just after the lines quoted above, Guardini notes that "in others this consciousness [of God] is less clear; in many it is entirely lacking." One may of course accept the testimony of others as the grounds of one's religious beliefs, but a reasonably critical person will eventually come to reflect on what authority these others have for their claims, and this inquiry will lead beyond them to the evidence for and against the claims themselves. It might seem that similar reflections will require even those whose religious beliefs are properly basic to search for *other* reasons for these same beliefs. This is due to the fact that most adults in contemporary Western societies encounter evidence or reasons to think that (1) religious beliefs are false (e.g., because of the problem of suffering) or that (2) their belief-forming faculties may not have been functioning properly (may not have been aimed at truth) when they brought about the basic beliefs in question (e.g., they may have been produced by other unnoticed psychological or emotional impulses such as wish-fulfillment, peer pressure, cultural pressures, aesthetic delight, etc.). If a person *does* come to have such doubts, then presumably that person will benefit from natural theology and apologetics. Interestingly, Christians have special reason to seek independent authority for their religious beliefs, due to their concern about the intellectual effects of sin. Guardini cautions, "Man is no pure reality capable of receiving divine truth without misunderstanding and distortion. Vanity, stupidity, and imagination use the flow of divine meaning for their own purposes, and not only in worldly things, but also in religious. We have good cause to remind ourselves constantly that our piety too is badly in need of redemption."[33]

What of the fortunate believer whose experiences of God are so forceful and undeniable that *no* later evidence she encounters is more plausible to her than her original belief? Alvin Plantinga sometimes writes as though this person is the paradigmatic Christian believer, so convinced of her experiences of God that no so-called defeaters of her beliefs can trouble her. Comparisons are often made to perceptual beliefs, where skeptical doubts about the external world are no match for our natural tendency to accept such beliefs. In the arena of religious beliefs, John Hick has forcefully pressed the argument that the phenomenon of religious pluralism should undermine one's confidence in the reliability of religious beliefs taken as basic. He focuses on the following facts: (P1) The content of basic religious beliefs varies predictably with the culture of the believer; (P2) persons in other cultures (and nonbelievers in

Western cultures) seem to be noetically on a par with Christian believers and yet do not find themselves with similar beliefs (they have no basic religious beliefs, or their basic religious beliefs are different from and incompatible with Christian beliefs); and (P3) whether any (or specific) religious beliefs are basic for one is (apparently) not within one's control. Hick draws many different lessons from (P1)—(P3), but the important ones for our purposes are these: (H1) The truth of (P1) and (P2) is strong prima facie grounds for doubting the reliability of whatever mechanism produced one's basic religious beliefs, and (H2) the truth of (P2) and (P3) is strong reason *for a theist* to doubt that Christianity is true in a way that excludes the truth of other religious traditions (Judaism, Islam, Buddhism, Hinduism, etc.).

Taking these conclusions in reverse order, it seems to me that (H2) is wrong, but not because involuntary ignorance and invincible ignorance are not a problem. If belief is at all important for salvation, and if (P2) and (P3) suggest that unbelief is not blameworthy, then it appears that certain persons (the elect?) are given this advantage and others are excluded from it through no merit or fault of their own. In other words, it looks as though for some (lucky) persons, true beliefs which are either necessary or at least sufficient for salvation get produced in them by a kind of irresistible grace or similar noetic mechanism which is not given to everyone. Such a view might be acceptable to those who accept strong doctrines of predestination or who believe that salvation is not genuinely offered to everyone, but these doctrines raise moral objections of a familiar sort.[34]

This line of criticism can be met in different ways. One might hold that specifically Christian beliefs are neither necessary nor sufficient for salvation, as is the official position of the Catholic Church. But if it is *any* kind of major advantage with respect to one's eternal destiny that one should have true religious beliefs, then the apparent absence of a voluntary element with respect to such beliefs remains troubling. Another possible response is to deny that believers and unbelievers are "noetically on a par." Thus Plantinga, in considering religious views incompatible with his own (Christian beliefs), says, "I believe (sometimes in fear and trembling) that they are not as well based, epistemically speaking, as my beliefs."[35]

Fair enough, but this does not remove Hick's difficulty altogether, since one wonders why non-Christians are in their unfortunate position. The Christian, says Plantinga, "believes that those who disagree with him lack some epistemic benefit *or grace* he has; hence he isn't being merely arbitrary."[36] If the epistemic advantage Christians have is due to grace, then why isn't it bestowed on everyone? On the other hand, if the advantage is offered to everyone and some willingly reject it, why are they not aware of any such resistance on their part? Unconscious resistance to grace seems no more blameworthy than a simple absence of grace. What exactly is the epistemic benefit Christians enjoy? If it is simply a matter of possessing more true beliefs about God, this does nothing to explain (P2) and (P3). On the other hand, Plantinga's descriptions of benefits that would explain differences in religious or moral beliefs tend to emphasize involuntary factors—the person with a given (wrong) view might be a "victim of bad upbringing," it may be that she "suffers from a cognitive glitch" or from a "congenital moral blind spot," or just an unnamed "epistemic impediment." Other descriptions of the obstacle here *allow* for a voluntary element, though they don't explicitly require it—the person is "blinded by ambition" or "doesn't have friends and confidants of the right sort."[37]

One reason to stay with these involuntary factors is that they help rebut the charge that the exclusivist believer is arrogant, since if one can't be faulted for one's unbelief, neither can one be praised for believing. On the other hand, including a voluntary component in religious beliefs enables one to overcome the charge of arbitrariness. I believe that Newman's view of faith, as described above, can help to exonerate exclusivist religious believers on both counts. The voluntary elements in faith, including the kind of purity of heart of which Newman speaks, are primarily a matter of cooperation with God's grace rather than of unaided achievement. And if sufficient graces are given to each person to enable him to achieve his supernatural end, no one can complain of arbitrariness. With respect to attaining salvation, it could be that the response of mind and heart to the truth one has is more important than the percentage of truth to which one has access. It may also be that to the one who has, more will be given, and that those who seek *with all their hearts* will find what they are seeking. The fact that not everyone is in the same epistemic position is more palatable, I think, if there is a sense that our epistemic position is in some important respects up to us—particularly with regard to these existentially important truths.

Newman's account suggests, I think, that properly basic religious beliefs, taken in isolation, rarely retain the kind of certitude that would overcome typical defeaters of such beliefs. His remarks about the illative sense evoke a more contextual and cumulative approach, in which so-called implicit reasons are combined with evidences of a more objective and public sort to produce a high level of confidence in the truth of a claim to divine origins. Here I think that the analogy between religious beliefs and perception has been something of a conversation-stopper, since perceptual beliefs seem involuntary *in excelsis*.

More recently Plantinga has shifted to an analogy with moral or philosophical beliefs, and this has more promise, I think. But this analogy does seem to open up a role for natural theology and apologetics, since few of us think that *each* of our moral beliefs or intuitions is impervious to doubt or that independent reasons to accept them wouldn't be desirable.

Indeed, though philosophical conversation might begin from such intuitions (even when these are basic beliefs), it cannot stop there. Even if everyone shares the same intuition, we will wonder how it is justified—what leads us to think that it is true. In morality, politics, philosophy, etc., if one refuses to offer grounds other than one's own personal experiences or intuitions, insisting that other parties suffer from unknown epistemic defects, this would be taken as insulting and unjustified. Even if such a posture isn't irrational, it makes rational discussion of the issue impossible. It's not so much that Reformed approaches are incompatible with these claims, as that they omit discussion of them. Suppose it's conceded that religious belief *can* be properly basic. The fact of religious pluralism will continue to raise a challenge to religious believers, whether their beliefs are basic or not, and this challenge cannot be met simply by assuming the veridicality of those beliefs. Certainly this won't help anyone else, but it's not that satisfying even to oneself.

This brings us to Hick's conclusion in (H1) above, that the facts about religious pluralism (especially that one's beliefs seem to track one's own culture and that those in other cultures seem noetically similar to ourselves) cast doubt on the reliability of the mechanism which produces basic religious beliefs. Even if Plantinga is correct in arguing that neither of these facts about pluralism is incompatible with the reliability of that mechanism, they do in fact raise a question as to what can be said in favor of its reliability. With respect to our moral beliefs, when we find that a large number of others who seem to be similarly situated with regard to these matters nevertheless reject one of these beliefs, our usual reaction is to look into our grounds for that belief. If we find no objective reasons to retain it and instead are relying on the fact that we have simply found ourselves with this belief that continues to seem obvious to us, etc., then this does raise a question as to the reliability of the sources of that belief. Guardini's point can be made here as well, in that there may be factors operating to obscure our vision of the truth in moral matters. Plantinga's philosopher is always on the right side (believing, say, that racism is wrong), but someone might find himself with equally strong intuitions that members of a given race are inferior.[38] This is not a proof that the moral sense mechanism (or whatever it is that produced this belief) is faulty, but it does point to the desirability of something more publicly accessible. It is one of the strengths of Calvinism that it draws our attention to the noetic effects of sin, as well as its effects on the will and the passions. As McInerny once said, anyone who believes in total depravity can't be all bad.

Still, these remarks may indicate a divergence between Protestant and Catholic approaches to nature and grace.[39] Following St. Thomas, Catholic teaching has it that grace perfects nature, and that there is a natural access to moral truth and even some truth about God, however partial and imperfect. Even Newman's illative sense is described as a natural faculty whose operations are familiar to us in reasoning about everyday matters, though it is one that can be developed and improved. Such development cannot take place in a vacuum, however, which is another reason for religious believers to be open to correction by sources external to their basic-religious-belief-producing mechanisms—the teaching of the Church, the Scriptures, one's spiritual director, etc. At the close of a recent essay on the problem of evil, Plantinga asks, "But *is* there such a thing as the Internal Testimony of the Holy Spirit, and *is* there such a thing as the *Sensus Divinitatis?* And do they teach us what Christians take them to teach? These are the important questions; but they take us well beyond epistemology into metaphysics, or religion, or theology, or all three. To determine whether there is nonpropositional warrant for Christian and theistic belief, we have to determine whether Christian and theistic beliefs are true."[40] Indeed. Of course we can simply decide to start from these beliefs, but we might also decide to take up the recently neglected projects of natural theology and apologetics and see if we can give Professor Hick a reason to believe.

### NOTES

1. John Hick, "The Epistemological Challenge of Religious Pluralism," *Faith and Philosophy* 14 (1997), p. 285.

2. Notably by William Alston, "Response to Hick," ibid., pp. 287–288; George Mavrodes, "A Response to John Hick," ibid., pp. 289–294; and especially Kelly James Clark, "Perils of Pluralism," ibid., pp. 303–319.

3. Linda Zagzebski, *The Virtues of the Mind* (Cambridge University Press, 1996).

4. To take just one example, McInerny argues in a chapter on "Christian Philosophy" that defenses of the rationality of belief in God (or in Christianity) are helpful, but that something more is needed. "To settle for them would be to abandon one of the essential features of Christian Philosophy, viz. that there are sound and valid proofs for God's existence and of other *praeambula fidei* and that this provides a basis for the argument that it is reasonable to accept the *mysteria fidei* as true." *Art and Prudence: Studies in the Thought of Jacques Maritain* (Notre Dame: University of Notre Dame Press, 1988), p. 43. (Here the *praeambula fidei* are those articles of the faith that are knowable independently of being

specially revealed by God, while the *mysteria fidei* are those articles of faith that could only be known on the basis of revelation.)

5. This type of virtue theory is articulated and defended by J. L. A. Garcia in a series of published articles. See especially "Interpersonal Virtues: Whose Interest Do They Serve?" *American Catholic Philosophical Quarterly* 71 (1998), pp. 31–60, and "Anti-Consequentialist Moral Theory," *Philosophical Studies* 71 (1993), pp. 1–32.

6. See Zagzebski, *The Virtues of the Mind*, pp. 61–72.

7. For a fuller discussion of these points, see J. L. A. Garcia, "Interpersonal Virtues."

8. George Mavrodes makes a similar point in "Intellectual Morality in Clifford and James," in *The Ethics of Belief Debate*, ed. Gerald D. McCarthy, AAR Studies in Religion 41 (Atlanta: Scholars Press), p. 219: "Once we recognize that not all truths are created equal, as it were, then it seems evident that we cannot express the goal of the cognitive life simply in terms of truth."

9. McInerney, *Art and Prudence*, p. 36.

10. Zagzebski, *The Virtues of the Mind*, p. 175.

11. See for example John Greco, "Natural Theology and Theistic Knowledge," in *Rational Faith: Catholic Responses to Reformed Epistemology*, ed. Linda Zagzebski (Notre Dame: University of Notre Dame Press, 1993), p. 185: "The first kind of objective merit that knowledge requires is truth. In order for a belief to be knowledge, it must have the distinction of being true." Greco lists as other virtues of beliefs: de facto reliability, epistemic praiseworthiness, internal coherence, etc.

12. Van Harvey, "The Ethics of Belief Reconsidered," in *The Ethics of Belief Debate*, ed. Gerald D. McCarthy, AAR Studies in Religion 41 (Atlanta: Scholars Press, 1986), p. 195.

13. W. K. Clifford, "The Ethics of Belief," in *The Ethics of Belief Debate*, p. 24.

14. John Locke, quoted in John Henry Cardinal Newman, *An Essay in Aid of a Grammar of Assent* (Notre Dame: University of Notre Dame Press, 1979), p. 138.

15. Ibid., p. 294, emphasis mine.

16. Ibid., p. 230.

17. Ibid., p. 253.

18. Ibid., p. 281.

19. William George Ward defends Newman's position against a published attack by James Fitzjames Stephen in which Stephen complains of the illative sense that "the 'function' of this 'new faculty' 'appears to be to draw positive conclusions from insufficient premises.'" See Ward, "The Reasonable Basis of Certitude," in *Ethics of Belief Debate*, p. 181.

20. See Thomas Sullivan, "Adequate Evidence for Religious Assent," in *Thomistic Papers IV*, ed. Leonard A. Kennedy, C.S.B. (Houston: Center for Thomistic Studies, 1988), pp. 73–99; "The Problem of Certitude: Reflections on the Grammar of Assent," in *Thomistic Papers V*, ed. Thomas A. Russman, O.F.M.Cap. (Houston: Center for Thomistic Studies, 1990), pp. 63–79; "A Reply to Russman," in *Thomistic Papers V*, pp. 91–95; and "Resolute Belief and the Problem of Objectivity," in *Rational Faith*, pp. 110–25.

21. Sullivan, "Resolute Belief and the Problem of Objectivity," pp. 125–26.

22. Sullivan, "The Problem of Certitude," p. 76.

23. James Ross, "Believing for Profit," in *The Ethics of Belief Debate*, pp. 221–35.

24. I assume here that evidence can include the kinds of nonpropositional grounds (experiences) appealed to by Alston, Plantinga, and others as support for (or as triggering mechanisms for) religious beliefs.

25. This assumes that what God reveals will not conflict with naturally known truths, though it may conflict with what we mistakenly believe to be true. That is, there's an implicit assumption that God is perfectly good and so would not give us cognitive faculties that deceive us, regardless of what he wishes to tell us by other (supernatural) means.

26. One of the great contributions of Cardinal Newman to this conversation has been to point this out. "Even as regards what are commonly called Evidences, that is, arguments *a posteriori*, conviction for the most part follows, not upon any one great and decisive proof or token of the point in debate, but upon a number of very minute circumstances together, which the mind is quite unable to count up and methodize in an argumentative form." From "Implicit and Explicit Reason," a sermon preached on St. Peter's Day, 1840, in Ian Ker, ed. *The Genius of John Henry Newman: Selections from His Writings* (Oxford: Clarendon Press, 1989), p. 68.

27. "Faith and Reason, Contrasted as Habits of Mind," a sermon preached on the Epiphany, 1839, in *The Genius of John Henry Newman*, p. 46.

28. McInerny, *Art and Prudence*, p. 185.

29. Alvin Plantinga uses the latter criterion as part of a definition for *warrant*, the property of a true belief that converts it into knowledge (see his *Warrant and Proper Function* (New York: Oxford University Press, 1993)). I use it here instead as a defeater for *justification*; when one reasonably believes that this condition is *not* met with respect to some belief, then that belief will not be justified.

30. The notion of proof is left vague—presumably it means that one has (and is aware of having) stronger grounds to doubt or deny the claim than one's grounds in its favor.

31. For an example of this view, see William J. Abraham, "The Epistemological Significance of the Inner Witness of the Holy Spirit," *Faith and Philosophy* 7 (1990), pp. 434–50.

32. Romano Guardini, *The Lord* (Chicago: Regnery, 1954), p. 505. Cardinal Newman speaks similarly of those who "are brought into [God's] presence as that of a Living Person, and are able to hold converse with Him, and that with a directness and simplicity, with a confidence and intimacy, *mutatis mutandis*, which we use toward an earthly superior; so that it is doubtful whether we realize the company of our fellow-men with greater keenness than these favoured minds are able to contemplate and adore the Unseen, Incomprehensible Creator." *An Essay in Aid of a Grammar of Assent*, p. 107.

33. Guardini, *The Lord*, p. 506.

34. Though the doctrine of irresistible grace is endorsed by some in the Calvinist theological tradition, there are also some in this tradition who reject it. In what follows I mean to defend a confidence in natural reason that is more characteristic of Catholic than of Reformed theology, but I would not want to overstate the differences. Surely the areas of agreement among Christian philosophers are much greater (and more central) than the areas of disagreement.

35. Alvin Plantinga, "Ad Hick," *Faith and Philosophy* 14 (1997), p. 297.

36. Ibid., p. 298; emphasis added.

37. Ibid., p. 297.

38. Using a religious example, Guardini notes: "It is not uncommon for someone particularly honored for his profundity and natural piety to suddenly break out with statements about God and Christ that are so false, so incomprehensibly distorted, that one is stricken by the heaven-shocking questionableness and unredeemed preposterousness of his views" (*The Lord* p. 507).

39. For further comparisons between Reformed and Catholic approaches to epistemological issues, see Linda Zagzebski, "Religious Knowledge and the Virtues of the Mind" in *Rational Faith*, pp. 199–225.

40. "On Being Evidentially Challenged," in Daniel Howard-Snyder, ed. *The Evidential Argument from Evil* (Bloomington: Indiana University Press, 1996), p. 260.

# 12

# Reid, Hume, and God

*Alvin Plantinga*

It gives me great pleasure to take part in this effort to honor Ralph McInerny, who deserves honor if anyone does. What would be most appropriate, obviously, would be a paper either on McInerny or on Aquinas. The problem here, however, is that much or most of what McInerny writes is on Aquinas, so the first option reduces to the second. The problem with the second, furthermore, is that I don't know much about Aquinas—and that, as Ralph once said in a different context, is no idle boast. In desperation, therefore, I shall write on Thomas Reid: perhaps you may think of him as a poor man's Aquinas.

The fact is, Reid is one of history's under-appreciated philosophers. In terms of sheer philosophical acumen and insight, he belongs in a very small, very select company. His response to Hume, at any rate to the Hume he thought he was addressing, is ingenious, insightful, and, best of all, *right*. Both Reid and Kant can be seen as replying to Hume; I think we can appreciate Reid's response when we compare it with Kant's. Their replies differ in several ways. Reid says that where philosophy appears to controvert long-standing and deep-rooted common human opinion (as in the opinion that there has really been a past, that there are other persons, there is an external world) he will throw in his lot with long-standing common opinion. On matters of common sense, he says, "the learned and the unlearned, the philosopher and the day-labourer, are upon a level, and will pass the same judgment, when they are not misled by some bias" (*Works*, p. 438).[1] Kant, on the other hand, seems to think this sentiment beneath the dignity of real philosophers like himself, saying, though not apparently with Reid in mind, that Reid's way of thinking is "but an appeal to the opinion of the multitude, of whose applause the philosopher is ashamed, while the popular charlatan glories and boasts in it."[2]

A second difference: Reid's work has all the qualities we try to encourage in ourselves and our graduate students. He writes clearly: one can ordinarily tell which opinion or topic it is Reid intends to address in any given passage, and more or less precisely what it is he proposes to say about it. One reason so much less is written about Reid than Kant is just that you can read Reid for yourself to see what he meant. There is no need for uncountably many commentaries with their endless wrangling as to what he really must have meant. This can hardly be said for Kant. Unlike Kant, furthermore, Reid writes with grace and style, introducing no more by way of complication, architectonic, neologism, and technicality than the work at hand requires. Still further, there is in Reid a certain humility, or at least modesty—in his attitude toward his nonphilosophical peers, of course, but also, despite the occasional gentle gibe, in his stance towards other philosophers. And finally, Reid, unlike Kant, doesn't join the game, common in modern philosophy since Descartes, of declaring that now, finally, with one's own work, we have arrived at the truth or at least are on the right road, the firm path, after all these centuries of wandering in darkness. Among Reid's virtues, therefore, are insight and acumen, clarity, forthrightness, relevance, a certain plainspokenness, modesty, brevity, and wit—and, as I'll argue, *truth*.

### REID, HUME AND SKEPTICISM

I had almost said these virtues are just a reflection of the fact that Reid was a Scot; but some of these virtues are clearly missing in David Hume, that other (modern) great philosophical Scot. Hume is in fact a black enigma: a certain surface clarity masks a deep underlying murkiness that makes confident interpretation impossible. Still, there is a strong and continuing tradition of interpretation that sees Hume as a serious skeptic, and Reid belongs to this tradition; he took Hume to be a skeptic with respect to external objects, an enduring self, other minds, causality, the past, and so on. And one of Reid's most notable accomplishments, I think, was his reply to what he saw as this dominant skepticism in Hume.[3] As Reid sees him, Hume's view is that there is something *wrong* in believing the things we ordinarily do: it isn't as if Hume simply announces that as a matter of fact we don't really know all we think we know about external objects, causal relations, our own selves. Perhaps that would be bad enough; but there is something much deeper here.

We can see what Reid has in mind by considering the Hume of the conclusion of Book I of the *Treatise*.[4] Here he isn't coolly announcing, as a sort of mildly interesting fact, about us, that fewer of our beliefs constitute knowledge than we ordinarily think; instead he finds himself in a sort of existential crisis. He simply doesn't know what to believe. When he follows out what seem to be the promptings and leading of reason, he winds up time after time in a black coal pit, not knowing which way to turn:

Where am I, or what? From what causes do I derive my existence, and to what condition shall I return? Whose favour shall I court, and whose anger must I dread? What beings surround me? and on whom have I any influence, or who have any influence on me? I am confounded with all these questions, and begin to fancy myself in the most deplorable condition imaginable, inviron'd with the deepest darkness, and utterly depriv'd of the use of every member and faculty.[5]

Of course this is Hume in his study, sometime before he emerges for that game of backgammon. Nature herself, fortunately, dispels these clouds of despair: she "cures me of this philosophical melancholy and delirium, either by relaxing this bent of mind, or by some avocation, and lively impression of my senses, which obliterate all these chimeras. I dine, I play a game of backgammon, I converse, and am merry with my friends"(269).

Still, the enlightened person, Hume thinks, holds the consolations of nature at arm's length. She knows she can't help acquiescing in the common illusion, but she maintains her skepticism of "the general maxims of the world" and adopts a certain ironic distance, a wary doublemindedness: "I may, nay I must yield to the current of nature, in submitting to my senses and understanding; and in this blind submission I shew most perfectly my sceptical disposition and principles" (269). This is the irony of the human condition: those who are really in the know can see that what nature inevitably leads us to believe is false, or arbitrary, or at best extremely dubious; but they also see that even the best of us simply don't have it in them to successfully reject her blandishments. We can't help believing those "general maxims" or if we can, it is only for brief periods of time and in artificial situations. No one can think Humean thoughts about, say, induction, when under attack by a shark, or when clinging precariously to a rock face high above the valley floor. (You won't find yourself saying "Well, I do of course believe that if my handhold breaks out I'll hurtle down to the ground and get killed, but [fleeting ironic smile] I also know that this thought is just a deliverance of my nature and is therefore not really to be taken seriously.") Still, in other circumstances one can take a sort of ironic and dismissive stance with respect to these promptings of nature. Perhaps I can't really help thinking these ways on some occasions, but on others, in reflective moments in my study, I see through them. As a rational creature I can rise above them, recognizing that they have little or nothing to be said for them. Indeed, I see more: this skepticism is itself a reflexive skepticism; it arises even with respect to this very thought; this very doubt, this feeling of superiority, this seeing through what our natures impose on us, is itself a deliverance of my nature and is thus as suspect as any other. The true skeptic, says Hume, "will be diffident of his philosophical doubts, as well as of his philosophical conviction" (273).

In these passages, therefore, Hume isn't shamefacedly confessing an epistemic weakness or flaw, rather as a victim of neurosis or mental disease might. ("Doctor, I find that I simply can't bring myself to believe that induction will continue to work, or that I myself have existed for a good long time, or that there really are other people.") No; this multiply skeptical position, he thinks, is somehow the *right* one, the one that the man of sense (or at least the man of philosophic sense) will adopt. The rest of us who unthinkingly acquiesce in the promptings of nature, who without a thought believe in causal connection, induction, persistent selves, external objects—the rest of us are naive or foolish, unwitting dupes of our own nature. Hume is a sort of Presbyterian of the intellect; we are all, sage and ingenue alike, enmeshed in the toils of an original sin of the mind (and here perhaps we can see a lingering influence of the Calvinism of his youth). Of course Hume at least has the advantage of knowing that for the bulk of his life he *is* a dupe. In this regard he may seem like the publican in Jesus' parable, who at any rate had the grace to confess that he was indeed a sinner. But the fact is Hume is really more like the Pharisee. He isn't confessing a fault or frailty or shortcoming, hoping for a cure; he is arguing, as he sees it, from a position of strength; the rest of us who unthinkingly accede to the promptings of nature are the ones who suffer from intellectual shortcoming. More than that, we are irrational, in the Humean view, in that reason, carefully preserved from the corrupting influence of everyday affairs, enjoins this skepticism upon us. To fail to accept it is to fail to follow reason, to go against its teachings, and in that sense to fall into irrationality.

Now it is at precisely this last point that Reid joins issue with Hume (at any rate Hume as he sees him). Reid's view is that there is nothing at all irrational, substandard, or epistemically second-rate, in my taking it utterly for granted, as we all ordinarily do, that, for example, there are external objects, that I myself have existed for a good long time, that there are other people who similarly endure, that most of us have hands and feet, and a thousand other Moorean truisms. Reid casts his lot with ordinary folk who hold these Moorean beliefs without so much as a second thought.

> On the one side stand all the vulgar, who are unpractised in philosophical researches, and guided by the uncorrupted primary instincts of nature. On

the other side stand all the philosophers. . . . In this division, to my great humiliation, I find myself classed with the vulgar. (176)

Of course this "humiliation" is irony of his own. Reid sees Hume as standing with Descartes in thinking that the deliverances of perception, memory, induction, sympathy, testimony, and any other faculty we might have must be validated before the bar of reason and consciousness. That is, none of these faculties can reasonably be trusted until it has been shown to be reliable by an argument that meets two conditions. First, the argument in question must start from premises that are either self-evident, like elementary truths of arithmetic, or else deliverances of consciousness: such propositions about my own mind as that I seem to see a horse or am appeared to redly. And second, the argument must be such that each of its steps is self-evidently valid.

Now Descartes thought that in fact the other sources of belief *could* be legitimated by reason and consciousness; he thought to establish the reliability of reason itself by giving a reasoned (rational) proof that we have been created by a benevolent God who is nondeceptive (and here, of course, we fall into that distressing Cartesian circle). As Reid sees it, Descartes is mistaken at several points; the point of present interest, however, is Descartes' confidence that the reliability of those other sources *can be* established by reason. It took the work of modern philosophy from Descartes to Hume, so Reid thinks, to show that in fact this is a chimera, a will-o'-the-wisp; this simply can't be done. The inevitable failure of this Cartesian project was therefore wholly evident to Reid some two hundred years or so before Richard Rorty and W. V. Quine took this failure as a reason for proclaiming the death of epistemology [Rorty][6] or its transfiguration into empirical psychology [Quine][7] Now one reaction would be to see this condition as interesting and perhaps even mildly regrettable, but of no real importance: these other sources of belief are perfectly acceptable, whether or not we can find arguments of the above sort for their reliability. But of course Reid's Hume takes quite a different tack: he takes it to be a sign of foolishness or error or dupery or perhaps just part of the deplorable human condition to accept the testimony of any source whose veracity hasn't been or can't be established by way of consciousness and reason. And he concludes that the *rational* course is to reject these beliefs, even if, due to nature's imperious edicts, we can't in fact really follow that austere prescription.

Now this strikes Reid as a piece of consummate arbitrariness:

> The sceptic asks me, Why do you believe the existence of the external object which you perceive? This belief, sir, is none of my manufacture; it came from the mint of Nature; it bears her image and superscription; and, if it is not right, the fault is not mine: I even took it upon trust, and without suspicion. Reason, says the sceptic, is the only judge of truth, and you ought to throw off every opinion and every belief that is not grounded on reason. Why, sir, should I believe the faculty of reason more than that of perception?—they came both out of the same shop, and were made by the same artist; and if he puts one piece of false ware into my hands, what should hinder him from putting another?[8]

And Reid is prepared to say the same thing with respect to our other faculties—memory, sympathy, testimony, induction, the lot. The skeptic thinks we can't properly accept the deliverances of any of these unless we can show by reason that it is reliable; Reid's response is that there is nothing but arbitrary partiality to support this discrimination among our faculties. All bear the same mint; all came from the same shop; all are gifts of the same Maker. So why this original prejudice in favor of some of our faculties as opposed to others? Why should reason and consciousness sit in judgment on the rest? Why should the latter have to prove themselves at the bar of the former? It isn't as if questions can never sensibly arise with respect to the deliverances of reason and consciousness. Indeed, a question with respect to the latter lies at the root of this very dispute between Hume and Reid. Hume apparently thinks it is a deliverance of reason that consciousness is reliable; Reid thinks not. He argues in more than one place that consciousness can't be proven to be reliable:

> If I am asked to prove that I cannot be deceived by consciousness—to prove that it is not a fallacious sense—I can find no proof. I cannot find any antecedent truth from which it is deduced, or upon which its evidence depends. It seems to disdain any such derived authority, and to claim my assent in its own right. (267)[9]

And isn't Reid right? Consciousness delivers such beliefs as that I am now being appeared to redly, that I believe that 7+5 = 12, that I seem to see a pair of hands, and the like. We might think that the reliability of consciousness *is* guaranteed by reason: doesn't the latter teach us (e.g.) that it isn't so much as possible that I believe that I am being appeared to redly when I am not being thus appeared to? Let's concede (what is in any event controversial) that reason *does* teach this: the objector is still mistaken. For what reason teaches here is a truth about certain beliefs: that they can't be false. But of course it doesn't teach me that I *have* that belief. *Given* that I believe that I am being appeared to redly, that belief—that I am being appeared to redly—is bound to be true. But to draw the conclusion that I am indeed being appeared to redly, I must have the premise that I *believe* that I am being appeared to redly. *This* premise is not a deliverance of reason, but of consciousness; and reason doesn't guarantee its truth. What reason guarantees here, at most, is that if I *believe* that I believe that I am being appeared to redly, then it is true that I believe I am being appeared to redly. And so on. Reason is always a day late, if not a dollar short.

So reason can't prove consciousness reliable, and of course it can't prove its own reliability either.[10] Indeed, things are even worse; it isn't merely that we can't prove that reason is reliable: reason seems to teach us propositions such that when we reason from them in the manner approved by reason, we wind up with propositions reason explicitly teaches us to reject. For example it is to at least some degree self-evident both that there is such a property as self-exemplification, and that every property has a complement, so that there is such a property as non-self-exemplification: which, sadly enough, according to reason, both does and does not exemplify itself.

So Reid's view is that the skeptic's procedure is arbitrary:[11]

> Thus the faculties of consciousness, of memory, of external sense, and of reason, are all equally the gifts of nature. No good reason can be assigned for receiving the testimony of one of them, which is not of equal force with regard to the others. The greatest sceptics admit the testimony of consciousness, and allow that what it testifies is to be held as a first principle. If, therefore, they reject the immediate testimony of sense or of memory, they are guilty of an inconsistency (261).

### REID, GOD, AND RELIABILITY

Here we must note a crucially important but so far unremarked feature of Reid's thought. This is the idea that it is a wise, benevolent, and providential *God* who has furnished us with these faculties: with consciousness and reason, indeed, but equally with perception, memory, induction, sympathy, and all the rest. Speaking of perception, he says:

> I find that without it I must have perished by a thousand accidents. I find that without it I should have been no wiser now than when I was born. I should not even have been able to acquire that logic which suggests these sceptical doubts with regard to my senses. Therefore, I consider this instinctive belief as one of the best gifts of Nature. I thank the Author of my

being, who bestowed it upon me before the eyes of my reason were opened, and still bestows it upon me, to be my guide where reason leaves me in the dark. And now I yield to the direction of my senses, not from instinct only, but from confidence and trust in a faithful and beneficent Monitor, grounded upon the experience of his paternal care and goodness. (86–87).[12]

Of memory, he says

... it appears, that memory is an original faculty, given us by the Author of our being, of which we can give no account, but that we are so made. ... I believe most firmly, what I distinctly remember; but I can give no reason of this belief. It is the inspiration of the Almighty that gives me this understanding. (209)

Of our faculties more generally:

Our Maker has provided ... means for giving us the knowledge of these things—means which perfectly answer their end, and produce the effect intended by them. (211)

Reid expresses similar gratitude for our disposition to believe what our elders and others tell us: the principle of credulity, as he calls it. Without this principle, he says, "Children ... would be absolutely incredulous, and, therefore, absolutely incapable of instruction" (96); without the operation of this principle, he says, he himself would be as a mere changeling. Still further, God (or nature: in this context they are interchangeable, since it is God who orders nature) has even given us the means whereby we can resolve disagreements about first principles (57).

The rational course, then, is to treat our major faculties alike: each should be trusted, at least until there appears a contrary reason; none should be given a priori pride of place; and none should be taken to be suspect until certified by others.[13] This is the reasonable course, he thinks, because our maker has given us these faculties as a way of coming to know what we need to know to achieve the ends for which he has created us and which he sets before us. The rational course is to take all of our faculties at face value and treat them as innocent until proven guilty. Given traditional theism, Reid thinks, skeptics like Hume display a silly and arbitrary partiality in insisting that some of these faculties can't properly be trusted until they are proved reliable by others; they also display a sort of ingratitude towards their maker. And again, isn't Reid right? According to traditional theism—Christian, Jewish, Muslim—we human beings and our faculties have been designed and created by God, an omnipotent, omniscient, wholly loving being who has *created us in his image*. We resemble him in certain crucial respects. Like him, for example, we are actors who aim at ends and take measures to achieve those ends. More relevant in the present context, he has created us in such a way that we resemble him with respect to *knowledge:* hence we can know something about ourselves, each other, our world, right and wrong, and God himself.[14] God could have accomplished this creation in more than one way: perhaps, as traditionally thought, he directly created an original pair of human beings from whom we have all sprung. On the other hand, perhaps we have evolved from nonhuman forms of life and have been produced by the mechanisms to which contemporary evolutionary theory directs our attention—guided and orchestrated, of course, by God. In either case, God aimed at producing creatures of a certain sort, and what God aims at, happens.

Of course a theist can't sensibly *argue* from these beliefs, taken as premises, to the conclusion that our faculties are in fact reliable. Any such argument would be epistemically circular; it would presuppose a trust in the very faculties whose reliability is to be the conclusion of the argument. Here Reid chides Descartes:

> Des Cartes certainly made a false step in this matter, for having suggested this doubt among others—that whatever evidence he might have from his consciousness, his senses, his memory, or his reason, yet possibly some malignant being had given him those faculties on purpose to impose upon him; and, therefore, that they are not to be trusted without a proper voucher. To remove this doubt, he endeavours to prove the being of a Deity who is no deceiver; whence he concludes, that the faculties he had given him are true and worthy to be trusted.
>
> It is strange that so acute a reasoner did not perceive that in this reasoning there is evidently a begging of the question.
>
> For, if our faculties be fallacious, why may they not deceive us in this reasoning as well as in others? (276)

So a theist can't sensibly argue that her cognitive faculties are reliable: but Reid's injunction to trust our natural cognitive inclinations seems eminently sensible in the context of theistic belief. These cognitive powers and faculties have all been given us by the same powerful and loving creator, and given to us to make it possible for us to attain shalom, to achieve our ends as God's creatures. The sensible attitude, in this context, then, is to accede to our natural tendency to think (or think as if) our faculties are in fact trustworthy.[15]

## HUME, GOD, AND RELIABILITY

So Reid is right. But perhaps Hume is also right. I think he has good reason for that complex skepticism of his, a reason in addition to his sometimes specious arguments. For suppose, for one reason or another, you give up this idea that we have been created by a benevolent deity. With Hume, perhaps you adopt instead a thoroughgoing agnosticism: there is simply no way to know whether there is any being at all like God, no way to know whether there is a divine being who created the world, no way, indeed, to know anything about the ultimate origin of the world or of the ultimate origin of ourselves and our cognitive faculties. "Our experience, so imperfect in itself and so limited both in extent and duration, can afford us no probable conjecture concerning the whole of things."[16] *Perhaps* the world owes its existence to intelligent design: just as likely, though, it owes it to animal or even vegetative generation (perhaps comets are seeds and our world has arisen from one); and there are a thousand other possibilities, some of them canvassed with grace and style in the *Dialogues Concerning Natural Religion*. Hume's conclusion there, it seems,[17] is that

> In such questions as the present [cosmogony, the origin of the universe], a hundred contradictory views may preserve a kind of imperfect analogy, and invention has here full scope to exert itself. Without any great effort of thought, I believe that I could, in an instant, propose other systems of cosmogony which would have some faint appearance of truth: though it is a thousand, a million to one if either yours or any one of mine be the true system. (p. 49)

He adds a bit later that on this topic, "A total suspense of judgment is here our only reasonable resource" (p. 53). Hume so understood has no idea at all how the world got here, how rational creatures such as we ourselves have arisen, and what the origin and provenance of our rational or belief-producing faculties might be.

And now turn to the question whether our cognitive faculties are in fact reliable, do in fact produce for the most part true belief. Given the kind of complete agnosticism in which Hume finds himself enmeshed, something like his deeply agnostic attitude to that question seems to me to be the sensible attitude. For suppose Hume asks himself how likely it is that our cognitive faculties are reliable, given his views (or rather lack of views) about the origin and provenance of ourselves and those faculties. What is the probability that our faculties produce the enormous preponderance of true belief over false required by reliability, given his views of their origin and purpose (if any)? I should think he would have to say that this probability is either low or inscrutable—impossible to determine. From his point of view, there are innumerable scenarios, innumerable ways in which we and our cognitive faculties could have come into being: perhaps we have been created by God, but also perhaps we and the world are the result of some kind of vegetative principle, or of copulation on the parts of animals we have no knowledge of, or the result of Russell's accidental collocation of atoms, or of. . . . On many of these scenarios, our cognitive faculties wouldn't be reliable (although they might contribute to fitness or survival); perhaps on others they would be reliable; but on balance one just wouldn't know what to think about this probability.

We can see this more fully as follows. Let R be the proposition that our cognitive faculties are reliable: now what is the likelihood of R? As Reid points out, of course, we all instinctively believe or assume that our cognitive faculties are indeed reliable; but what is the probability of that assumption, given the relevant facts? Well, what are the relevant facts? First, of course, they would be facts about those faculties: the probability of R given (relative to) the population of China would not be relevant. And presumably the relevant facts would be facts about how these faculties originated, whether they were designed, if so, by whom and with what end in view, what constraints governed their development, and what their purpose and function is, if indeed they have a purpose and function. Were they, as Reid thought, created in us by a being who intends that they function reliably to give us knowledge about our environment, ourselves, and God himself? On that scenario, the purpose of our cognitive faculties would be (in part, at least) to supply us with true beliefs on those topics, and (given that they are functioning properly) there would be a high probability of their doing just that. Did they, on the other hand, arise by way of some chance mechanism, something like the mindless swerve of atoms in the Democritian void? What is the likelihood, on that possibility, that our cognitive faculties are reliable? Well, you might think it pretty low. More likely, you may think that you simply can't say what that probability is: perhaps it is high (though presumably not very high), perhaps it is low: you simply can't tell.[18] There will be many more such scenarios, says Hume, some involving vegetative origin, some copulative origin, some still other kinds of origin; with respect to them too, the probability that our cognitive faculties are reliable is simply inscrutable. So first, Hume thinks his grasp of the whole set of relevant scenarios is at best infirm; second, with respect to many of these scenarios, those possible origins, the probability of R is inscrutable; and finally, the probability with respect to any of these scenarios that it is in fact the truth of the matter is also, as far as Hume is concerned, quite inscrutable.

But that means that the probability of R, given Hume's agnosticism, is also inscrutable for Hume. Let F be the relevant facts about their origin, purpose, and provenance: my claim is that, for Hume, P(R/F) is inscrutable. He simply doesn't know what it is, has no opinion about its value, although presumably it wouldn't be very high. Another way to put it: the probability of R, given Hume's agnosticism, is inscrutable.

But that gives Hume a reason to be agnostic with respect to R as well; it gives him a reason to doubt that R is in fact true. We can see this as follows. Our cognitive faculties, our belief-producing mechanisms, are a bit like measuring instruments (more exactly, measuring instruments under an interpretation). Our faculties produce beliefs; for each belief there is the content of that belief, the proposition believed, a proposition that is true if and only if the belief is true. Now a state of a measuring instrument (relative to a scheme of interpretation) can also be said to have content. For definiteness, consider a thermometer and suppose its pointer is resting on '70'. Given the natural scheme of interpretation, this state can be said to have the content that the ambient temperature is 70 degrees F. And of course a thermometer is *reliable* only if the propositions it delivers in this way are for the most part true, or nearly true.

Now suppose you embark on a voyage of space exploration and land on a planet revolving about a distant sun. This planet has a favorable atmosphere, but you know little more about it. You crack the hatch, step out, and find something that looks a lot like a thermometer. (It is about as large as a medium-sized pocket watch, has what looks a bit like a pointer and a dial with inscriptions that slightly resemble Arabic numerals (proceeding counterclockwise) going from -40 up to 120.) Relying on past experience with things that look like that, you initially form (no doubt a bit hastily) the opinion that this instrument reliably indicates the ambient temperature in degrees Fahrenheit. But then it occurs to you that you really haven't the faintest idea how this apparent instrument came to be, what its purpose is, whether it *has* a purpose, and so on. Then (in the absence of investigation) you have a *defeater* for your initial belief that the thing does in fact reliably indicate the temperature, a reason to reject that belief, a reason to give it up, to be agnostic with respect to it. Relative to your beliefs about the origin, purpose, and provenance of this apparent instrument, the probability that it is in fact a reliable thermometer is low or (more likely) inscrutable. But that gives you a defeater for your original and hasty belief that the thing really does reliably indicate the temperature. If you don't have or get further information about its reliability, the reasonable course is agnosticism about that proposition.

But the same goes, I think, in the case of Humean views (or nonviews) about our origins, and the origins and purpose, if any, of our cognitive faculties. Suppose I join Hume in his agnosticism. Then P(R/F) is for me inscrutable (as for Hume); I have no idea what the probability of my faculties being reliable is, given the relevant facts about their origin and purpose. But then I have a defeater for my original belief or assumption that my faculties are in fact reliable. If I have or can get no further information about their reliability, the reasonable course for me is agnosticism with respect to R, giving it up, failing to believe it. It isn't that rationality requires that I believe its *denial;* but it does require that I not believe *it.*

Suppose, therefore, that I *am* agnostic with respect to R: I believe neither it nor its denial. And now consider any belief B I have: that belief, of course, will be a deliverance of my cognitive faculties. But I don't believe that my cognitive faculties are reliable—not because I've never thought about the question, but because I have thought about it, and seen that P(R/F) is inscrutable for me. Well, what does rationality require with respect to this belief B? The clear answer seems to be that I have a defeater for this belief too, a reason to withhold it, to be agnostic with respect to it. Perhaps it isn't in fact possible, given my nature, that I *be* agnostic with respect to it, at least much of the time; as Hume says, nature may not permit this. Still, this agnosticism is what reason requires, just as Hume suggests. And we can take one further step with Hume. Since B is just *any* belief I hold—since I have a defeater for just any belief I hold—I also have a defeater for my belief that I *have* a defeater for B. This universal, all-purpose defeater provided by my agnosticism is also a defeater for *itself,* a self-defeating defeater. And hence this complex, confusing, multilayered, reflexive skepticism Hume describes, a skepticism in which I am skeptical of my beliefs, of course, but also of my doubts, and of the beliefs that lead to those doubts, and of my doubts with respect to those doubts, and the beliefs leading to *them,* and so on: the true skeptic, says Hume, "will be diffident of his philosophical doubts, as well as his philosophical conviction."

Here we can imagine the following response: "Hey, hang on a minute! You said Hume and any similarly situated agnostic has a defeater for R, a belief to which he is inclined by nature—and you added that the rational course for them therefore is to give up belief in R—*provided they have no other information* about the reliability of their faculties. But what about that strong natural inclination to believe that our faculties are in fact reliable? Doesn't *that* count as "other information"? According to Reid (who might object to being pressed into service in defense of Hume) this belief in the reliability of our faculties is a *first principle:*

> Another first principle is—*That the natural faculties, by which we distinguish truth from error, are not fallacious.* (275)

He goes on:

> If any truth can be said to be prior to all others in the order of nature, this seems to have the best claim; because, in every instance of assent, whether upon intuitive, demonstrative, or probable evidence, the truth of our faculties is taken for granted.... (p. 277)

Surely there is truth here: this conviction is one normal human beings ordinarily have, and, as Reid gleefully points outs, even skeptics also seem to assume, in the course of ordinary daily living, but most poignantly when proposing their skeptical arguments, that their faculties are functioning reliably. Very few skeptics, in offering their skeptical arguments, preface the argument by saying something like, "Well, here is an argument for general skepticism with respect to our cognitive faculties, but of course I realize that the premises of this argument are themselves produced by cognitive faculties whose reliability the conclusion impugns, and of whose truth I am therefore extremely doubtful."

But our question is whether this belief can sensibly be pressed into service as information which can defeat the defeater provided for R by Hume's agnosticism about the origin and provenance of ourselves and our faculties. And of course it cannot, as Reid clearly sees. If the general reliability of our cognitive faculties is under question, we can't hope to answer the question whether they *are* reliable by pointing out that these faculties themselves deliver the belief that they are in fact reliable. "If a man's honesty were called into question," says Reid, "It would be ridiculous to refer it to the man's own word, whether he be honest or not" (276). Concede that it is part of our nature to assume R; concede further that it is part of our nature to take R in the *basic* way, so that this conviction is not given or achieved by argument and evidence but comes with our mother's milk; concede still further, if you like, that this belief is produced by our cognitive faculties functioning properly. None of this, clearly enough, can serve to defeat the defeater for R provided by Hume's agnosticism. For of course any doubt about our cognitive faculties generally is a doubt about the specific faculty that produces this conviction;

therefore we can't allay such a doubt by appealing to the deliverances of that faculty.

AGNOSTICISM AND SKEPTICISM

*Ordinary Naturalism*

There is another kind of agnosticism, both less global and presently much more popular, that leads to the same skeptical coal pit as Hume's; to see this point, however, we must first make a brief detour. Suppose you are a serious naturalist. You think there is no such person as God, nor anyone at all like him (it isn't that you believe, for example, that there are one or more finite gods). Perhaps your view is much like that of Bertrand Russell's: you think that "man is the product of causes which had no prevision of the end they were achieving; that his origin, his growth, his hopes and fears, his loves and his beliefs, are but the outcome of accidental collocations of atoms...."[19] Perhaps you even go so far as to add, with Richard Dawkins, that the very idea that there is such a person as God is really a kind of cognitive virus, an epistemic sickness or disease, distorting the cognitive stance of what would otherwise be reasonable and rational human beings.[20] Unlike Hume, therefore, you are not agnostic as to whether there is such a person as God or any being at all like him; you think there is not.

There is likely to be a further difference between you and Hume. Having rejected theism, Hume had no comparable story to put in its place: he was left with no idea as to how humanity arose, under what conditions our cognitive faculties came to be, and so on. The contemporary naturalist, however, is in a different condition; for naturalism now sports a shared myth or story about ourselves and our origins, a set of shared beliefs about who we are, where we come from and how we got here. The story is familiar; I shall be brief. We have arrived on the scene after millions, indeed, billions of years of organic evolution. In the beginning there was just inorganic matter: somehow, and by way of processes of which we presently have no grasp, life, despite its enormous and daunting complexity even at the simplest level,[21] arose from nonliving matter, and arose just by way of the regularities studied in physics and chemistry. Once life arose, random genetic mutation and natural selection, those great mechanisms of evolution, swung into action.[22] These genetic mutations are multiply random: they weren't intended by anyone, of course, were not directed by any sort of natural teleology, and do not arise at the behest of the design plan of the organism; they are "not in a response to the needs of the organism" (Ernst Mayr). They unaccountably appear. Some of them, happily enough, yield an adaptive advantage; their possessors come to predominate in the population and they are passed on to the next and subsequent generations. In this way all the enormous variety of flora and fauna we behold came into being.

Including, of course, we ourselves and our cognitive systems. These systems and the underlying mechanisms have also been selected for, directly or indirectly, in the course of evolution. Consider, for example, the mammalian brain in all its enormous complexity. It could have been directly selected for in the following sense: at each stage in its development, the new stage (by virtue of the sort of behaviors it helps confer) contributed to fitness and conferred an evolutionary advantage, giving its possessors a better chance of surviving and reproducing. Alternatively, at certain stages new structures (or new modifications of old structures) arose, not because that structure itself was selected for, but because it was genetically associated with something else that was selected for (pliotropy). Either way, of course, these structures were not selected for their penchant for producing true beliefs in us. Instead, they conferred an adaptive advantage or were genetically associated with something that conferred such an advantage. And the ultimate purpose or function, if any, of these belief-producing mechanisms will not be the production of true beliefs, but *survival*, of the gene, genotype, individual, species, whatever.

If you are a naturalist and also believe these things, then you are what I shall call an ordinary naturalist. I've argued elsewhere that an ordinary naturalist is like Hume in that she has a defeater for any belief she holds—including, ironically enough, naturalism itself.[23] Here I shall briefly recapitulate that argument and then go on to argue my main point here: even if you aren't an ordinary naturalist but are *agnostic* as between theism and ordinary naturalism, then too you have such a defeater. Then too you have a reason for withholding, failing to accept the beliefs you ordinarily do accept; then too you have a good reason to join Hume in his complex, reflexive, multilayered skepticism.

For what is the probability that our cognitive faculties are *reliable*, given the ordinary naturalist account of their origin? Note first that reliability is a fairly demanding condition: most of my beliefs being as a matter of fact true may be necessary but isn't sufficient for reliability. There are deep questions here: but a reliable faculty or mechanism must be one that produces a large preponderance of true beliefs, not just in the actual world, as we say, but in nearby worlds as well. (A thermometer stuck on 72 degrees in San Diego isn't automatically reliable, even if it is always 72 degrees in San Diego. Also relevant is what would happen if we moved the thermometer to Death Valley, say, or Aberdeen.) So what are the chances, given this story about the origin and development of us and our cognitive faculties, that the latter are reliable? What is P(R/N), where N is ordinary naturalism? What is at issue, of course, is the likelihood (on N) that these faculties reliably produce *true beliefs;* the fact that they produce or help produce behavior that is adaptive is neither here nor there.

Well, can we mount an argument from the evolutionary origins of the processes, whatever they are, that produce these beliefs to the reliability of those processes? Could we argue, for example, that these beliefs of ours are connected with behavior in such a way that false belief would produce maladaptive behavior, behavior which would tend to reduce the probability of the believers surviving and reproducing?[24] I don't think so. For first, false belief doesn't by any means guarantee maladaptive action. Perhaps a primitive tribe thinks that everything is really alive, or is a witch, or a demon of some sort; and perhaps all or nearly all of their beliefs are of the form *this witch is F* or *that demon is G: this witch is good to eat,* or *that demon is likely to eat me if I give it a chance.* Clearly these beliefs could be adaptive while nonetheless false. Also, of course, there is the fact that behavior, if it is partly produced by belief, is also partly produced by desire: it is belief and desire, together with other things, that together produce behavior. But then clearly there could be many different systems of belief and desire yielding the same given bit of adaptive behavior, where in many of those systems the belief components are largely false; there are many possible belief-desire systems yielding the whole course of my behavior, where in each system most of the beliefs are false. But then the fact that my behavior (or that of my ancestors) has been adaptive is at best a third-rate reason for thinking my beliefs mostly true and my cognitive faculties reliable. So we can't sensibly argue from the fact that our behavior (or that of our ancestors) has been adaptive, to the conclusion that our beliefs are mostly true and our cognitive faculties reliable.

We can go further. We can't sensibly argue for R in this way; more distressing, however, is the fact that ordinary naturalism gives its devotee a defeater for R. We can see this as follows. In the last paragraph we were assuming that belief and behavior are connected in the commonsense way we ordinarily think: belief serves as a (partial) *cause* or *explanation* of behavior. I want a beer and believe there is one in the fridge; that belief, we ordinarily think, partly explains the movements of that large lumpy object that is my body as it heaves itself out of the armchair, moves over to the fridge, opens it, and extracts the beer. As we ordinarily think of the matter, belief plays a role in the *causation* of behavior. But of course (given naturalism) we can't just assume that belief *is* connected with behavior in this commonsense way: there are other possibilities. One is *epiphenomenalism,* the proposition that belief (conscious belief) isn't involved in the causal chain leading to behavior at all. This view was suggested by T. H. Huxley[25] ("Darwin's bulldog"). Although epiphenomenalism runs counter to our commonsense ways of thinking, it is nonetheless widely popular among those enthusiastic about the scientific study of human beings. According to *Time,* a few years ago the eminent biologist J. M. Smith "wrote that he had never understood why organisms have feelings. After all, orthodox biologists believe that behavior, however complex, is governed entirely by biochemistry and that the attendant sensations—fear, pain, wonder, love—are just shadows cast by that biochemistry, not themselves vital to the organism's behavior."[26]

But the same can be said for conscious belief: if "behavior, however complex, is governed entirely by biochemistry," there seems to be no room for conscious belief to become involved in the causal story, no way in which conscious belief can get its hand in; it will be causally inert. If this possibility were in fact actual, furthermore, then evolution would not have been able to mold and shape our beliefs, or belief-producing structures, weeding out falsehood and encouraging truth; for then our beliefs would be, so to speak, *invisible* to evolution. Which beliefs (if any) an organism had, under this scenario, would be merely accidental as far as evolution is concerned. Belief, under this scenario, would be a mere accident. It wouldn't make any difference to behavior or fitness what beliefs our cognitive mechanisms had produced, because under this scenario those beliefs play no role in the production or explanation of behavior.

But then what is the probability of R on this scenario? What reliability requires, of course, is that an enormous preponderance of our beliefs be true. Now most large sets of propositions do not meet that condition; but one large set of beliefs would seem to be about as likely as any other on this scenario. But then we couldn't claim with a straight face that there is a probability, on this scenario, that most of our beliefs are true. Perhaps the verdict is that this probability is less than a half; more likely the right attitude here would be that the probability in question is inscrutable, such that we really can't come up with much of a sensible estimate at all as to what it is.

A second possibility as to the relation between belief and behavior: *semantic* epiphenomenalism. From a naturalistic point of view, it is natural to think of human beings as material objects.[27] Well suppose that's what they are: then what sort of thing will a belief be—perhaps the belief that Cartesian dualism is false? Presumably a long-standing neural or neuronal event of some kind. This neural event will have *electrochemical* properties: the number of neurons involved; the way in which the neurons involved are connected with each other, with other neuronal events, with muscles, with sense organs, etc.; the average rate and intensity of neuronal firing in various parts of this event and the ways in which this changes over time and with respect to input from other areas. Now of course it is easy to see how *these* properties of this neuronal event should have causal influence on behavior. A given belief is of course neurally connected both with other beliefs and with muscles; we can see how electrical impulses coming from the belief can negotiate the usual neuronal channels and ultimately lead to muscular contraction.

But if this belief is really a *belief,* then it will also have other properties, properties in addition to its electrochemical properties. In particular, it will have *content;* it will be the belief that *p*, for some proposition *p*—in this case, the proposition that Cartesian dualism is false. But how does the *content* of this neuronal event—that *proposition*—get involved in the causal chain leading to behavior?[28] Under this scenario, it will be difficult or impossible to see how a belief can have causal influence on our behavior or action *by virtue of its content*. Suppose the belief had had the same electrochemical properties but some entirely different content—perhaps the proposition *Cartesian dualism is true;* would that have made any difference to the behavior it causes? It is certainly hard to see how. The electrochemical properties seemed to have swept the field when it comes to the causation of behavior; there seems to be no way in which content can gets its foot in the door. But of course it is the *content* of my beliefs, not their electrochemical properties, that is the subject of truth and falsehood: a belief is true just if the proposition which constitutes its content is true. As in the epiphenomenalist scenario, then, the content of belief would be invisible to evolution and the fact that we have survived and evolved, that our cognitive equipment was good enough to enable our ancestors to survive and reproduce—this fact would tell us nothing at all about the *truth* of our beliefs or the reliability of our cognitive faculties. It would tell something about the *electrochemical* properties of our beliefs (their *syntax*, as it is sometimes put); it would tell us that by virtue of this syntax these beliefs played a role in the production of adaptive behavior. But it would tell us nothing about the *contents* of these beliefs, and hence nothing about their truth or falsehood. On this scenario as on the last, therefore, we couldn't sensibly claim a high probability for R. As with the last scenario, the best we could say, I think, is that this probability is either low or inscrutable.

Note that the two brands of epiphenomenalism unite in declaring or implying that the content of belief lacks causal efficacy with respect to behavior; the content of belief does not get involved in the causal chain leading to behavior. So perhaps we can reduce these two to one: the possibility that the content of belief has no causal efficacy. Call this possibility '–C'. What we have so far seen is that the probability of R on –C (and N) is low or inscrutable. Earlier on we noted that the probability of R on C is also inscrutable or at best moderate. And of course what we are looking for is P(R/N). Since C and –C are jointly exhaustive and mutually exclusive, the calculus of probabilities tells us that

P(R/N) = P(R/N&C) × P(C/N) + P(R/N&–C) × P(–C/N),

i.e., the probability of R on N is the weighted average of the probabilities of R on N&C and N&–C—weighted by the probabilities of C and –C on N.

Consider the left-hand terms of the two products on the right side of the equality: the first probability, as we have seen, is either moderate or inscrutable; the second is either low or inscrutable. What remains is to evaluate the weights, the right-hand terms of the two products. So what is the probability of –C, given ordinary naturalism, the probability that one or the other of the two epiphenomenalistic scenarios is true? Note that according to Robert Cummins, semantic epiphenomenalism is in fact the received view as to the relation between belief and behavior.[29] That is because it is extremely hard to envisage a way, given materialism, in which the *content* of a belief—the proposition that Cartesian dualism is false, say—could get causally involved in behavior. If a belief is not a material structure at all, but a nonphysical bit of consciousness, it is hard to see that there is any room for it in the causal chain leading to behavior; what causes the muscular contractions involved in behavior will be states of the nervous system, with no point at which this nonphysical bit of consciousness makes a causal contribution. On the other hand, if a belief is just a neural structure of some kind—a structure that somehow possesses content—then it is exceedingly hard to see how that content can get involved in the causal chain leading to behavior: had a given such structure had a different content, the causal results, one thinks, would be the same. So it is exceedingly hard to see, given N, how the content of a belief can have causal efficacy.

It is exceedingly hard to see, that is, how epiphenomenalism—*simpliciter* or semantic—can be avoided, given N. (There have been some valiant efforts—for example, by Fred Dretske[30]—but things don't look hopeful.) Of course the fact that it seems hard to see how, from that point of view, content could be causally efficacious with respect to behavior is far from a conclusive argument for the claim that if naturalism is true, then so is epiphenomenalism. Accordingly, perhaps on balance the sensible thing to say here is that, given current knowledge, P(C/N) is low or inscrutable. Given what we know or think we know, it looks as if this probability is low; but we could easily be wrong. We don't really have a solid way of telling. And so perhaps the conservative position here is that this probability is inscrutable. One simply can't tell what this probability is.

If P(C/N) is inscrutable, then the same goes, naturally enough, for P(−C/N); that means that the weights in the above expression—the second terms in each of the sums—are inscrutable. As we saw, the same goes for the left-hand term of the second product. What does that mean for the sum of these two products, i.e., P(R/N)? What it means is that no number in the unit interval can be ruled out: that sum could be as high as 1 or as low as 0; one simply can't tell. That is, this probability is inscrutable. P(R/N), therefore, is inscrutable.

But doesn't that give the devotee of N&E a defeater for R, and for the proposition that his own cognitive faculties are reliable? I say it does. Suppose once more (above, p. 212) you embark on a voyage of space exploration and land on some planet revolving about a distant sun. This time you find something that looks a lot like a radio; it periodically emits strings of sounds that, oddly enough, form sentences in English. The sentences emitted by this instrument express propositions only about topics of which you have no knowledge: what the weather is like in Beijing at the moment, whether Caesar had eggs on toast on the morning he crossed the Rubicon, whether the first human being to cross the Bering Straits and set foot on North America was left-handed, and the like. Unduly impressed with your find, you initially form the opinion, perhaps again unwisely, that this quasi-radio speaks the truth: i.e., the propositions expressed (in English) by those sentences are true. But then you recall that you have no idea at all as to what the purpose of this apparent instrument is, whether it *has* a purpose, or how it came to be. You see that the probability of its being reliable, given what you know about it, is for you inscrutable. Then you have a defeater for your initial belief that it is reliable, a reason for being agnostic with respect to that belief, a reason for giving it up, for withholding it.

And doesn't the same hold for R and the ordinary naturalist who sees that P(R/N) is for him inscrutable? With respect to these factors crucially important for coming to a sensible view of the reliability of his belief-producing mechanisms—how they were formed and what their purpose is, if any—he must concede that the probability that those faculties are reliable is inscrutable. Unless he has some other information,[31] the right attitude here would be to withhold R. It isn't required, for me to have a defeater here, that I think the probability in question be low; it is sufficient if that probability is inscrutable for me. But then something like Hume's attitude towards my beliefs would be the appropriate one. I recognize, of course, that I can't help forming most of the beliefs I do form; for example, it isn't within my power, just now, to withhold the belief that there are trees and grass outside my window. But since I now do not believe that my cognitive faculties are reliable (I withhold that proposition), I also realize, no doubt a bit ruefully, that these beliefs produced by my cognitive faculties are no more likely to be true than false: I therefore assume a certain skeptical distance with respect to them. And, since my doubts about my beliefs themselves depend upon my beliefs, I also assume a certain skeptical distance with respect to these doubts, and with respect to the beliefs prompting *those* doubts, and with respect to the beliefs prompting. . . . [32] What we have so far seen is that the ordinary naturalist should take this same skeptical, ironic attitude toward his beliefs—including N itself; for this reason we might say that N is self-defeating, in that if it is accepted in the ordinary way, it provides a defeater for itself, a defeater that can't be defeated.[33]

*Agnosticism*

So Hume's multiply skeptical attitude is the rationally appropriate one, given his agnostic views about the origin and purpose (if any) of his cognitive faculties; and the same attitude is rationally appropriate for the ordinary naturalist, who isn't agnostic at all on this topic but accepts the currently popular story about the evolutionary origins of ourselves and our faculties. We now turn (finally) to another kind of agnosticism, a kind with respect to which, as I said several pages back, Hume's skeptical attitude is also appropriate. This version of agnosticism is much more limited than Hume's: it is one in which, for all you know, ordinary naturalism is true. More exactly, you are an agnostic of this sort if you think the probability of ordinary naturalism, given what you know or firmly believe, is either inscrutable or in the neighborhood of 1/2.

We may see this as follows. Suppose you are agnostic as between, say, theism and N&E: you think one or the other is true, but you can't say which. Given what you know or firmly believe, so you think, the probability of theism and of ordinary naturalism are each either about .5 or inscrutable. Then too, I think, you have a defeater for R, a reason to doubt or withhold it, and a reason to accept that multiple reflexive Humean skepticism. Again, consider an analogy, and just to preserve continuity, make it another instrumental analogy. You are confronted with a measuring instrument of some kind—for definiteness, a barometer. You believe that this barometer could be in either of two conditions, C1 or C2; the probability that it is in either is for you either inscrutable or about .5. The probability of its being reliable, given that it is in C1, is high, certainly high enough so that if you believed that it was in C1 you would unhesitatingly accept its deliverances. On the other hand, the likelihood that it is reliable, given that it is in condition C2, is inscrutable so far as you are concerned: it could be high, but it could also be low; you just don't know what to think about that probability. Would it be reasonable to accept the deliverances of this instrument? I should think not. You know that if it is in C1, it is reliable; but the probability that it *is* in C1 is (for you) either about .5 or inscrutable. Either way, the rational attitude is to withhold the belief that it is reliable, accepting neither it nor its denial. And then (given that you have no other source of information) the same goes for the output of the barometer: for any proposition in its output, the rational course for you would be agnosticism with respect to that proposition. The pointer points to 30 inches; but (if you have no other information) you will not believe that the ambient atmospheric pressure is 30 inches. Of course you won't form a belief inconsistent with that one either: you will withhold the proposition.

The application to the case of agnosticism as between theism and ordinary naturalism is easy to make. If I am such an agnostic, the probability of ordinary naturalism is either in the neighborhood of .5 or inscrutable for me. Suppose the former: what attitude should I take towards R? Well, there is a 50–50 chance that my cognitive faculties were produced in a way with respect to which the probability of R is inscrutable; but if so, I have a defeater for R, good reason to withhold. Suppose the latter: then I can't rule out any probability for ordinary naturalism. But since the probability of R on ordinary naturalism is also inscrutable, I can't rule out any probability for R; in particular, I can't rule out a low probability for R. But again, that gives me a defeater for my ordinary and instinctive belief that R. In either case, therefore, I acquire a defeater for R; unless I have or can come up with a defeater-defeater for this defeater,[34] I should be agnostic with respect to R. But if I am agnostic with respect to R, then just as Hume sees, the rational attitude is to be agnostic with respect to any of the deliverances of my cognitive faculties. I may not in fact *be able* to be agnostic with respect to them, but agnosticism is what rationality requires. But of course I recognize that the beliefs involved in my coming to this agnosticism—e.g., the belief that the relevant probabilities are inscrutable—are themselves products of my cognitive faculties, and no better off than any other such products. Hence that multilayered reflexive Humean skepticism.

In conclusion, therefore: Reid is right in rejecting Hume's skepticism, but only because Reid is a theist. But Hume is also right: given his agnosticism with respect to the origin and purpose of his cognitive faculties, his sort of skepticism is the appropriate attitude. Further, the ordinary naturalist should also (in the interest of rationality) join Hume in this skepticism. And finally, the same goes even for someone who doesn't accept ordinary naturalism but is agnostic about it in the sense that he takes its probability to be inscrutable or, as far as he can see, 50–50.

### NOTES

1. Thomas Reid, *The Works of Thomas Reid* (Edinburgh: Maclachlan and Stewart, 1863), p. 438.

2. Immanuel Kant, *Prolegomena to any Future Metaphysics*, ed. L. W. Beck (New York, 1950) p. 7.

3. I don't mean to join the discussion as to whether Hume was or wasn't a real skeptic; this is an example of where Hume, despite a certain pleasing superficial appearance of clarity, is in fact desperately difficult to figure out.

4. David Hume, *Treatise of Human Nature*, ed. L. A. Selby-Bigge (Oxford: Clarendon Press, 1951 [first published in 1739]), pp. 263 ff.

5. Ibid. p. 269.

6. Richard Rorty, *Philosophy and the Mirror of Nature* (Princeton: Princeton University Press, 1979).

7. W. V. Quine, "Epistemology Naturalized," in *Ontological Relativity and Other Essays* (New York: Columbia University Press, 1969).

8. Reid, *Works*, pp. 84–85.

9. See also 56–57: "The author of the *Treatise of Human Nature* appears to me to be but a half-sceptic. He hath not followed his principles so far as they lead him; but, after having, with unparalleled intrepidity and success, combated vulgar prejudices, when he had but one blow to strike, his courage fails him, he fairly lays down his arms, and yields himself a captive to the most common of all vulgar prejudices—I mean the belief of the existence of his own impressions and ideas.

"I beg, therefore, to have the honour of making an addition to the sceptical system, without which I conceive it cannot hang together. I affirm, that the belief of the existence of impressions and ideas, is as little supported by reason, as that of the existence of minds and bodies. No man ever did or could offer any reason for this belief....

" ... of the semisceptics, I should beg to know, why they believe the existence of their impressions of ideas. The true reason I take to be, because they cannot help it; and the same reason will lead them to believe many other things."

10. Compare here Reid's strictures on Descartes' attempt to give a rational proof of

the reliability of reason, and compare the following Reidian first principle: "Another first principle is—*That the natural faculties, by which we distinguish truth from error, are not fallacious.* If any man should demand a proof of this, it is impossible to satisfy him. For, suppose it should be mathematically demonstrated, this would signify nothing in this case; because, to judge of a demonstration, a man must trust his faculties, and take for granted the very thing in question" (275).

11. Here we do need a couple of qualifications. First, it isn't true that Reid sees no sense *at all* in the skeptic's procedure in giving more credit to reason and consciousness than the others: "When I compare the different kinds of evidence above-mentioned, I confess, after all, that the evidence of reasoning, and that of some necessary and self-evident truths, seems to be the least mysterious and the most perfectly comprehended; and therefore I do not think it strange that philosophers should have endeavoured to reduce all kinds of evidence to these" (204–5).

There are properties of reason (and consciousness, as I think Reid would concede) that distinguish them from the other faculties and by virtue of which it is not unreasonable to trust them more than those others. And second, Reid's view of Hume may be at times a bit unnuanced. As I have already argued, Hume isn't holding simply that these other sources must be attested by reason before they can be trusted; his thought is more like the idea that when we follow reason itself we wind up in anomalies, antinomies, paradox. But these qualifications aren't particularly relevant to my present point. Suppose we take things in Reid's terms: he is at any rate objecting to the view (whether precisely held by Hume or not) that reason and consciousness are innocent until proven guilty, while the other faculties and sources of belief are guilty until proven innocent; and he goes on to add that this position displays arbitrary partiality.

12. Elsewhere, on perception: "Shall we say, then, that this belief is the inspiration of the Almighty? I think this may be said in a good sense; for I take it to be the immediate effect of our constitution, which is the work of the Almighty" (203).

13. For a powerful contemporary development of this theme specified to perception and religious belief, see William Alston's *Perceiving God* (Ithaca: Cornell University Press, 1991), esp. chaps. 5 and 6.

14. Thus, for example, Thomas Aquinas: "Since human beings are said to be in the image of God in virtue of their having a nature that includes an intellect, such a nature is most in the image of God in virtue of being most able to imitate God" (*ST* Ia q. 93 a. 4); and "Only in rational creatures is there found a likeness of God which counts as an image. . . . As far as a likeness of the divine nature is concerned, rational creatures seem somehow to attain a representation of [that] type in virtue of imitating God not only in this, that he is and lives, but especially in this, that he understands" (*ST* Ia Q.93 a.6).

15. From a Christian perspective, this sunny sanguinity must be tempered by a recognition of sin and its noetic effects; but our created nature persists despite sin, and we remain human beings created in the epistemic image of God himself.

16. David Hume, *Dialogues Concerning Natural Religion*, ed. Richard Popkin (Indianapolis: Hackett, 1980), p. 45.

17. I make no pretense to settle the question of who speaks for Hume in the dialogue, something Hume artfully conceals.

18. So of course we aren't thinking here of the Bayesian personal probability, but

of either objective probability or epistemic probability: the sort of probability Hume has in mind when he says that "it is a thousand, a million to one if either yours or any one of mine be the true system."

19. Bertrand Russell, "A Free Man's Worship," in *Why I Am Not a Christian* (New York: Simon and Schuster, 1957), p. 107.

20. Richard Dawkin, "Viruses of the Mind," in *Dennett and His Critics: Demystifying Mind*, ed. Bo Dahlbom (Oxford: Blackwell, 1993), p. 13 ff. As evidence for the virulence and tenacity of this virus, Dawkins cites the fact that it took Sir Anthony Kenny (as learned and sapient a person as we can easily find), a very long time to fight his way clear of it. Others may wonder whether the virus is all Dawkins says it is, given that Dawkins himself, clearly no match for Kenny in learning or sapience, apparently escaped it long ago.

21. See Robert Shapiro, *Origins* (New York: Summit Books, 1986).

22. Various other mechanisms (e.g., genetic drift) are proposed, but these two remain the most popular.

23. "An Evolutionary Argument Against Naturalism," *Logos* (1992), and chap. 12 of *Warrant and Proper Function* (New York: Oxford University Press, 1993).

24. Thus Quine: "There is some encouragement in Darwin. If people's innate spacing of qualities is a gene-linked trait, then the spacing that has made for the most successful inductions will have tended to predominate through natural selection. Creatures inveterately wrong in their inductions have a pathetic but praiseworthy tendency to die before reproducing their kind" ("Natural Kinds," in *Ontological Relativity, and Other Essays* [New York: Columbia University Press, 1969] p. 126).

25. "It may be assumed . . . that molecular changes in the brain are the causes of all the states of consciousness. . . . [But is] there any evidence that these stages of consciousness may, conversely, cause . . . molecular changes [in the brain] which give rise to muscular motion? I see no such evidence. . . . [Consciousness appears] to be . . . completely without any power of modifying [the] working of the body, just as the steam whistle . . . of a locomotive engine is without influence upon its machinery" (T. H. Huxley "On the Hypothesis That Animals Are Automata and Its History" [1874], chapter 5 of his *Method and Results* [London, Macmillan, 1893] pp. 239–40). Later in the essay: "To the best of my judgment, the argumentation which applies to brutes holds equally good of men; and therefore . . . all states of consciousness in us, as in them, are immediately caused by molecular changes of the brain-substance. It seems to me that in men, as in brutes, there is no proof that any state of consciousness is the cause of change in the motion of the matter of the organism. . . . We are conscious automata" (243–44). (Note the occurrence here of that widely endorsed form of argument, "I know of no proof that not-*p*; therefore there is no proof that not-*p*; therefore *p*".) However I am here using the term to denote *any* view according to which belief isn't involved in the causal chain leading to behavior, whether or not that view involves the dualism that is apparently part of Huxley's version.

26. Dec., 1992

27. It isn't easy to say just what a material object *is*. Still, I think it can be done (though this is not the place to do it); as far the present argument is concerned, however, we can narrow our focus just to the claim that beliefs are neural processes of some sort.

28. A question just as pressing, of course, is How does this neuronal event *have* a content at *all?* What is it that assigns to this neuronal event the proposition that Cartesian

dualism is false, as opposed, e.g., to the proposition that it is true, or interesting, or obsolete, or vaguely obscene?

29. Robert Cummins, *Meaning and Mental Representation* (Cambridge: MIT Press, 1989), p. 130.

30. In *Explaining Behavior* he makes a heroic but (as far as I can see) unsuccessful effort to show how the content of belief could be causally involved with behavior.

31. And how could he have or get other information? Any such information would of course consist in beliefs that were a product of his cognitive faculties: but he has a defeater for the reliability of those faculties, and hence for any belief produced by them.

32. See the reply to the Dreaded Loop objection in my "Naturalism Defeated" (which may be difficult, because it is so far unpublished).

33. See chap. 12 of Plantinga, *Warrant and Proper Function*, and "Naturalism Defeated."

34. And again, how could I? In *Warrant and Proper Function* I argue that I couldn't have such a defeater-defeater. I won't repeat the argument here, but in essence it goes like this. A defeater-defeater would be or involve an *argument* of some sort against some proposition involved in the defeater of R. But of course any such argument would have premises—which premises would be subject to the very same defeater as is R itself.

# 13

# Two Roles for Catholic Philosophers

*Alfred J. Freddoso*

In his treatise on justice St. Thomas points out that the virtue of filial piety (*pietas*), by which we render honor to our parents, fails to satisfy the proper definition of justice because we cannot fully repay our debt to them. The same holds true of the virtue of respectfulness (*observantia*), by which we render honor to our teachers and guides, all the more if they themselves are virtuous. Ralph McInerny has been teacher and guide to me, and a virtuous one at that. Still, it would be deplorably small-minded merely to call Ralph virtuous without noting the sheer magnificence of his moral and intellectual contributions to the building up of the Kingdom of God on earth. As is only fitting in the Christian dispensation, these contributions have made him an object of scorn in the eyes of some who are less magnanimous than he. But, like Peter and the apostles before him, he has rejoiced at being "judged worthy of ill-treatment for the sake of the Name."

In the present paper I begin to come to grips with a question inspired by Ralph's example as well as by his writings: how to understand the nature of Catholic philosophy and the mission of the Catholic philosopher.[1] I offer this reflection to him in partial payment for the ineliminable debt I have incurred; and if some of my views make him a bit uneasy, then I offer it too as the basis for what I hope will be a long-lived and lively future discussion.

In what follows I will describe the two principal roles that, as I see it, are incumbent upon Catholic philosophers. In a certain respect, there is nothing new in what I have to say on this topic, since the two roles correspond exactly to the two separate tasks that St. Thomas Aquinas, the prototypical Catholic philosophical inquirer, takes up in the *Summa Theologiae* and the *Summa Contra Gentiles*. Still, in light of recent philosophical developments, especially the many trenchant critiques of modernist conceptions of rationality and philosophical inquiry, we are in a position to challenge some deeply entrenched ways of thinking about the distinction between philosophy and theology, the division of labor among Catholic philosophical inquirers, and the self-conception that Catholic philosophers should take to their interactions with nonbelieving philosophers. I intend to press this challenge here, if only inchoately.

Though everyone is of course welcome to listen in, my remarks are addressed principally to philosophical inquirers for whom fidelity to the teachings of the Catholic Church, as propounded by the magisterium, functions as a central intellectual commitment. I do not preclude the possibility that others, Catholic or non-Catholic, might contribute—intentionally or unintentionally, directly or indirectly—to the project of articulating Catholic wisdom and of clarifying and defending it within a wide variety of cultural and intellectual settings. But conformity to the teachings of the Church is a nonnegotiable constraint on what is to count as a substantial and enduring contribution to that project, and this constraint will operate most effectively in the minds and hearts of those who in their own intellectual undertakings gratefully embrace the teachings of the Church and are motivated by the conviction that one must cleave to those teachings in order to find the Way, the Truth, and the Life.

To be sure, even this relatively straightforward sentiment would in the proper context require an extensive commentary. I will mention in passing just three relevant considerations. First, I am not suggesting that it is always easy to ascertain with precision just what the teaching of the Church is in a given case, or to determine exactly the degree of theological certitude possessed by one or another doctrine. This is a point worth emphasizing, even if dissidents have used it of late to cast doubt upon what ought not to be doubted. Second, a survey of the Catholic intellectual tradition makes it clear that many premises, arguments, and conclusions in metaphysics and moral theory are underdetermined by the teachings of the Church and that, more broadly, the articulation of Catholic wisdom admits of a plurality of potentially fruitful approaches, each of which must stand or fall on its own intellectual merits. Third, the history of the Church reveals that tensions between Catholic philosophical inquirers and members of the hierarchy have been present even in the best of times, when Catholic thinkers for their part have been concerned not only to appear orthodox but to be orthodox, and when bishops for their part have been concerned to preserve the rightful autonomy of scholarship in the various intellectual disciplines that touch upon the faith. Even under such relatively ideal conditions, there are likely to be—and legitimately so—differences of emphasis and perspective issuing in conflicting prudential judgments.

I mention such complications in order, first, to make it clear that I have no interest in suppressing them and, second, to assert that they do not in any way constitute obstacles to the main claims I wish to press here. I turn now to those claims themselves.

I will first introduce and defend the thesis that one role of Catholic philosophical inquirers is to articulate and transmit Catholic wisdom in its entirety. Then I will address various aspects of the second role of Catholic philosophers, which is engagement with nonbelieving fellow philosophers. Finally, I will make a few remarks about the present separation between the theology and philosophy curricula in Catholic colleges and universities.

ROLE ONE: ARTICULATION AND TRANSMISSION

The first role of Catholic philosophers is to articulate the Catholic faith (or, better, Catholic wisdom) in a comprehensive, systematic, and intellectually rigorous manner and to transmit this articulation at appropriate levels of sophistication to other members of the Church—especially, but not only, to those who themselves aspire to be Catholic philosophical inquirers. The *Summa Theologiae* serves as an obvious paradigm here, both structurally and substantively. But the *Summa* itself does not treat in detail every important metaphysical, moral, or epistemological issue. What is more, since the teachings of the Church leave plenty of room for fruitful disagreement about particular conclusions and about particular ways of arguing to incontrovertible conclusions, and since philosophical, scientific, social, and cultural developments constantly present new opportunities for extending and deepening and recovering various aspects of the Catholic wisdom-tradition, there will always be new intellectual challenges to be met.

In order to flesh out more fully my conception of this first role, I will now consider two objections; the first and most important of these objections is theoretical, while the second is practical.

*Theoretical objection*

Upon hearing the claim that a central role of Catholic philosophers is to articulate and transmit Catholic wisdom, someone familiar with the Catholic intellectual tradition might object as follows: "Wait just a minute! You are running roughshod over the distinction between philosophy and theology that was formulated with precision by St. Thomas and has been institutionalized in Catholic colleges and universities by the strict separation of philosophy faculties from theology faculties. According to this distinction, the domain of philosophy as an intellectual discipline is limited to principles and conclusions that are or can be made evident to natural reason, whereas theology counts among its principles the mysteries of the faith, which *ex professo* are not evident by the light of natural reason. More loosely, one can say that philosophy studies the natural, whereas theology studies the supernatural. Thus, the idea that Catholic philosophers should be in the business of articulating and teaching specifically Catholic wisdom violates the integrity of natural reason and conflates philosophy with theology."

My reply is that this objection not only distorts St. Thomas's intention but proceeds from an inadequate or, at any rate, nonmandatory conception of the nature of philosophical inquiry.

Let me begin with the second prong of this reply. The term "philosophy" will, because of its etymology and its original historical denotation, always admit of a sense according to which the genuine philosopher is willing to entertain all claims to ultimate wisdom, regardless of their source. What, after all, is the purpose of the philosophical life and of philosophical inquiry? Suppose we accept the classical answer that the aim of an intellectually, morally, and spiritually integrated philosophical life is the attainment of wisdom—that is, the attainment of a comprehensive and systematic elaboration of the first principles of being that provides definitive answers to fundamental questions about the origins, nature, and destiny of the universe and about the good for human beings and the ways to attain it. This conception of the goal of philosophical inquiry puts no a priori restrictions on possible sources of cognition, but ostensibly invites us as philosophers to draw upon *all* the cognitive resources available to us in constructing a complete and coherent set of answers to the deepest human questions. But Catholic philosophers of the sort I am addressing believe that the most indispensable of all our cognitive resources is divine revelation as communicated to us through Sacred Scripture and the teachings of the Church.

What is more, according to the classical conception of philosophical inquiry, the pursuit of wisdom will prosper only insofar as rigorous intellectual training and practice are embedded within a well-ordered program of moral or spiritual development consonant with the attainment of complete wisdom. That is, successful philosophical inquiry presupposes a way of life that fosters rectitude of affection, where such rectitude is deemed essential for one's having a clear cognitive grasp of first principles, especially (but not only) moral first principles. But, again, Catholic philosophers of the sort I am addressing take the appropriate way of life to include reception of the sacraments, personal prayer, intense intellectual work done for the glory of God, and, more generally, the practice of sacrificial self-giving rooted in the supernatural virtue of charity.

It was precisely this conception of philosophical inquiry and of the philosophical life that St. Thomas had in mind when he identified absolute wisdom, the self-avowed goal of the classical philosophical inquirers, with *sacra doctrina* or Catholic systematic theology.[2] I conclude that, far from being separate from philosophical inquiry, systematic theology—in both its metaphysical and moral dimensions—is the central component of philosophical inquiry for Catholics.

This will undoubtedly sound shocking to some, but I have no desire to shock just for the sake of shock. So let me restate the claim as carefully as I can: If we take the classical view that the ultimate aim of philosophical inquiry is wisdom, where wisdom includes, in the first place, a comprehensive and intellectually rigorous understanding of the First Cause of all being and, derivatively, a similarly comprehensive and intellectually rigorous understanding of all dependent beings insofar as they originate from the First Cause as their source and are ordered to the First Cause as their end, then systematic theology lies at the pinnacle of philosophical inquiry for Catholics. Another way to put this is as follows: If we construe wisdom to include both metaphysics and moral theory, then for a Catholic philosopher of the sort I am addressing, to do metaphysics and moral theory is to do systematic theology.

In saying this, I do not mean to deny the existence of ancillary philosophical disciplines that are in some sense epistemically prior to, and hence distinct from, metaphysics and moral theory. I have in mind disciplines such as logic and certain parts of epistemology, as well as philosophy of nature and some aspects of philosophical anthropology (including philosophy of mind), which are closely tied to the natural and human sciences. To the extent that such disciplines study created entities in their own right or "from below," they are distinct from metaphysics. Yet it is important to remember that classical philosophical inquiry has as an abiding regulative ideal the integration of the ancillary philosophical disciplines and the natural and human sciences into a comprehensive account of reality.[3] That is, a full understanding of the objects of the natural and human sciences can be had only when the sciences themselves are integrated "from above" by metaphysics and moral theory. One corollary of this classical vision for Catholic philosophical inquiry is that the objects of the natural and human sciences can be *fully* understood only from a supernatural perspective that takes into account, but is not exhausted by, what the sciences tell us about them. I will return to this general theme below.

Again, in claiming that, for Catholic philosophers, to do metaphysics and moral theory is just to do systematic theology, I do not mean to subvert the distinction between faith and natural reason or to cast aspersions on attempts to show that various elements of Catholic wisdom can in principle be arrived at without direct appeal to Christian revelation. I simply mean to point out that if we conceive of wisdom and the philosophical pursuit of wisdom in the classical sense, then—like many Fathers of the Church and almost all the important Catholic medieval thinkers—we will find it easy to identify Christian wisdom, personified in the incarnate Son of God and articulated systematically by Catholic theology, as the real (albeit hidden) object of the quest for wisdom that the classical philosophical inquirers had initiated but had been incapable of bringing to fulfillment in the absence of Christian revelation. In fact, as I understand it, the main medieval dispute over faith and reason had to do not with the question of whether Catholics should avail themselves of revelation in conducting philosophical inquiry, but rather with the question of how exactly to spell out the successor-relation that Catholic philosophers, gifted with divine revelation, bear to the classical philosophers, who lacked that revelation.[4]

Had we not been bombarded in the last twenty years with so many convincing critiques of modernist epistemology—in both its rationalist and empiricist manifestations and in both its more optimistic early versions and its more chastened later versions—we might by force of habit still be worried about the propriety of allowing cognitive claims involving affective commitments to function as starting points and first principles in philosophical inquiry.[5] But such critiques, coming from sources as varied as Nietzscheans on the one hand and Christians such as Alvin Plantinga and Alasdair MacIntyre on the other, have exposed as irremediably defective the modernist tenets that individual philosophical inquirers, precisely as philosophical inquirers, must ideally begin in absolute neutrality by setting aside affective commitments to any intellectual or moral traditions that have emerged from the shared beliefs and practices of particular historical communities, and must ideally proceed only from starting points that are acknowledged as evident by all philosophical inquirers regardless of their moral and spiritual condition and regardless of the moral and spiritual condition of the cultural communities within which they practice philosophical inquiry. These same critics have likewise called into question the tendency, typical of later and more skeptical brands of modernism, to value brilliance, cleverness, and novelty over genuine intellectual virtue—an inevitable development once intellectual prowess has been severed, in the manner of Gorgias and his friends, from moral integrity and a single-minded devotion to truth.[6]

Let me return now to the first prong of my reply, namely, that the objection under consideration distorts the intention of St. Thomas. I recognize, of course, that St. Thomas normally uses terms such as "philosopher" and "philosophical discipline" in a more specialized and less proper sense than the one I have just sketched. What he has in mind is fairly obvious. Among those intellectual predecessors whom he especially admires are many who had searched for wisdom without the aid of Christian revelation, either because they had never come into contact with the Christian claim to wisdom or because, having learned of it, they had rejected it. Yet St. Thomas held that, despite this grave impediment, these philosophical inquirers had as a group established—or had at least come close to establishing—many metaphysical and moral truths that are in fact contained in Christian revelation. Such truths he labeled *preambles* of the faith in order to distinguish them from those revealed truths which, though necessary for genuine human happiness, cannot even in principle be discovered without the aid of divine revelation. And he used the term "philosophers" to designate precisely these non-Christian seekers after wisdom. (We might imagine St. Thomas ostensively defining the term *philosophi* by pointing to the group of intellectually and morally well-disposed classical philosophical inquirers whom Dante would later place in the first circle of his Inferno.)

Yet it goes without saying that St. Thomas does not deny that intellectually sophisticated Christians may themselves seek the very same wisdom that the classical philosophers had sought; indeed, in his own work he attempts to show that Christian theology, as the highest science, is exactly the wisdom that the *philosophi* had at least implicitly desired.[7] So, for example, when St. Thomas invokes the distinction between the *philosophi* and the *fideles* (the faith-filled) in *Summa Contra Gentiles* 2, chap. 4, he is not pointing to a contrast between two irreducibly distinct types of highest wisdom, one of which is properly pursued only by the light of natural reason and the other of which is properly pursued with the aid of divine revelation. Rather, the contrast is between two classes of intellectually sophisticated human beings, the first consisting of those philosophical inquirers (the *philosophi*) who are destined for one reason or another to pursue wisdom without the aid of Christian revelation, and the second consisting of those philosophical inquirers (the *fideles*) who, because they possess Christian revelation, are alone in a position—perhaps with ample help from the *philosophi*—to articulate that highest science (*sacra doctrina*) which all seekers after wisdom desire.[8]

But if this is so, then it seems clear that St. Thomas himself did not intend that his distinction between philosophy and theology should be used to divide future generations of Christian or Catholic philosophical inquirers into some individuals who would avail themselves of the sunlight of faith in their search for philosophical wisdom and other individuals who would pursue philosophical wisdom merely by the candlelight of natural reason. To think otherwise seems plainly misguided. Joseph Ratzinger has put the point this way:

> With the terminology which began with St. Thomas, philosophy and theology were distinguished as the study of the natural and supernatural, respectively. These distinctions received a particular sharpness in the modern era. This was then read back into Thomas and the distinction began to be presented in a way cut off from the earlier tradition and in a more radical manner than the texts themselves would justify.[9]

The "particular sharpness" Ratzinger alludes to stemmed in large measure from various modernist conceptions of rationality and philosophical inquiry which, though differing in detail, shared in common a devotion (I know of no better word for it)[10] to "pure" reason and/or "pure" experience unadulterated by affectivity, along with the resulting injunction that genuine philosophical inquiry (even in ethics!) must proceed only from universally evident and affectively neutral starting points. Somehow the idea got out, and was accepted by many Catholic philosophers, that it would be intellectually dishonest to let philosophical inquiry, the search for ultimate truth and wisdom, be "contaminated" by any direct appeal to the certitude of faith.[11]

Ratzinger goes on to lament the sharp opposition that has developed in modern times between philosophy and theology. As he sees it, the result of this opposition is that philosophy, having despaired of ever finding genuine wisdom, has devolved into a technical academic discipline cut off from the persistent metaphysical and moral questions that inspired philosophical inquiry in the first place; whereas theology, having repudiated systematic metaphysics and with it the claim to absolute truth, has lost its missionary character and thus become isolated from the other intellectual disciplines. Ratzinger's remedy is to reconceive philosophy and theology, along with the relation between them, in a way reflective of the early Christian identification of Christian doctrine with the true philosophy that fulfills the hopes of the ancient wisdom-traditions. He even goes so far as to speculate that only Christian theology, rightly construed as a hope-filled inquiry into the deepest metaphysical and moral questions, will keep philosophy itself alive as the search for wisdom.

Be that as it may, it is at least clear that St. Thomas did not mean to urge Catholics to pursue wisdom as if the Son of God had not come to expel sin and ignorance from their hearts and minds, or to conduct their philosophical inquiries with the light of faith formed by charity hidden under a bushel basket, so to speak. What would be the point of doing this, given that our goal as philosophers is to attain and to live in accord with ultimate metaphysical and moral truth, and given that we believe Jesus Christ to be the Way, the Truth, and the Life? Is revealed Wisdom somehow beyond the pale for those who profess to be *philoi sophias*, lovers of wisdom? Aristotle and Plato had no choice but to practice philosophical inquiry without the aid of special divine revelation. But what excuse could we as Catholics possibly have? As Alvin Plantinga has remarked in a similar context: "I could probably get home this evening by hopping on one leg; and conceivably I could climb Devil's Tower with my feet tied together. But why should I want to?"[12]

I do not deny that it might sometimes be rhetorically or dialectically inappropriate to invoke propositions or models not accepted by one's philosophical interlocutors, but this is a general point that applies to *every* philosophical inquirer, believer or nonbeliever, and to *every* philosophical conversation, whether or not it involves revealed truths; and even here, as I will indicate below, there is flexibility about what can count as an effective and intellectually virtuous dialectical strategy.

Nor do I mean to deny that it is both intrinsically and apologetically valuable to show that some element or other of Catholic doctrine can in principle be made evident by the light of natural reason; indeed, a central goal of the philosophical inquirer is to make every conclusion as evident as possible or, in Aristotle's words, to "seek exactness in each area to the extent that the nature of the subject allows."[13] But this consideration is wholly consonant with the claim that one role of Catholic philosophers is to contribute to the systematic articulation and transmission of Catholic wisdom as a whole and in all its ramifications.

Finally, if we think of all philosophical inquiry as aimed ultimately at metaphysics and moral theory, then we can add that work by Catholic intellectuals even in the ancillary philosophical disciplines and in the sciences can count as an integral part of, or at least as a necessary propaedeutic to, the systematic articulation of Catholic wisdom, and thus in that sense can count as a contribution to systematic theology.

*Practical objection*

Now that I have addressed the main theoretical objection to what I have called the first role of Catholic philosophers, let me turn briefly to a practical objection, namely, that under the present dispensation we Catholics who are professional philosophers are not adequately equipped to articulate and transmit Catholic wisdom as a whole because we lack the right sort of training in Sacred Scripture, patristics and Church history, liturgical theology, the history of Catholic theology, and contemporary systematic theology (both theoretical and practical).

To begin with, this objection is at best only partly true, since many of us have formally studied, or at least read widely in, one or more of the areas just listed. But the obvious "low-road" response is that by this very same criterion not many Catholic professional theologians—and this holds especially for those who have received their advanced degrees in the last twenty years or so—are adequately equipped to articulate and defend Catholic wisdom. For one thing, most of them are woefully undertrained in the history of philosophy and in philosophical subdisciplines such as logic, ontology, philosophy of mind, philosophy of science, ethics, and epistemology. Even more to the point, their advanced theological training itself has almost certainly been focused on just one or perhaps two of the areas noted above to the virtual exclusion of the others.[14] What's more, many younger Catholic systematic theologians have received their doctoral degrees from programs which put no emphasis at all on the specifically Catholic theological tradition.

So what conclusion should we draw? The first role I have set for Catholic philosophers is a collaborative one that requires rectitude of will, a spirit of cooperation, and various types of intellectual expertise on the part of many thinkers who see themselves as engaged in a common project. In short, we must communicate with one another and learn from one another despite the institutional and curricular barriers that have been interposed between theology and philosophy. In particular, we must become more creative in devising interdisciplinary courses and research programs. (I will return briefly to curricular matters at the end of this paper.)

The need for rectitude of will and a spirit of cooperation is symptomatic of the fact—noted above and emphasized by the classical philosophers themselves within their own context—that our common philosophical enterprise has moral and spiritual dimensions that cannot be divorced from its intellectual dimension. In short, the success of Catholic philosophical inquiry depends as much on the exercise of the theological and moral virtues as on the exercise of the intellectual virtues. Only a moral and spiritual effort of this sort will enable us to hone our philosophical insights and to keep constantly in mind that our intellectual endeavors, including our disagreements, will be fruitful only if we desire above all, in Etienne Gilson's words, to put our intelligence at the service of Christ the King.

ROLE TWO: INTELLECTUAL ENGAGEMENT
WITH NONBELIEVING PHILOSOPHERS

The second role of Catholic philosophers is to engage nonbelieving philosophers in intellectual exchanges, and to do so with charity, courage, and integrity, in order to learn and in order to teach.[15] This claim, taken generally and in the abstract, is very nearly uncontroversial, since sympathetic and intellectually rigorous interaction with philosophically sophisticated nonbelievers has been a staple of the Catholic tradition from the very beginning, despite periodic protests from those who see the Gospel as a wholesale replacement for, rather than the perfection and completion of, the philosophical inquiry of nonbelievers.

In the remainder of this section I will examine the theoretical underpinnings for this second role, make two brief comments about the division of labor with regard to it, and then discuss in general terms the prospects for fruitful engagement between Catholic philosophers and our nonbelieving fellow philosophers. This will lead us back to a few closing comments about the relation between philosophy and theology as they are situated in the curriculum of the Catholic university.

*Theoretical underpinnings*

St. Thomas was confident that those nonbelieving philosophical inquirers who are intellectually and morally virtuous can be led, by standards of successful philosophical inquiry they themselves accept, toward recognizing Catholic theology as a viable candidate for the absolute wisdom they are seeking.[16] As he saw it, the classical philosophers had already taken significant steps in this direction and could have gone even further had they done better by their own standards. (This I take to be the main thrust of the first three books of the *Summa Contra Gentiles*.) Then, too, he showed by example that Catholic philosophical inquirers can in favorable circumstances adopt substantive theoretical claims proposed by nonbelieving philosophers or at least make extensive use of conceptual resources developed by them. Moreover, he held that even though the dim light of natural reason pales by comparison with the radiant light of faith, and even though the certitude attainable by reason is markedly inferior, absolutely speaking, to the certitude of faith, nonetheless, the demanding intellectual activity by which a wide range of philosophical principles and conclusions are rendered progressively more evident to natural reason is perfective of the philosophical inquirer as such and hence valuable to the Catholic philosopher in itself and not just for whatever apologetic usefulness it might have. These were among the factors that led St. Thomas, as noted above, to distinguish philosophy (narrowly conceived) from theology (likewise narrowly conceived) and to attribute a limited autonomy to those "philosophical disciplines" that had been developed by the classical philosophers without the aid of special Christian revelation.

At this point I want to reiterate that what I said above about the first role of Catholic philosophers does nothing to undermine either the distinction between faith and reason or the distinction between the natural and the supernatural; nor does it in any way derogate the many impressive attempts by Catholic philosophical inquirers to show that a wide range of revealed truths (the preambles of the faith) can be made as evident as any other significant conclusions established by nonbelieving philosophers. Indeed, mainstream Catholic philosophy, while openly acknowledging the limitations and deficiencies of natural reason, has always insisted that some revealed metaphysical and moral truths are such that every human being of normal intelligence has a natural inclination to assent to them, especially under the guidance of wise teachers—and this, despite the fact that personal sin and cultural corruption can render us blind to what should have been obvious to us even in the absence of Christian revelation. In this way, the standard of natural reason serves as a regulative ideal which can guide Catholic philosophers both in their efforts to develop their own intellectual virtues by rendering Catholic teaching as evident as possible and in their efforts to lead nonbelieving philosophers toward that teaching. I will return to this theme in a moment.

*The division of labor*

Before that, though, I want to make two points about the division of labor appropriate to this second task of the Catholic philosopher. I take these points to be nearly self-evident and would not even bother to mention them explicitly if contrary views were not currently in the air.[17]

First, it is important for the Catholic philosophical community *as a whole* to be engaged *both* in exegetical research projects aimed at deepening our understanding of historically important philosophical traditions—especially, but not only, the medieval and early modern Catholic subtraditions—*and* in systematic research projects aimed at pushing forward discussions currently at the forefront of philosophical interest among both believers and nonbelievers. But it is not necessary that *each* Catholic philosopher should excel at both types of research. This general point seems uncontroversial, even given the obvious fact that the division between exegetical projects and systematic projects is not as neat as the above characterization might suggest.

Still, unfortunate tensions exist here: exegetes often chide systematicians for being short-sighted and ahistorical, while systematicians often chide exegetes for not having their interests sufficiently shaped by contemporary philosophical discussions. Needless to say, Catholic philosophy will flourish only if both types of research project are carried out at a very high level of intellectual excellence and only if both types are valued highly by all Catholic philosophers. Moreover, it would be disastrous for exegetical projects either to be wholly shaped by contemporary philosophical problematics or to be carried out in virtually total ignorance of those problematics; and it would be unfortunate if systematic projects were historically uninformed, as they often are, especially in analytic philosophy.

Second, while it is important for the Catholic philosophical community *as a whole* to be intimately familiar with, and in many cases engaged in, the important research programs currently being carried out by nonbelieving philosophers, this is not incumbent upon *each* Catholic philosopher. Catholic philosophical inquiry is, once again, a communal project that admits of and in fact demands a prudent division of labor. But this division of labor itself is likely to produce tensions among us, and we will be successful only to the extent that what we share predominates over our philosophical differences in those many matters that the faith allows us to disagree about. The differences I have in mind here include some that stem from divergent philosophical styles imported from the broader philosophical world (especially "analytic" vs. "continental"), as well as the more parochial ones that have developed internally within our own tradition (e.g., among competing forms of Thomism or among Augustinians, Thomists, Scotists, Suarezians, etc.).

*The prospects for fruitful engagement*

Even though fruitful engagement with nonbelieving philosophers, especially with regard to matters that bear on the faith, should be an abiding goal for the Catholic philosophical community, we must not be naive in our assessment of the prospects for success in this venture.

St. Thomas felt a special kinship with the classical philosophers and their later commentators (including several Jews and Muslims) not only because they were intellectually and morally well-disposed seekers after wisdom, but also because by his lights they had hit upon many important truths or insights which could be incorporated into a comprehensive Christian articulation of absolute wisdom. We cannot take it for granted that *every* philosophical system or research program will be as congenial to Catholic doctrine as, say, Platonism and Aristotelianism turned out to be in many important respects. In his Gifford Lectures Alasdair MacIntyre faults "much nineteenth- and early twentieth-century Thomism" for not appreciating just how disparate its own first principles and conception of philosophical inquiry were from those of Cartesianism, Humeanism, and Kantianism, and thus for not understanding just how different its relation to these philosophical systems was from St. Thomas's relation to Aristotelianism.[18] To the extent that Catholic philosophers differ from nonbelieving philosophers in both substantive and methodological assumptions, fruitful interchange will be difficult, especially in circles dominated by scientific naturalism or postmodern antirealism. In short, even if our intellectual work is excellent by generally accepted standards, often the best we will be able to hope for is the grudging respect of our nonbelieving colleagues. This is not a counsel of despair so much as an indication of how arduous and delicate the second role of Catholic philosophers is likely to be over the next few decades—and probably beyond that as well.

Indeed, the present, somewhat inhospitable, climate of secular philosophy underscores the importance of our maintaining centers of learning and research in which Catholic philosophical inquiry has the freedom to develop and flourish without constantly having to justify its very existence. Recently I had the opportunity to hear a group of senior professors from Belgium and the Netherlands lament their marginalization as self-professed Catholic scholars in both the state-run and Catholic universities of their native countries. Yet despite fretting about their own isolation and about the secularization of their universities, some of them seemed even more haunted by the specter of the "intellectual ghetto" they describe Catholic thought as having occupied before Vatican II—so much so that they cannot even now bring themselves to embrace the idea, set forth boldly in Pope John Paul II's Apostolic Constitution *Ex Corde Ecclesiae*, that Catholic universities must be places of "rigorous fidelity" and "courageous creativity" where distinctively Catholic learning can flourish even within otherwise hostile secular intellectual climates.[19] Perhaps Catholic philosophers before the council were to some extent responsible for their own isolation from the secular intellectual mainstream, though it is worth remembering that at that time professional philosophy in England and the United States was dominated by logical positivism, pragmatism, and ordinary-language philosophy, three of the most harshly antimetaphysical movements in the history of philosophy. In any case, what Catholic philosophers require now are environments in which we can carry out our work with freedom and confidence, independently of how we are received in the wider philosophical world.

On the other hand, even if many of our fellow philosophers will simply ignore us or deem us peculiar and even dangerous, we must not be deterred from reaching out to them in charity. As noted above, the light of natural reason has traditionally functioned as a normative ideal for Catholic philosophical inquiry, in the sense that an intrinsic goal of such inquiry is to render Catholic wisdom as evident as possible by the light of natural reason and, in particular, to establish the preambles of the faith with a high degree of evidential certitude.[20] To reiterate, this project is important both because it leads to intellectual perfection for Catholic philosophers themselves and also because it promises to establish common ground with nonbelieving philosophers. Notice, however, that even within the Catholic philosophical tradition there has been significant disagreement about the material content of this normative ideal; that is, Catholic philosophical inquirers have differed over just how extensive in principle the range of the preambles of the faith is and over just how evident in principle those preambles can be rendered. St. Thomas, deeply impressed by the accomplishments of his nonbelieving philosophical predecessors, was a cautious optimist on this score, as have been most important Catholic thinkers since his time; by contrast, other Catholic philosophical inquirers have tended to be more pessimistic.

The issues upon which this disagreement focuses, though not settled by what I have said about the two roles of Catholic philosophers, are obviously pertinent to the decisions that Catholic philosophers must make about how they are to deal with their nonbelieving counterparts in discussions bearing on matters of the faith. Still, we should not exaggerate the importance of these issues, since, for reasons of the sort adumbrated above, premises that given philosophical interlocutors *should* assent to by the standard of natural reason are very often such that they *do not in fact* assent to them. Sometimes the relevant disputes are amenable to further analysis or to deeper probing for shared assumptions, sometimes not. In the latter type of case, direct appeals to the authority of natural reason are likely to be no more successful than direct appeals to divine revelation. After all, even if one might in appropriate circumstances be warranted in chiding one's interlocutors for not seeing what they should see, doing so is not generally an effective dialectical strategy. As in any other instance of philosophical dialectic, we must be sensitive to the beliefs of our intended audience.

However, standoffs regarding basic principles are fairly widespread in the world of philosophy, and it is instructive to look at one popular strategy philosophers deploy in their attempts to make progress in the face of such fundamental disagreements. What I have in mind is the common practice of indirectly countering an objection to one's theory by exhibiting the internal conceptual resources by which the theory as a systematic whole can either render the objection irrelevant or accommodate its thrust without falling prey to it. Such replies are indirect because they do not appeal immediately to premises or assumptions accepted by the objector; rather, they invite the objector to look more closely at the systemic virtues of the disputed theory and to compare it in that light to alternatives.

Here are two examples relevant to the present topic. Bare classical theism, the usual target of atheistic arguments from evil, has far less impressive resources at its disposal for dealing with such arguments than does full-fledged Catholic theology—or so, at least, I would contend.[21] On the surface, this sounds paradoxical, since Catholic theology includes classical theism as a proper part and, one might infer, is therefore more difficult to defend. But the fact is that the complete Christian story, centered around the death and resurrection of Christ, transforms our ordinary understandings of suffering, death, and moral evil in such a profound and striking way that it might very well be more attractive—or at least more intriguing—to the atheistic or agnostic philosopher than is bare classical theism. At the very least, the Catholic philosopher engaged in discussions of the problem of evil should be conversant with the best expositions of the Christian understandings of suffering and evil and should be prepared to deploy such understandings if this seems the best way to move the debate forward.[22]

Similarly, I cannot as a Catholic philosopher intelligently discuss moral theory with nonbelieving philosophers unless I understand deeply the ways in which Catholic belief and practice shed a distinctive light on the moral life in general and the moral virtues in particular. Think, for instance, of the fascinating confluence of magnanimity and humility which the eyes of faith see in the life of every great saint, but which is very nearly incomprehensible, at least at first sight, to many nonbelievers. More generally, as St. Thomas teaches by example, Catholic philosophers of the sort I am addressing cannot responsibly do moral theory without explicitly investigating the theological virtues, the infused moral virtues, the gifts of the Holy Spirit, original sin, the New Law, the nature of grace, etc. For Catholic philosophers to give the impression that moral philosophy is a "merely natural" discipline that can prescind from these realities without gravely distorting our understanding of the moral life is intellectually irresponsible as well as a culpable disservice to our nonbelieving colleagues, not to mention our students. Once again, I do not claim that these supernatural realities must be invoked in every conversation about moral theory that a Catholic philosopher might have with a nonbelieving counterpart, or in every lecture or article intended for a general audience.

But I do mean to insist that no Catholic philosopher should pretend, for fear of crossing some inviolable boundary between philosophy and theology, that moral theory can be adequately or successfully pursued without reference to such realities.

Similar examples are easy to produce along a whole front of metaphysical, epistemological, and moral topics which impinge directly on the deliverances of the faith. In short, when we engage in discussions with nonbelieving fellow philosophers, we should keep close at hand the full array of the principles and conclusions that we hold as believers. Otherwise we will be, and will likely be perceived as being, insincere and intellectually dishonest. Or so at least it seems to me.

Such examples help drive home two further points. First, they make it crystal clear that we must resist the temptation to turn the distinction between theology and philosophy into a distinction between individuals who articulate and transmit Catholic wisdom (role one) and individuals who engage in active interchanges with nonbelieving philosophers (role two). The two roles simply cannot be divorced in this way. On the one hand, engagement with nonbelieving philosophers presupposes a thorough understanding of the claim to wisdom which we bring to that engagement. On the other hand, an articulation of Catholic wisdom that is oblivious to the best of non-Christian philosophical inquiry is likely to be superficial and merely transitory.

Second, the above examples should make us wary of the claim that philosophy has the natural as its object, whereas theology has the supernatural as its object. I do not deny—in fact, I would insist—that the Catholic perspective must preserve a sharp *metaphysical* distinction between the natural and the supernatural; but it does not follow from the recognition of this distinction or of its importance that we can understand the natural fully in all its aspects (especially with regard to the human person) without seeing it in the supernatural light of faith. Servais Pinckaers has put the point aptly as follows:

> In starting out from natural reason, we shall often have to recall St. Thomas's saying that grace does not destroy nature but perfects it. This could be seen to imply that we should first study and acknowledge natural gifts in human beings and in moral theory, and then move on to grace and the supernatural. This implication is not the only possible one, however; we could as well, perhaps better, conclude that since grace perfects nature, the more we study human nature in the light of faith, the better we will understand its essence and potential.[23]

As I have tried to show, if Catholic philosophers come to conversations with nonbelievers equipped with deep knowledge only of principles, arguments, and assumptions that a nonbeliever is or "should be" prepared to accept, they will fail to recognize opportunities for driving philosophical discussions to deeper levels. Again, this is not to say that Catholic philosophers must invoke the articles of the faith in every such situation or even in most such situations; it is just to say that we should be prepared to do so when the time is ripe.

### PHILOSOPHY, THEOLOGY, AND THE CURRICULUM

I have argued that to draw St. Thomas's distinction between philosophy narrowly conceived and theology narrowly conceived is not at all to encourage faithful Catholics to practice philosophical inquiry as if their faith were an obstacle to their being genuine philosophers, or as if it would be inappropriate for them to invoke the mysteries of the faith in their articulation of wisdom. I now want to add that, as far as I can tell, St. Thomas's distinction does not by itself provide any *theoretical* justification at all for the sharp separation of the philosophy and theology curricula that one finds today in most Catholic colleges and universities.[24] To the contrary, his narrow use of the term "philosophy" seems to function merely as an ostensive designator for what Plato, Aristotle, and other classical "gentile" philosophers actually accomplished without the aid of divine revelation by way of attaining wisdom—or, perhaps better, what they could have accomplished without divine revelation had they done better by their own standards of successful philosophical inquiry. There is no suggestion at all that Catholic philosophers themselves should put their faith aside when they pursue wisdom as classically defined. It follows straightforwardly that they should not put their faith aside in the classroom, either.

I acknowledge—and indeed have already asserted—that at least some Catholic philosophical inquirers should explicitly take on the task of studying in depth what the best philosophers, believers or nonbelievers, have said in the past and are saying in the present, so as to learn from them, criticize them, cooperate with them in mutually advantageous research projects, and help educate fellow Catholic intellectuals about them. Indeed, embracing this task enthusiastically is for us a core demand of supernatural charity, which militates against our assuming a smug intellectual complacency and thereby being content to abandon the souls of secular philosophers and their students to falsehood, unhappiness, and despair. But, once again, acknowledging this point does nothing at all to justify a sharp separation between philosophy and systematic theology within educational institutions that are meant to embody St. Thomas's conviction that *sacra doctrina* brings classical philosophical inquiry to perfection by standards of intellectual perfection that nonbelieving philosophers themselves can recognize, or be led to recognize, as legitimate.

As I see it, the only remotely plausible justifications for such a separation are purely *practical* ones—for example, that the cultures of theology and philosophy are at present too diverse to tolerate any attempt at a merger; or that given the disdain for religion and theology characteristic of top-rated graduate programs in philosophy, Catholic colleges will be unable to place their philosophy majors in such graduate programs unless they clearly distinguish them from theology majors.

But it is not at all clear how serious these problems really are. The cultures of both professional philosophy and professional theology seem especially fluid at the present time in North America. In addition, within academia there is a general recognition of—and dissatisfaction with—the artificiality of disciplinary boundaries in the humanities.

As for the second worry, the prejudice against those who have graduated from Catholic colleges with joint philosophy/theology degrees may not be any worse than the current prejudice against those who have graduated from Catholic colleges with "straight" philosophy degrees. (At Notre Dame we are now running a successful joint undergraduate program in philosophy and theology, and some of its graduates have gone on to advanced studies in philosophy, including a Rhodes scholar who is presently at Oxford University.)

Moreover, even if these problems are in fact serious, they are by no means insurmountable. I for one have no doubt that if we are sufficiently creative and self-confident, we can find ways to resolve or at least circumvent them without abandoning a distinctively Catholic vision of the nature of philosophical inquiry. In this connection it is worth noting Alasdair MacIntyre's observation that the biggest obstacle facing St. Thomas and later Thomists in the thirteenth and fourteenth centuries was precisely "the power of the institutionalized curriculum," and that the truly amazing thing is "the way in which Aquinas was repeatedly revived and invoked after that initial rehabilitation which led to his canonization."[25] Perhaps another radical revolt against the "institutionalized curriculum" is in order.[26] Why, after all, should we rest easy with a situation in which undergraduate philosophy majors in many Catholic colleges and universities receive a philosophical formation that is virtually indistinguishable from what they would have received in secular schools? Indeed, even though the sharp separation between philosophy and theology predates the ravages of secularization in Catholic colleges and universities, the prevailing idea that philosophy is independent of the faith has in its own way facilitated that secularization.

I am under no illusion that Catholic colleges and universities, especially those presently headed toward becoming second- or third-rate imitations of their more prestigious secular counterparts, will any time soon voluntarily undertake to restructure their philosophy and theology curricula in ways consonant with our distinctive intellectual tradition.[27] But the present time is rife with possibilities, and like-minded faculty on both sides of the divide should be looking for opportunities to subvert the "institutionalized curriculum."

### CONCLUSION

It hardly needs saying that I have merely skimmed the surface in these brief reflections, and I do not claim to have addressed every issue that needs to be addressed or to have answered every objection that needs to be answered. Still, I believe that it is a propitious time for us as Catholic philosophers to stop worrying about crossing some imaginary boundary between philosophy and theology, and to be forthright and creative in presenting the Catholic claim to wisdom in as attractive a light as we can to our students as well as to intellectually sophisticated nonbelievers. In this we will only be following in the footsteps of our most illustrious predecessor.[28]

### NOTES

1. The writings range from *Thomism in an Age of Renewal* (Garden City: Doubleday, 1966), which continues to reward rereading even thirty years later, to *The Question of Christian Ethics* (Washington, D.C.: Catholic University of America Press, 1993), along with many less extensive pieces in between.

2. See *Summa Theologiae* 1, q. 1, art. 6, and *Summa Contra Gentiles* 1, chaps. 1–9.

3. The aspiration to exhibit the "unity of truth" across the liberal arts and sciences is a defining characteristic of the Catholic university according to Pope John Paul II's Apostolic Constitution *Ex Corde Ecclesiae* (1990). In contrast, today's typical big university is a knowledge factory shattered into many fragmentary units, each motivated almost exclusively by narrow self-interest. And because they have lost, or despaired of, or grown skeptical of the ideal of the unity of truth, university administrators find themselves unable to articulate a coherent vision of the whole that is capable of uniting their disparate constituencies under the flag of a common project.

4. I develop this line of thought at more length in "Faith and Reason," in Paul V. Spade, ed., *The Cambridge Companion to Ockham* (Cambridge: Cambridge University Press, 1998).

5. John Crosby has posed this challenge: "Isn't it obviously the case that, say, the

metaphysics of first principles offered by Aristotle in *Metaphysics* 4 is more properly philosophical than a treatise on Eucharistic theology?" I concede that most professional philosophers would answer affirmatively; but the reasons for this are contingent. First, in our culture most philosophers are not Catholics and hence are not tempted, say, to offer courses on Eucharistic theology. (In contrast, at my own university I teach philosophy courses on St. Thomas's moral theory—something that cannot be done responsibly without including the order of grace and salvation.) Second, many of today's philosophers operate with a conception of philosophy that a priori excludes revealed truths from the domain of philosophical inquiry. But this, too, is a contingent matter. Remember that in the heyday of logical positivism, metaphysics and "normative" moral theory were excluded by the prevailing conception of philosophy.

6. This "Gorgian" valuation is suggested by the ubiquitous claim that the main justification for requiring philosophy courses in the undergraduate curriculum is that they help students think clearly and convincingly about significant metaphysical and moral issues. One sometimes gets the impression that the question of just which conclusions students reach with their newly enhanced powers of reasoning and persuasion falls outside of the proper purview of teachers of philosophy. On such a view, we may *prefer* that our students hold one set of beliefs rather than another, but we will have succeeded *qua* teachers of philosophy as long as they can argue well for whatever beliefs they might adopt.

7. See especially *Summa Contra Gentiles* 1, chaps. 1–3, and 9, where wisdom in the sense expounded above is explicitly set forth as the goal of philosophical inquiry. We must, of course, keep in mind St. Thomas's distinction between being wise *by way of inclination* and being wise *by way of cognition* (see *Summa Theologiae* 1, ques. 1, art. 6, and 2-2, ques. 45, art. 2). All devout Christians possess the gift of wisdom, which enables them to order and judge things correctly by way of inclination and to act promptly on those judgments; this is the wisdom that accompanies the supernatural love of God and is especially well developed in those who lead saintly lives. On the other hand, those versed in sacred doctrine acquire through study the ability to make wise judgments about divine things by way of cognition. As with other good habits, it is better, all other things being equal, to have wisdom in both ways than to have it in just one; but given that one has it in only one way, it is better to be wise by way of inclination than merely by way of cognition.

8. This interpretation of chapter 4 might not at first be obvious, because St. Thomas initially characterizes the philosophers as those who study created things in terms of "their own proper causes," thus suggesting that "human philosophy" is exhausted by what I have called the ancillary philosophical disciplines. But he then adds: "Sometimes divine wisdom results from the principles of human philosophy. For even among the philosophers First Philosophy uses the teachings of all the sciences to prove what it intends." The idea is that even though metaphysics integrates all human philosophy "from above," the only *access* that the *philosophi* had to metaphysical wisdom was "from below." The *fideles*, in contrast, have an added route to that wisdom through divine revelation.

9. Joseph Cardinal Ratzinger, "Faith, Philosophy, and Theology," *John Paul II Lecture Series* (St. Paul: College of St. Thomas, 1985), p. 11.

10. As Chesterton aptly remarks, "Reason is itself a matter of faith. It is an act of faith to assert that our thoughts have any relation to reality at all." See *Orthodoxy* (San Francisco: Ignatius Press [1908], 1995), p. 38.

11. Given my own fondness for Francisco Suarez and the seeming penchant of

some contemporary Catholic authors to blame every historical distortion of St. Thomas's thought on the Jesuits in general and on Suarez or his progeny in particular, I hasten to point out that the mere fact that Suarez authored the *Disputationes Metaphysicae* as a "narrowly" philosophical work is not a sufficient reason for imputing to him the idea that philosophy and philosophical inquiry are strictly independent of theology. First of all, the *Disputationes Metaphysicae* were explicitly intended to provide students of theology with what the study of Aristotle's *Metaphysics* was supposed to be providing them with, but was not in fact doing so in Suarez's estimation. Second, Suarez goes out of his way in the Preface to make clear to the reader that the *Disputationes Metaphysicae* are ordered toward the articulation of Christian doctrine: "In this work I am doing philosophy in such a way as to keep always in mind that our philosophy should be Christian and a servant to divine Theology. I have kept this goal in view, not only in discussing the questions but also in choosing my views or opinions, inclining toward those which seem to comport better with piety and revealed doctrine."

12. Alvin Plantinga, "Advice to Christian Philosophers," *Faith and Philosophy* 1 (1984): 253–71. Over the past twenty years, Plantinga's has been the most eloquent and compelling voice within analytic circles urging Christian philosophers to stand firm as articulators of the faith in their philosophical endeavors and not to accommodate themselves to the many current philosophical trends and research programs that are deeply anti-Christian in their root assumptions. To be sure, "Advice to Christian Philosophers" could perhaps have been more accurately entitled "Advice to Theistic Philosophers." However, in "Christian Philosophy at the End of the 20th Century," in Sander Griffioen and Bert Balk, eds., *Christian Philosophy at the Close of the Twentieth Century* (Kampen: Kok, 1995), pp. 29–53 (available on the worldwide web at www.faithquest.com/philosophers/plantinga/20th.html), and in his latest book, *Warranted Christian Belief* (New York: Oxford University Press, forthcoming), Plantinga goes beyond mere theism to defend the epistemic credentials of faith in revealed Christian doctrines.

13. *Nicomachean Ethics* 1.3 1094b24. This passage is cited by St. Thomas in *Summa Contra Gentiles* 1, chap. 3, just before he introduces the distinction between the preambles of the faith and the mysteries of the faith.

14. For instance, Notre Dame's doctoral program in theology is divided into five semiautonomous areas: (1) Christianity and Judaism in Antiquity, (2) the History of Christianity, (3) Liturgical Studies, (4) Moral Theology/Christian Ethics, and (5) Philosophical and Systematic Theology. A student may get a doctorate in theology by taking advanced graduate courses in just three—and in some cases two—of these five areas.

The best theologians are themselves well aware of the deleterious consequences of the fragmentation of their discipline. See, e.g., Servais Pinckaers, O.P., *The Sources of Christian Ethics* (Washington, D.C.: Catholic University of America Press, 1995), esp. chapters 1 and 2, where Pinckaers decries the relatively recent separation of moral theology from the "spiritual" theology of the Church Fathers, a separation that occurred in the Renaissance when morality ceased to be thought of as a road to happiness (or salvation) and came to be thought of instead as mainly a matter of not violating negative moral precepts. From the other side, some powerful Catholic philosophical voices have been raised in protest against the bifurcation of philosophy (especially metaphysics and moral theory) from theology. See, e.g., Frederick Wilhelmsen, *The Metaphysics of Love* (New York: Sheed and Ward, 1962), esp. pp. 13–19; Josef Pieper, *Problems of Modern Faith* (Chicago: Franciscan Herald

Press, 1985), esp. pp. 265–76; and Adriaan Theodoor Perperzak, "Philosophia," *Faith and Philosophy* 14 (1997): pp. 321–33.

15. In this paper I am addressing just the issue of how Catholic philosophers should think of their relation to non-Christian philosophers, since contemporary philosophers are predominantly non-Christians. Still, a complete treatment of the relevant issues would also address the question of how Catholic philosophers should think of their relation to philosophers who are non-Catholic Christians. I will postpone that discussion until a later time.

16. In "Faith and Reason" I argue at length for this and the other claims made in this paragraph.

17. What I have to say here is prompted in part by John Haldane's "What Future Has Catholic Philosophy?" *American Catholic Philosophical Quarterly* (Annual Proceedings of the American Catholic Philosophical Association) 77 (1997): 79–90. In the first few pages of his essay Haldane consigns all of "continental philosophy" to the scrap heap and singles out Heidegger, Sartre, Derrida, and Foucault as "examples of intellectual corruption" (p. 81)—a judgment that he assumes his audience of Catholic philosophers will unreservedly concur with. He then urges all Catholic philosophers to embrace the "analytical tradition" of twentieth-century philosophy as the fitting contemporary manifestation of "the spirit of scholastic Aristotelianism." While I have little problem with the idea that some Catholic philosophers should be active in the mainstream of analytic philosophy, I believe that (1) Haldane misunderstands the saga of philosophy departments in Catholic universities over the past thirty years, that (2) his estimation of the virtues of the "analytical tradition" is myopic, and that (3) implementing his suggestion would worsen an already lamentable situation. Some of what I say below will at least hint at my reasons for making this judgment, but I will defer to a later time a full response to Haldane's paper.

18. Alasdair MacIntyre, *Three Rival Versions of Moral Inquiry: Encyclopedia, Genealogy, and Tradition* (Notre Dame: University of Notre Dame Press, 1990), pp. 145–48.

19. See John Paul II, *Ex Corde Ecclesiae*, #8. Ironically, at a time when certain American philosophers are making bold to echo aloud Daniel Dennett's sentiment that "safety demands that religions be put in cages," some Catholics who should know better are still persisting in the adolescent antipapalism of the 1960s and 1970s. The world seems to have passed them by and, as I can attest from personal experience, many of today's Catholic college students are not failing to notice this.

20. I call the relevant type of certitude "evidential" in order to distinguish this certitude, which constitutes a natural intellectual perfection for us, from the "certitude of adherence" proper to our grasp of the objects of Christian faith. See *Summa Theologiae* 2-2, ques. 4, art. 8, and *De Veritate*, ques. 14, art. 2, ad 7.

21. By "bare classical theism" I mean the thesis that there is an absolutely perfect being and, more specifically, that there is an omnipotent, omniscient, and perfectly good God.

22. For instance, I would not hesitate for a moment to insist that contemporary Catholic philosophers writing or lecturing on the problem of evil should study carefully Pope John Paul II's magnificent Apostolic Letter *Salvifici Doloris* as part of their intellectual preparation.

23. Pinckaers, *The Sources of Christian Ethics*, p. 292.

24. Interestingly, the separation of philosophy departments from theology depart-

ments that one finds in some denominationally Protestant colleges appears to have a rather different genesis. When I asked my colleague Alvin Plantinga about this, he surmised that the philosophy departments in such colleges had their origins in the conviction, deeply felt in at least some Reformed circles, that students of theology should be acquainted with the history of philosophy. Later, because of pressures to prepare promising students for graduate work in philosophy, the philosophy curriculum evolved from its primarily historical orientation to something more in tune, both substantively and methodologically, with what was going on in the most prestigious graduate programs in philosophy. Still, Plantinga remarked, evangelical Christians who choose careers in academic philosophy have always been encouraged and even expected to use their philosophical training as a tool for articulating and defending the Christian faith.

25. MacIntyre, *Three Rival Versions of Moral Inquiry: Encyclopedia, Genealogy, and Tradition*, p. 151.

26. In the spring of 1998 a group of over twenty Notre Dame students, predominantly philosophy and theology majors, wanted to study the encyclicals *Veritatis Splendor* and *Evangelium Vitae* along with the parts of St. Thomas's moral theory pertinent to them. Since no such course was contained in the philosophy or theology curriculum, they simply prevailed upon the man to whom this paper is dedicated to meet with them once a week for credit in a readings course. Upon hearing about this, a colleague remarked to me that it reminded him of the 1960s. Such is the stuff of radical curricular reform.

27. Just for the record, I admit that in some ways the separation of philosophy departments from theology departments has been a blessing over the last twenty-five years, given the culture of dissent that has permeated many theology departments at major Catholic institutions of higher learning. Some of us who profess fidelity to the magisterium of the Church have found the philosophy departments in such institutions to be places of refuge where we can carry on our research and teaching with freedom. However, my argument is predicated on the assumption that this deplorable situation is a temporary aberration.

28. Earlier versions of this paper were delivered at the 1997 Patristic, Medieval, and Renaissance conference at Villanova University and at the Franciscan University of Steubenville. I am grateful for the many helpful comments I received on both occasions, as well as for the comments of my colleague Thomas Flint.

# 14

# From Analogy of "Being" to the Analogy of Being

*David B. Burrell, C.S.C.*

Ralph McInerny's philosophical reflection has been framed by careful and subtle probings into the analogous uses of language, where the inquiry has been motivated by an irenic yet persistent corrective to the tradition which has called itself "Thomist," taking issue first with the sixteenth-century commentator par excellence of Thomas Aquinas, Thomas de Vio Cajetan.[1] From *The Logic of Analogy* (1961) and *Studies in Analogy* (1968) to *Aquinas and Analogy* (1996), his goal has been consistent and unyielding: to show how Aquinas managed to articulate the logical and semantic structure of language in such a way as to display its analogical reaches. Hence his untiring emphasis: analogy is a logical doctrine in Aquinas. That is not to say, however, that attention to analogical uses of language has no metaphysical payoff; it is simply to note that conflating the two risks harming both. More precisely, a precipitate move to metaphysical assertion without careful preliminary attention to language will invariably overlook Aquinas's reminder that the "mode proper to metaphysical inquiry is logical" and so unwittingly resolve to the imagination.[2] This animadversion captures the point of McInerny's most mature reflections on these matters:

> if the "analogy of being" refers to real relations, so that what is first is the cause of what is secondary, and if "analogous names" involve an ordered plurality of meanings of a common name in which the first, controlling meaning, the *ratio propria*, is not the cause of the rest, the difference is as important as the difference between logical and real orders. Thomas Aquinas took this difference between the order of our knowledge and the order of being to be decisive as between Plato and Aristotle. He accuses Plato of confusing these two orders and assuming that what is first in our knowing is first in being. Any confusion of the logical and real orders comes under the same criticism. A correct understanding of Thomas on

analogy saves him from the grievous mistake he attributed to Plato. (*Aquinas and Analogy,* 162–63)

The Plato whom Aquinas knew, of course, was the one whom Aristotle criticized and the one filtered through Proclus in the *Liber de Causis,* on which Aquinas commented.[3] So McInerny's criticism is not of Plato but of Thomists who either confused these two orders or presumed a ready parallel between them, thereby constructing an "analogy of being" which was touted as the keystone of Aquinas's metaphysical "system."

Yet of course there is a parallel between real and logical orders for Aquinas, assured by the originating fact of creation. Its apprehension by us, however, will always be inverted, as "we are aware that what we last name is what is ontologically first," so that "knowledge of the source of all being of whom finally we know what he is not rather than what he is, ... is the ultimate point of philosophizing" (160–61)—not its beginning. Words like these would have warmed Karl Barth's heart, for the *analogia entis* which he found anathema to authentic Christian theology claimed that sort of parallelism between real and logical orders which McInerny is anxious to subvert by inverting. Moreover, this was claimed in the name of the real Aquinas, to whom it had been unwarrantedly attributed. Yet these summary remarks are dense, offered by McInerny as a valedictory to his latest clarifications of Aquinas's teaching regarding analogous uses of language. The standard set by these clarifications is exceedingly high, representing as they do some thirty-five years of sifting and of simplifying by a mind as subtle as it is witty; and subtlety and wit are the very stuff of recognizing and employing the analogous reaches of language. I shall be arguing that McInerny's reflections have as much to do with doing philosophy as they have with Thomas Aquinas's teaching; indeed, that analogy is at the very heart of doing philosophy, especially of a philosophy which seeks to integrate the Jewish, Christian, and Muslim conviction that the universe is freely created by one God. If it is that belief which assured Aquinas that the order of logic and of reality are indeed isomorphic, it is the same teaching which reminds us that we know God better the more we realize that we do not know our creator, as Aquinas frequently put it. So the two orders, of logic and of reality, will be the inverse image of each other in these reaches.

### CREATION AND PARTICIPATION

The remarks we have identified as valedictory to McInerny's treatment of analogy represent a fine specimen of philosophy serving as handmaid to faith, for the philosophizing in this book stops short of what is identified as philosophy's "ultimate point: knowledge of the source of all being of whom finally we know what he is not rather than what he is" (*Aquinas and Analogy*, 161). One explicit point of McInerny's book is to show that identifying the activity of analogous naming with "the causal dependence in a hierarchical descent of all things from God" (162) could mislead others about that source of all being. How so? It could, for example, lead one to suspect that we could know the character of that hierarchical descent, or that such a descent might already be inscribed in our language, so that we would feel no need to learn the specific practices associated with using terms of God that we have learned to use in our context. In other words, we might be tempted to turn philosophy into a proto-theology which could give us an adequate understanding of God—exactly Barth's complaint about *analogia entis* as it had been presented to him. Indeed, philosophy's preferred way of accounting for the origination of all things, the necessary emanation scheme of al-Farabi, which Aquinas came to know in Avicenna's amended version, promises just such a knowledge. Moreover, Aquinas was sufficiently taken with it to have recourse to it as an image for the unimaginable act of creating, yet only after he had shown it to be both false and redundant as an explanatory scheme.[4] False, because the model of logical deduction which animated the scheme assured that the First in such a scheme could not adequately be distinguished from the premises which followed from it; redundant, because the act of creation must be the act of a cause of being whose effect follows immediately from it, absent any motion or mediation. Indeed, this is a paradigmatic instance of Aquinas's philosophical inquiry being shaped by premises from faith. The telling text is imbedded in a question regarding God's triunity, where it is asked whether the trinity of the divine persons can be known by natural reason. Aquinas captures the opportunity offered by a sophistical objection—that knowledge of the trinity must be accessible to reason since it would be superfluous to teach what cannot be known by natural reason, yet it would hardly be becoming to say that the divine tradition of the trinity was superfluous—to offer "two reasons why the knowledge of the divine persons was necessary for us," and the first envisages "the right idea of creation: the fact of saying that God made all things by His Word excludes the error of those who say that God produced things by necessity, [a corollary of the emanation scheme. Moreover,] when we say that in Him there is a procession of love, we show that God produced creatures not because He needed them, nor because of any other extrinsic reason, but on account of the love of His own goodness" (*Sum. Theol.* [=*ST*] 1.32.1.3).

Philosophy could lead one, Aquinas thought, to understand that the universe must have been originated, but the prevailing schemes for elucidating that origination had dire consequences for a proper conception of the First as well as for human freedom, so the findings of faith will be required—"necessary," as he puts it—to have the "right idea of" this origination, as an utterly free creation. As Josef Pieper has remarked, creation is the "hidden element in the philosophy of St. Thomas"—perhaps hidden because, correctly understood, it requires a theological premise if it is to be properly understood.[5] This example offers us a tangible instance where philosophy can serve the faith yet cannot pretend to elucidate the entire story by its own resources. It bears on McInerny's treatment of analogy, for whatever exiguous knowledge we might have of God would be severely threatened without the resources of analogous language. The medieval witness to such a state of affairs was Moses Maimonides, who argued strenuously that no terms could be employed of both God and creatures, given the crucial "distinction" between creator and creatures.[6] His arguments did not turn on the immense "distance" between God and creatures so much as on what Kierkegaard would call "the infinite qualitative difference." It is not that God's justice far outstrips ours, but rather that any statement made about God's being just would be ill-formed, since it would presume by its very structure that justice is an attribute of God, whereas God—to be God—must be utterly simple (1.57). So there can be, "in no way or sense, anything common to the attributes predicated of God, and those used in reference to ourselves; they have only the same names, and nothing else is common to them." Otherwise, one might believe "that there is in God something additional to His essence, in the same way as attributes are joined to our essence" (1. 56). So the radical difference between the creator and creatures precludes any use of the same terms, since the very form of predication belies the manner in which God is just. This chapter (56) contains a passing reference to a set of terms which might so function, called "amphibolous" by Harry Wolfson, and ill-defined by Maimonides as "applied to two things which have a similarity to each other in respect to a certain property which is in both of them an accident, not an essential, constituent element."[7] Maimonides rejects such a suggestion, since "the attributes of God are not considered as accidental by any intelligent person." The idea seems to be that such terms could not be predicated properly of either creatures or creator, since the shared accidental feature is extrinsic to both.

If we prescind from his inadequate characterization of a usage which might have been identified as *analogous,* this observation of Maimonides is telling for our reflections on Cajetan and Aquinas, since Cajetan's insistence on *proportionality* as the normal form for properly analogous usage turns on whether or not the *ratio* can be predicated intrinsically of both subjects. Recalling Aquinas's favorite example of "health," it is easy to see that "healthy" can be attributed properly only to an organism, so there is no *something* which healthy medicine shares with a healthy organism. Rather, medicine is called "healthy" by virtue of its role in helping to cure a diseased organism. Yet Aquinas does not hesitate to offer this form of analogous usage as the model for our speaking of a just God. Note how Aquinas accepts Maimonides' criteria here: there is no *something*, no shared feature by which Socrates and God might each be said to be just.[8] As if to echo the Rambam, Aquinas eschews any similarity between God and creatures except for "the sort of analogy that holds between all things because they have existence in common" (*ST* 1.4.3). Yet *existence* (*esse*) cannot be a feature, so he goes on to specify: "this is how things receiving existence from God [*illa quae sunt a Deo*] resemble him; for precisely as things possessing existence [*inquantum sunt entia*] they resemble the primary and universal source of all existence [*esse*]." I have inserted the Latin here to illustrate how the Blackfriars translator, Timothy McDermott, has brought what Pieper called the "hidden element" in Aquinas's philosophical treatment into the clear light of day. There need not be any feature intrinsic to creator and creature to use the same term of both; indeed, there could be none such a priori if we are to respect "the distinction" between them; indeed, their "infinite qualitative difference." We are required, however, to advert to the foundational fact that whatever perfections creatures possess "must pre-exist in God in a higher manner . . . since God is the primary operative cause of all things" (*ST* 1.4.2). Without the offices of a creator, analogous predication would have to be assured by an inherent proportionality between the related uses of a term. Yet as we shall see, it is precisely recognition of God as the cause of being which allows that the same terms may be predicated of creator and of creatures, without thereby implying that there be *something* they both hold in common. Whatever *analogia entis* there may be has to be governed by the rules which Maimonides discerned, the "distinction" which Sokolowski has articulated, as well as the negation which "dialectical theology" demands—all of which is already present in Aquinas's insistence that "we cannot know what God is, but only what he is not" (*ST* 1.3., Prol.), articulated in McInerny's trenchant reminder of what knowledge we can expect to have of the "source of all being."

These summary remarks (of McInerny's) which we have been probing are contained in a chapter entitled "Analogy and Participation," as if to remind us that if Aquinas "does not call the real hierarchy of being an analogy of being" (156), he does structure it according to the Platonic notion of *participation*.[9] But that notion too is imported in an attempt to characterize the relation of creatures to the creator, once one has so accentuated their difference. So once again, *creation* emerges as the central, if unaccented, reality. It is as though we need to have a subset of terms—those intending *perfections*—which may be used of both creatures and creator, but we will use them properly only when "we are aware that what we last name is ontologically first" (160–61). That there be such a set of terms is, then, a necessary condition for their being used of both creator and of creature. What must be added to the terms (*parole*), however, is their use (*langue*) according to a heightened operative awareness that we are employing them here of beings and of the cause of being, of the One in whom they exist preeminently. Moreover, when said of the cause of being, they cannot be predicated as attributes, strictly speaking, but as part of what it is to be the One whose essence is simply to be. The role of *participation*, then, is to remind us that there could be no such set of terms were the universe not itself derived from a source from which all that is, and notably what is perfect about what-is, flows. So the ontological ground of the set of terms lies in the fact that all-that-is participates in the One from whom everything derives, and their proper use demands that we bring this grounding fact to awareness. Yet we can only assert it, knowing as little as we do how to express this all-important "distinction" and the consequent relations obtaining between creator and creatures.

What *participation* clarifies, however, is a crucial ambiguity in Cajetan's criterion that properly analogous usage demands that the feature in question be possessed inherently by each party of which it is predicated, albeit in a proportional manner. For if we fail to advert to creation, understood precisely as participation, then such a criterion will be read to imply that there can be no properly analogical predication unless there be a common feature, justice, itself predicable of both God and Socrates. But the presence of such a common feature would effectively deny "the distinction" of creator from creature, as Maimonides articulates so well: to treat the creator as an item in the universe, which a shared feature would imply, is to deny the basis of Jewish, Christian, and Muslim faith in the free creation of the universe by one God. Indeed, what the device of *participation* is designed to do is to show us how "just" can be attributed to creatures as well as to the creator *without* there being a feature, justice, common to both. *Pari passu*, the *res significata* of the analogous term, justice, need not be accessible to our understanding for us to use the term properly. We need only to be aware that it is a perfection, and so will outstrip any realization that we come across of it—indeed, it must do so if it is to function as it should, lest we have nothing but a conventional ethics, that is to say, no ethics at all! We will be more inclined to acknowledge that feature in practice the more we recognize that all such perfections have their preeminent source in a creator.

So here too, a properly analogous use of analogous terms demands an awareness that we are functioning as creatures ourselves in a created *order* whose principles remains unknown to us, yet whose lineaments can be glimpsed from time to time. Creatures can be just in their fashion, and hence properly be said to be so: the term "just" can be predicated of them inherently, without there being a proportional similarity between God's justice and theirs. For as the cause of being, the creator is not an extrinsic cause of creatures, since their very to-be is to-be-in-relation to the creator. That is why Aquinas can say that to-be [*esse*] is "more intimately and profoundly interior to things than anything else" (*ST* 1.8.1), and it is precisely this *esse* which accounts for whatever similarity can be had between creator and creature. Indeed, created *esse* brings them so close that the nonreciprocal relation of dependence, which is participated being, can be likened to Sankara's notion of *nonduality:* the distinction does not amount to a separation, as though God could be pictured as one more being over against the universe.[10] Ralph McInerny may never have suspected how his careful work in the semantics of analogous terms could facilitate moves so apparently radical as these; or again he may well have done so, but forbore drawing such conclusions, for they smack more of philosophical theology while he wished to underscore philosophy's ancillary role. Yet without such astute servants the fare which theology serves can be ill-chosen and underdone.

PRACTICES TO HEIGHTEN AWARENESS: LANGUE AND PAROLE

Keeping the orders of discourse and of being distinct is a taxing job, notably for philosophers whose very trade involves using discourse to articulate what-is by showing the way it must be! Here is where Etienne Gilson's observations that "'analogy' for Aquinas refers to our capacity to make the kind of judgments we do" can illuminate McInerny's strategy as well as help us spell out its implications for our practice in doing philosophical theology especially.[11] Whoever understands that analogy is to be explicated "on the level of judgment" and not of concepts, Gilson contends, has also grasped the real divergence between Aquinas and Scotus.[12] He corroborates his point by noting, as does McInerny, that all discussion of "analogy of being" or of "analogous concepts" is utterly foreign to Aquinas, who speaks rather of "terms used analogously." Judgment is indispensable precisely because responsible analogous usage requires that we assess the way in which a term is being used in relation to its primary analogate. Yet such an assessment demands both that we identify the primary analogate as well as grasp how the use in question relates to it, and each of these apperceptions involves judgment. In practice, this comes to adducing appropriate examples, like the ones needed to make this very point.[13] If we think of a relatively neutral but highly analogous term like "order," we can imagine any number of situations in which the term may be properly used, while each varies widely from the other. A compulsive personality may need a clean desk at work yet learn to tolerate a great deal of mess at home, especially when children are young. She could still find herself spontaneously "cleaning up" when she comes home, however, especially if she brings a colleague who has no children into her home. Yet if she relates appropriately to each environment, she knows that her own sanity demands that she respect the order proper to each. In such cases, the term is properly context-dependent, so there is no set "primary analogate"; each case establishes a base line for proper use, which can be formulated functionally: an environment is "in order" when we can interact appropriately in it.

When such a term is attributed to the creator, however, the issue of a prime analogate quickly becomes problematic. Consider Aquinas's insistence that "the order of the universe as a whole is the object proper to God's intention, ... the direct object of God's creating act and intended by God" (*ST* 1.15.2). Whatever uses of the term "order" may be functionally proper to environments in which we have come to be at home will doubtless fail when speaking of the "order of the universe," yet we do know that *order* must accompany intelligent agency. Here one's adeptness at shifting contexts in which the term can properly be used will doubtless help in assessing how little we can expect to understand the order God intends in a universe we apprehend so minimally. Our emerging consciousness of ecological realities, contrasted with the way in which we have proceeded to "improve" a natural order in the direction of serving human needs, yet quite oblivious to the complexities of that order itself, offer some salutary reminders of the difficulty of identifying the "order of creation." What we have discovered here is our endemic tendency to align the primary analogate with human needs as we perceive them; and a similar predilection clearly operates in the usual conundra spelled out with regard to human suffering or so-called "natural evil." Where these become ludicrous, indeed, is when any one of us attempts to "explain" to someone else the place their suffering holds in "God's plan." Indeed, the very use of the term "plan" to introduce the order the creator bestows in creating begs the question, since plans and planning must be part of our ordering process (and so belong to our *mode of signifying*) but need not characterize the way divine wisdom is operative in creating at all. So what we "intend to mean" (the *res significata*) in speaking of "the order of the universe [which] is the direct object of God's creating act" lies utterly beyond our conceptual capacities. We can at best use our practiced judgment to recognize that we do not and cannot know it, all the while trusting that the universe is ordered. So analogous usage, especially in such domains, demands that we eschew any straightforward grasp of the *res significata,* relying on an astute judgment regarding the direction of the pointers which we can articulate, much as Aristotle observed that properly metaphorical discourse required a deftness of judgment.[14]

Here is where we may have recourse to the work of Pierre Hadot to remind us that doing philosophy is ever a matter of the proper *exercises* and, in executing philosophical theology, of properly "spiritual exercises."[15] Indeed, it is questionable whether the reaches of analogical language can ever be appreciated so long as one identifies "philosophy" with a "set of propositional attitudes," effectively restricting philosophical inquiry to analyzing what can be formulated, abstracted from the form of life required to carry it out. Yet expressing the relationship between formulations and forms of life remains strangely elusive. Trying to do so, however, should illuminate Gilson's insistence that analogical usage involves exercising judgments regarding our use of the key terms in question, while identifying the character of those judgments will help us see how deeply faith is intertwined with carrying out philosophical inquiry. Trying to grasp this inner relation of formulation to practices may also clarify the way in which we are able to appreciate something about medieval philosophy which medievals themselves could not be expected to see, since they were immersed in it: the formative character of their particular world of faith, be it Jewish, Muslim, or Christian. When such forms of life take on the shape of intentional choices, as they must for us, their formative function is cast more clearly into relief, whereas so long as they remain the air one breathes, that crucial role will remain quite indiscernible.

Robert Sokolowski supplied me with the clue to this observation in his genial monograph, *The God of Faith and Reason,* where he introduces "the distinction" of God from creation as a decisively Christian achievement, "glimpsed on the margins of reason, . . . at the intersection of reason and faith."[16] By focusing on the key role which making *distinctions* plays in philosophical inquiry, and then turning the very notion of a *distinction* into a conceit or trope, he proceeds to identify just how unique is the relation of the creator-of-all with all that is created, something which Jewish and Muslim philosophers were also taxed to articulate.[17] "The distinction" then becomes a way of gesturing towards what indeed distinguishes those who believe the universe to be freely created by one God from those who do not. For the God in question would be God without creating all-that-is, so much so that everything-that-is adds nothing to the perfection of being of such a One. (To use a familiar abstract descriptor, that is what "monotheism" entails; not a simple reduction of the number of gods to one.) What makes this so significant philosophically is that it forbids any ordinary brand of "onto-theology" wherein a notion of *being* can be stretched to include the creator as well as creation.[18] Yet that is what philosophers seem to need: a univocal notion whereby we can find some sameness between creator and creatures, in order to predicate terms of God. That is what Scotus promised, in conjunction with his rejection of the analogical character of "being." And while it can be argued that the account of analogy which he rejected was that of Henry of Ghent and not that of Aquinas, the legacy stands, presumably because it answers so well to a standing predilection of philosophers.[19] What seems to defeat philosophers, ironically enough, is the practice of "Socratic unknowing." This practice of Plato's Socrates is linked with displaying a mode of discourse beyond the theoretical (Plato's *dianoia*), which Plato called "dialectic" and usually articulated in a mythic manner. What philosophical discourse could not realize had to be displayed in another idiom, gesturing towards something which language could only intimate.[20] Yet as Pierre Hadot reminds us, the intellectual exercise of dialogue itself could also be summed up as "dialectical," so the virtues which Socrates' interlocutors had to develop would have prepared them to respect the limits of the univocal discourse which theory (*dianoia*) requires, yet do so in such a way as to recognize that the very élan of their inquiry pointed beyond such language.

So philosophical dialogue, as exercised by Socrates, represents a mode of doing philosophy which is also a spiritual exercise, and which calls forth from its participants a palpable sense of "something more," something towards which the inquiry is directed and which can be said to guide it to the outcomes which it can attain. Plato called this lure "the Good," and the tradition which traced itself to Plato demanded of its adherents a way of living in relation to that Good which could not but affect the way in which they carried out intellectual inquiry. Medieval philosophers were often themselves participants in a vowed community life which made similar demands on them, demands which have also been called "spiritual exercises." How can we identify the connection between these ways of life and their use of philosophical discourse? In approaching Aquinas for an answer to this question, I have found it useful to attend to the matter-of-fact way in which he will put things which we find arresting. Consider, for example, the straightforward introduction to questions 3–11 at the outset of the *Summa Theologiae*, where he announces that "we cannot know what God is, but only what he is not, so we must consider the ways in which God does not exist, rather than the way in which he does." One could not, it seems, engage in "negative theology" so gracefully without having some other access to the One whose nature remains unknown to us, for philosophers trained in a modern idiom invariably find such statements utterly disconcerting. And that other access must be such that it does not reduce the "unknowing" but rather offers a way of living with it. In the terms which we have been using from Aquinas's treatment of discourse *in divinis*, we need not be able to articulate the *res significata* to assure ourselves that there is such. What we need to be able to do, however, is to recognize that the very terms we use have a reach beyond the *modus significandi* that is accessible to us. Indeed, their proper use in human contexts demands just that, as my allusion earlier to conventional morality suggested. Normative language needs to have a purchase on us which carries us beyond the descriptive domain of "everybody does it," and that must be inscribed in the key terms themselves, without our possessing a firm criterion for their transcendent use.[21] For that demand readily translates into asking one to articulate the *res significandi*, the prime analogate proper to the creator rather than the ones accessible to creatures.

Aquinas had explicit recourse to the creature/creator relation to respond to Maimonides' objections to our using our perfection terms of God: "any creature, in so far as it possesses any perfection, represents God and is like to him, for he, being simply and universally perfect, has pre-existing in himself the perfections of all his creatures. But a creature is not like to God as it is like to another member of its species or genus, . . . thus words like 'good' or 'wise' when used of God do signify something that God really is [*divinam substantiam*], but they signify it imperfectly because creatures represent God imperfectly" (*ST* 1.13.2). All of the semantic markers are here: the terms must be "perfection-terms," they cannot be univocal (pertaining to the same genus), and therefore they can "signify imperfectly" what they "intend to signify." Our capacity to do just that—intend to signify by the terms we employ—responds to the deeper objection of Maimonides, which Aquinas acknowledges: "when we say that a man is wise, we signify his wisdom as something distinct from other things about him—his essence, for example, his powers or his existence. But when we use this word about God we do not intend to signify something distinct from this essence, power or existence"

(*ST* 1.13.5). How can we do something like that? By the power of judgment which directs our use of the discourse we employ; Aquinas has recourse to this power in his final assessment of our ability to "name" the God we cannot know, a capacity that is displayed in the way we make statements: "God considered in himself is altogether one and simple, yet we think of him through a number of different concepts because we cannot see him as he is in himself. But although we think of him in these different ways we also know that to each corresponds a single simplicity that is one and the same for all. The different ways of thinking of him are represented in the difference of subject and predicate; his unity we represent by bringing them together in an affirmative statement" (*ST* 1.13.12). The translator (Herbert McCabe, O.P.) supplies "statement" here, but its addition is crucial for us to grasp how judgment enters in at this very point. Aquinas's term is *compositio*, which is the task he reserves to judgment, reminding us how, for Aristotle, propositions or sentences are parasitic upon the act of stating something to be the case, as *langue* is posterior to *parole*, to language in use.

So it is never enough to identify a subset of terms which are susceptible of analogous usage; one must always display them in use. And to do so will exhibit a judgment in operation; in this case, a judgment informed by "knowing that" in God a "single simplicity" corresponds to these distinct terms. It is this judgment which reminds us that the compositional form of the statements made is improper when used of God, so it belongs to judgment to factor such a "knowing that" into one's use, thereby offsetting the inherently misleading form of the statement itself. This will sound complicated to one who expects language to reflect on its face all that we accomplish when we use it properly; yet a bit of reflection shows that we make such subtle judgments all the time. In fact, when we cannot do so, our speech is justly described as "wooden." So analogous usage need not be justified; it only needs to be pointed out. Yet justifying using it with respect to God does require the explicit premise of creation. And Aquinas insists that we need a trinitarian revelation if we are going to get that relation right, so Pierre Hadot's observations about the need to understand philosophical inquiry in terms of the modes of life consonant with it are vindicated in Aquinas's case. For revelation can never be a simple fact; it always requires our commensurate response. Such at least is the testimony of any faith-tradition, to which we must have recourse to learn the proper use of a term like "revelation." Yet it should not appear all that strange that a thesis like Ralph McInerny's—that "analogy" is a linguistic doctrine—should lead to such consequences, for language in use can take many forms, and respecting them, as Aristotle and McInerny note, is the mark of a wise person.

### NOTES

1. *The Logic of Analogy* (1961) and *Studies in Analogy* (1968) (The Hague: Martinus Nijhoff) to *Aquinas and Analogy* (Washington, D.C.: Catholic University of America Press, 1996).

2. *In 4 Metaphysica* 4, 574.

3. See the recent English translation of Aquinas's *Commentary of the Book of Causes* by Vincent Guagliardo, O.P., Charles Hess, O.P., and Richard Taylor (Washington, D.C.: Catholic University of America Press, 1996).

4. This is the burden of my comparative study: *Knowing the Unknowable God: Ibn Sina, Maimonides, Aquinas* (Notre Dame: University of Notre Dame Press, 1986).

5. Josef Pieper, *The Silence of St. Thomas* (New York: Pantheon, 1957): "The Negative Element in the Philosophy of St. Thomas," 47–67.

6. See Maimonides, *Guide for the Perplexed* 1.51–60; for this use of "the distinction" see Robert Sokolowski, *The God of Faith and Reason* (Notre Dame: University of Notre Dame Press, 1981), and my interfaith commentary: "The Christian Distinction Celebrated and Expanded," in John Drummond and James Hart, eds., *The Truthful and the Good* (Boston: Kluwer, 1996), 191–206.

7. The Arabic term is *b'ishtarâk;* I tend to use Friedlander's translation (New York: Dover, 1956), corrected from the Arabic where needed, since his use of philosophical terminology is more predictable than Pines (Chicago: University of Chicago Press, 1963), whose translations are lexically correct but often oblivious to philosophical terminology.

8. See my *Knowing the Unknowable God* (note 4) and Alexander Broadie, "Maimonides and Aquinas on the Names of God," *Religious Studies* 23 (1987).

9. For a sterling treatment of this topic, see Rudi te Velde, *Participation and Substantiality in Thomas Aquinas* (Leiden: Brill, 1995); see my review in *International Philosophical Quarterly* 37 (1997): 101–4.

10. On this comparison, see Sara Grant R. S. C. J., *Towards an Alternative Theology: Confessions of a Nondualist Christian* (Bangalore: Asian Trading Corporation, 1991), and Kathryn Tanner, *God and Creation in Christian Theology* (Oxford: Blackwell, 1988).

11. Etienne Gilson, *Christian Philosophy of Saint Thomas* (New York: Random House, 1956) 105–7; *Jean Duns Scot* (Paris: Vrin, 1952), 101; the relevant texts he cites in Aquinas can be found in *ST* 1.13.5–6, 1.13.10.4; *Contra Gentiles* 1.34, 2.15.

12. See my "Aquinas and Scotus: Contrary Patterns for Philosophical Theology," in Bruce D. Marshall, ed., *Theology and Dialogue* (Notre Dame: University of Notre Dame Press, 1990), 105–29.

13. That such strategies are not foreign to McInerny can be gleaned from his reflections on Soren Kierkegaard's use of examples in philosophy, to say nothing of his prolific fiction!

14. Aristotle contends that being a "master of metaphor . . . is a sign of genius since a good metaphor implies an intuitive perception of the similarity in dissimilars" (1459a5).

15. For an illuminating introduction to the work of Pierre Hadot in English, see *Philosophy as a Way of Life*, ed. Arnold Davidson (Cambridge, Mass.: Blackwell, 1995); for a synopsis, see his *Qu'est-ce que la philosophie antique?* (Paris: Gallimard, 1995).

16. See Sokolowski, *The God of Faith and Reason*, p. 39.

17. See my "The Christian Distinction Celebrated and Expanded," note 6 above.

18. See J-L Marion, "Saint Thomas d'Aquin et l'onto-théologie," *Revue Thomiste* 95 (1995): 31–66, where he expands on his Preface to the English edition of *God Without Being* (Chicago: University of Chicago Press, 1991).

19. See my *Analogy and Philosophical Language* (New Haven: Yale University Press, 1973), 96, and on the larger point, Eric Alliez, *Capital Times*, trans. Georges Ven Den Abbeele (Minneapolis: University of Minnesota Press, 1996).

20. For a telling example, consider the words of Socrates which form a transition to the closing myth in the Phaedo: "if you analyze [the initial hypotheses] adequately, you will, I believe, follow the argument to the furthest point to which a human being can follow it up; and if you get that clear, you'll seek nothing further" (107b5–10).

21. The work of Julius Kovesi, *Moral Notions* (London: Routledge & Keegan Paul, 1971), continues to be fruitful here.

# INDEX

Abraham, W., 198
Achilles, 114
Adams, J., 158
Albertus Magnus, 15, 23
Albert of Saxony, 14–15
Allan, D. J., 105, 122
Allen, I., 174
Alliez, E., 266
Alston, W., 191, 196, 198, 225
Anaximander, 40
Anscombe, G. E. M., 48, 100
Antigone, 63–64
Aquilonis, F., 19, 23
Aquinas. *See* Thomas Aquinas
Arches, P., 17
Archimedes, 11, 13, 15, 17
Aristotle, 2–6, 11–18, 20–21, 25–26, 29, 31–34, 36–37, 39–40, 44, 57, 59–62, 65, 67, 71, 73–85, 87, 94, 99, 102–3, 105–8, 110–22, 124, 151, 166, 180–81, 186–87, 237, 241–42, 246, 249–51, 253–54, 261, 264–65
Armstrong, R. A., 118, 124
Audi, R., 104
Augustine of Hippo, 53–54, 56, 62, 64, 241
Avicebron (Ibn Gebirol), 41
Avicenna, 255

Bach, J. S., 114
Barnes, J., 72
Barth, K., 254–55
Beard, C., 147

Beato, F., 17
Beauchamp, T., 86, 90–91
Bellasco, G. B., 17
Benedetti, G. B., 16–18
Bentham, J., 84
Berrouard, M.-F., 64
Biancani, G., 13
Binns, J. W., 82
Boethius, 58
Bohr, N., 30–31, 33–34
Boileau, D., 25
Bonaventure, 41
Borro, G., 17
Bradley, D., 108, 115
Brandt, R., 87
Broadie, A., 265
Buridan, J., 76
Burrell, D., 7–8

Cajetan, T., 253, 256, 258
Case, J., 4, 72–81
Celaya, J. de, 14
Cephalus, 118
Chandler, R., 174
Charlemagne, 152
Chesterton, G. K., 6, 164–66, 169–70, 173, 249
Cicero, 75, 78, 80
Clark, K., 196
Clavius, C., 12–13, 19
Clifford, W. K., 183, 185
Comte, A., 2, 25–29, 35–36

267

Constant, B., 63
Cooper, J., 121
Cooper, S., 157
Copenhauer, B., 76
Crosby, J., 248
Cummins, R., 220
Curran, C., 140

d'Abano, P., 15
Dahl, N., 121
Dante, 235
Darwin, C., 226
Davidson, D., 3, 38–39, 46
Dawkins, R., 215, 226
DeKoninck, C., 57
DeKoninck, T., 3–4
Democritus, 211
Dennett, D., 251
De Pace, A., 22
Derrida, J., 251
Descartes, R., 6, 20–21, 42, 56–57, 65, 202, 205, 209, 218–20, 224, 226, 242
Devereux, Robert, 2nd earl of Essex, 79
Dewey, J., 36
Dexter, C., 172
Dostoevsky, F., 168, 174
Dougherty, J., 2–3
Dretske, F., 220
Dudley, R., 72
Dullaert, J., 14
Dummett, M., 66
Durkheim, E., 25, 36

Eco, U., 173
Edelman, G., 64, 67
Elisabeth (Queen of Sweden), 65
Elizabeth I of England, 78–79
Elyot, T., 75, 80
Engelhardt, H. T., 55–56, 58, 65
Essex, 2nd earl of. *See* Devereux, Robert
Eudaemon-Ioannes, A., 18–19

Fager, C., 174
al-Farabi, 255
Fermi, E., 31
Ferne, J., 80
Field, H., 42
Finnis, J., 143, 161
Flint, T., 252
Fodor, J., 42
Folscheid, D., 64
Foot, P., 100
Foucault, M., 251
Frankena, W., 93–99
Freddoso, A., 7
Freedman, S., 174
Frisch, O., 29–31
Fuchs, J., 137, 145

Gaffney, J., 145
Galilei, G., 13–21
Garcia, J., 179–80, 197
Garcia, L., 6
Gaustad, E., 160–61
Geach, P. T., 41, 100
Gebauer, G., 65
George III of England, 158
Gilbert, P., 172
Gilson, E., 25, 34, 238, 259, 261
Glendon, M. A., 161
Goethe, J., 63, 151
Goldwin, R., 160
Gorgias, 234, 249
Grant, S., 265
Greco, J., 197
Grimaldi, F. M., 19
Grisez, G., 143
Guardini, R., 191–92, 195, 199

Hadot, P., 261–62, 264, 266
Hahn, O., 29–31
Haldane, J., 3, 251
Hardie, W. F. R., 121

Hare, R. M., 104
Harré, R., 36
Harvey, V., 183
Hauerwas, S., 6
Hegel, G. W. F., 54
Heidegger, M., 251
Henry of Ghent, 262
Hick, J., 6, 179, 192–93, 195–96
Hill, T., 65
Hitler, A., 128, 148, 155, 173
Hittinger, R., 123–24
Hobbes, T., 80, 147
Holmes, S., 165
Hume, D., 6, 26–29, 95, 98, 114, 201–6, 208, 210–16, 222–26, 242
Hutson, J., 161
Huxley, T. H., 218, 226

Ignatius of Loyola, 20
Irwin, T., 108, 112, 115, 119, 121–23, 125
Isaiah, 64

Jaffa, H., 108, 115–16, 124
James, M., 82
James, P. D., 169, 174
James, W., 43, 184
Jefferson, T., 153, 158, 161
Jesus, 151–52, 171, 204, 234, 236–38
John Paul II (pope), 181, 248, 251
John of St. Thomas, 8
Jordanus, 15

Kamm, F. M., 65
Kant, I., 55, 65, 83–85, 87–91, 94–96, 103, 113, 151, 179, 201–2, 242
Kenny, A., 226
Kepler, J., 20
Kerr, F., 56
Kierkegaard, S., 256, 265
Kim, J., 46
Kirk, R., 149

Knox, R., 163
Kovesi, J., 266
Kraut, R., 123

Lancelot, 167
La Ramée, Pierre de, 76
Latini, B., 75
Lattis, J., 22
Laudan, L., 29
Lenin, V. I., 155
Levinas, E., 4, 63
Lévy-Bruhl, L., 36
Lindberg, D., 23
Livesey, S., 21
Locke, J., 25, 27, 42, 56–57, 147, 183, 185
Lombard, P. *See* Peter Lombard
Louden, R., 104
Lowe, J., 47
Lowery, M., 143

Mach, E., 29
MacDonald, S., 108, 122, 124
MacIntyre, A., 4, 100, 102, 123, 125, 161, 234, 242, 247
Madison, J., 153
Maier, D., 160
Maimonides, 256–58, 263, 265
Major, J., 14
Malik, C., 155
Marion, J.-L., 65, 266
Maritain, J., 5, 147–57, 159–61
Mather, C., 160
Mavrodes, G., 196–97
May, W., 143
Mayr, E., 215
McCabe, H., 264
McCormick, R., 132, 138, 141–46
McDermott, T., 257
McDowell, J., 43, 50
McInerny, D., 4–5
McInerny, R., 1–2, 5–8, 37, 49, 83–84,

101–2, 122–23, 125, 147–49, 155, 159–61, 163–65, 170, 173–74, 179, 182, 190, 196, 201, 229, 253–57, 259, 264–65
McLaughlin, B., 47
Meitner, L., 29–31
Meno, 116
Menu, A., 13
Mercier, D., 25, 27, 36
Mill, J. S., 26, 36, 87
Miller, F., 124
Moletti, G., 17
Moore, G. E., 103, 204
Moore, R., 30
Mullady, B., 143–44

Napoleon, 152
Nemorarius, J., 13
Newman, J. H., 183–86, 190, 194, 196–98
Newton, I., 18, 20
Niebuhr, H. R., 67
Nietzsche, F., 234
Novak, M., 5
Nuñez, P., 12
Nussbaum, M., 60–61, 67, 100, 121–22

O'Connor, F., 173
O'Donovan, O., 175
Oresme, N., 15

Pascal, B., 53
Paul, Saint, 181
Paul of Venice, 15
Pellegrino, E., 86
Peperzak, A., 251
Pereira, B., 13
Perry, A., 175
Peter, Saint, 229
Peter Lombard, 58
Phillipson, N., 160
Philiponus, J., 15

Piccolomini, A., 13
Pieper, J., 124, 250, 256–57
Pinckaers, S., 66, 245, 250
Pius V (pope), 78
Plantinga, A., 6, 191–96, 198, 234, 237, 250, 252
Plato, 26, 173, 237, 241, 246, 253–54, 258, 262
Poincaré, H., 29
Pritzl, K., 123
Proclus, 254
Putnam, H., 3, 29, 33, 43–44, 50, 60–61, 67
Pythagoras, 40, 61

Quine, W. V. O., 33, 205, 226

Rahner, K., 144
Railton, P., 104
Ramsey, P., 174
Ramus. *See* La Ramée, Pierre de
Ratzinger, J., 236
Rawls, J., 89–90
Reid, T., 6, 50, 201–2, 204–11, 214, 224–25
Rescher, N., 33
Riccioli, G., 13
Richards, D., 89–90
Romulo, C., 155
Rorty, R., 151, 205
Ross, J., 187
Rugerius, L., 13–14
Russell, B., 151, 211, 215

Sandoz, E., 157
Sankara, 259
Sartre, J. P., 251
Sayers, D., 6, 166–69, 171–73
Schindler, D., 159
Schmitt, C., 72, 76
Scotus, J. D., 123, 241, 259, 262
Sidgwick, H., 92

Sidney, P., 4, 71–74
Simmons, L., 143
Sherman, N., 121
Smith, A., 150, 160
Smith, J. E., 4–5
Smith, J. M., 218
Socrates, 59, 118, 151, 173, 257–58, 262, 266
Sokolowski, R., 257, 261, 265–66
Solomon, W. D., 4
Sophocles, 4, 63
de Soto, D., 11–12, 14–18, 20, 23
Spaemann, R., 66
Springer, J., 182
Stalin, J., 155
Stecker, R., 50
Stephen, J., 197
Strassman, F., 29–31
Strauss, L., 147
Strawson, P. F., 34
Struever, N., 76
Suarez, F., 124, 241, 249–50
Sullivan, T., 186–87, 197

Tacelli, R., 143
Taine, H., 25, 36
Tanner, K., 265
Taylor, C., 65
Thomas Aquinas, 5, 7, 15–16, 20, 25, 37, 40–41, 43, 55–56, 58–62, 66, 76–78, 83–84, 102, 105–9, 111–25, 127–29, 131, 133–34, 137, 143–45, 148–49, 155, 173–74, 180–81, 187–88, 196, 201, 225, 229, 231–36, 239–47, 249–50, 252–57, 259–60, 262–65
Toledo, F., 12
Tooley, M., 55, 57
Toqueville, A. de, 154, 160
Trianosky, G., 104

Upfield, A., 164, 172

Vacek, E., 132
Vallentyne, P., 103
Vallius, P., 13, 17
van Fraassen, B., 226
Varchi, B., 17
te Velde, R., 265n9
Villey, M., 161
Vitelleschi, M., 13, 15, 16
Vuillemin, J., 65

Wallace, W., 2, 36
Walsh, J., 171, 173
Walters, J., 65
Ward, W., 197
Washington, G., 153
Weisheipl, J., 23
Wells, H. G., 28
Westberg, D., 123
Wiggins, D., 105–9, 112, 121–22
Wilhelmson, F., 250
Wilkinson, J., 75
Williams, B. A. O., 100, 110–11
Winthrop, J., 154
Wittgenstein, L., 56–57
Wolfson, H., 256
Wolpert, L., 64, 67
Wood, A., 78
Wotyla, K. *See* John Paul II
Wrong, E. M., 173

Yoder, J. H., 174
Yordy, L., 172–73

Zabarella, J., 15–16, 20–21
Zagzebski, L., 179–80, 182–83, 197, 199
Ziggelaar, A., 23
Zimara, M., 15

www.ingramcontent.com/pod-product-compliance
Lightning Source LLC
Chambersburg PA
CBHW030613230426
43661CB00053B/1969